Project 2016

FOR DUMMIES®
A Wiley Brand

by Cynthia Snyder

FOR DUMMIES®
A Wiley Brand

Project 2016 For Dummies®

Published by: **John Wiley & Sons, Inc.,** 111 River Street, Hoboken, NJ 07030-5774, www.wiley.com

Copyright © 2016 by John Wiley & Sons, Inc., Hoboken, New Jersey

Published simultaneously in Canada

For general information on our other products and services, please contact our Customer Care Department within the U.S. at 877-762-2974, outside the U.S. at 317-572-3993, or fax 317-572-4002. For technical support, please visit www.wiley.com/techsupport.

Wiley publishes in a variety of print and electronic formats and by print-on-demand. Some material included with standard print versions of this book may not be included in e-books or in print-on-demand. If this book refers to media such as a CD or DVD that is not included in the version you purchased, you may download this material at http://booksupport.wiley.com. For more information about Wiley products, visit www.wiley.com.

Library of Congress Control Number: 2016932541

ISBN 978-1-119-22451-8 (pbk); ISBN 978-1-119-22452-5 (ebk); ISBN 978-1-119-22453-2 (ebk)

Manufactured in the United States of America

10 9 8 7 6 5 4 3 2 1

Contents at a Glance

Introduction 1

Part I: Getting Started with Project 2016 5
Chapter 1: Project Management, Project 2016, and You 7
Chapter 2: Starting the Project 19
Chapter 3: Becoming a Task Master 39
Chapter 4: The Codependent Nature of Tasks 53
Chapter 5: Estimating Task Time 65
Chapter 6: Check Out This View! 81

Part II: Managing Resources 101
Chapter 7: Creating Resources 103
Chapter 8: Working with Calendars 119
Chapter 9: Assigning Resources 133
Chapter 10: Determining a Project's Cost 145

Part III: Before You Baseline 155
Chapter 11: Fine-Tuning Your Plan 157
Chapter 12: Negotiating Project Constraints 171
Chapter 13: Making the Project Look Good 185
Chapter 14: It All Begins with a Baseline 201

Part IV: Staying on Track 211
Chapter 15: On the Right Track 213
Chapter 16: Project Views: Observing Progress 237
Chapter 17: You're Behind — Now What? 251
Chapter 18: Spreading the News: Reporting 267
Chapter 19: Getting Better All the Time 289

Part V: The Part of Tens 299
Chapter 20: Ten Golden Rules of Project Management 301
Chapter 21: Ten Cool Shortcuts in Project 2016 309

Appendix: Glossary 315

Index 325

Table of Contents

Introduction *1*

About This Book 1
Foolish Assumptions...2
Icons Used in This Book 2
Beyond the Book 3
Where to Go from Here..3

Part I: Getting Started with Project 2016 .... *5*

Chapter 1: Project Management, Project 2016, and You............7

Introducing Project Management...7
Defining project manager...8
Identifying what a project manager does 9
Introducing Project 2016...10
Getting to Know You 11
Navigating file tabs and the Ribbon.............................14
Displaying more tools 17
Tell Me What You Want to Do...18

Chapter 2: Starting the Project...19

Creating the Project Charter 20
Introducing the Work Breakdown Structure (WBS)...............21
Organizing the Work 22
Starting the Project 24
Entering project information...24
Weighing manual scheduling versus automatic scheduling 26
Entering the WBS 28
Entering tasks 30
Importing tasks from Outlook 32
Promoting and demoting: The outdent-and-indent shuffle 35
Saving the Project..36

Chapter 3: Becoming a Task Master......................................39

Creating Summary Tasks and Subtasks................................39
How many levels can you go? 41
The project summary task..41

Moving Tasks Up, Down, and All Around 43
    Moving tasks with the drag-and-drop method 44
    Moving tasks with the cut-and-paste
    (or copy-and-paste) method 44
Now You See It, Now You Don't: Collapsing and
    Expanding the Task Outline 45
Showing Up Again and Again: Recurring Tasks 48
Setting Milestones 49
Deleting Tasks and Using Inactive Tasks 50
Making a Task Note 51

Chapter 4: The Codependent Nature of Tasks 53

How Tasks Become Dependent 54
    Dependent tasks: Which comes first? 54
    Dependency types 55
    Allowing for Murphy's Law: Lag and lead time 57
Setting the Dependency Connection 58
    Adding the dependency link 58
    Extending your reach with external dependencies 61
    Words to the wise 61
    Understanding that things change: Deleting dependencies 62

Chapter 5: Estimating Task Time 65

You're in It for the Duration 66
    Tasks come in all flavors: Identifying task types 66
    Effort-driven tasks: $1 + 1 = \frac{1}{2}$ 67
Estimating Effort and Duration 70
    Estimating techniques 70
    Setting the task duration 72
Controlling Timing with Constraints 73
    Understanding how constraints work 73
    Establishing constraints 74
    Setting a deadline 75
Starting and Pausing Tasks 76
    Entering the task's start date 77
    Taking a break: Splitting tasks 78

Chapter 6: Check Out This View! 81

A Project with a View 81
    Navigating tabs and views 82
    Scrolling around 84
    Reaching a specific spot in your plan 85

More Detail about Views..86
    Home base: Gantt Chart view..86
    Resourceful views: Resource Sheet and Team Planner.................88
    Getting your timing down with the Timeline.................................88
    Going with the flow: Network Diagram view.................................89
    Calling up Calendar view...90
Customizing Views...91
    Working with view panes..92
    Modifying Network Diagram view..96
    Resetting the view...100

Part II: Managing Resources.. 101

Chapter 7: Creating Resources 103
Resources: People, Places, and Things..103
Becoming Resource-Full...104
    Understanding resources...104
    Resource types: Work, material, and cost....................................105
    How resources affect task timing...105
    Estimating resource requirements...106
The Birth of a Resource..107
    Creating one resource at a time..108
    Identifying resources before you know their names....................109
    Many hands make light work...110
Managing Resource Availability...111
    Estimating and setting availability...111
    When a resource comes and goes...112
Sharing Resources...114
    Skimming from resource pools..114
    Importing resources from Outlook..116

Chapter 8: Working with Calendars 119
Mastering Base, Project, Resource, and Task Calendars.................119
    How calendars work...120
    How one calendar relates to another...121
Scheduling with Calendar Options and Working Times...................122
    Setting calendar options..122
    Setting exceptions to working times..124
Working with Task Calendars and Resource Calendars...................126
    Setting resource calendars..126
    Making the change to a resource's calendar................................127
Creating a Custom Calendar Template..129
Sharing Copies of Calendars..130

Chapter 9: Assigning Resources **133**

Finding the Right Resource 133
Needed: One good resource willing to work 134
Custom fields: It's a skill 135
Making a Useful Assignation 136
Determining material and cost-resource units 137
Making assignments 137
Shaping the contour that's right for you 140
Benefitting from a Helpful Planner 142

Chapter 10: Determining a Project's Cost **145**

How Do Costs Accrue? 146
Adding up the costs 146
When will this hit the bottom line? 147
Specifying Cost Information in the Project 148
You can't avoid fixed costs 148
Entering hourly, overtime, and cost-per-use rates 149
Assigning material resources 151
How Your Settings Affect Your Costs 152

Part III: Before You Baseline **155**

Chapter 11: Fine-Tuning Your Plan **157**

Everything Filters to the Bottom Line 157
Setting predesigned filters 158
Putting AutoFilter to work 159
Creating do-it-yourself filters 161
Gathering Information in Groups 163
Applying predefined groups 163
Devising your own groups 164
Figuring Out What's Driving the Project 166
Inspecting tasks 166
Handling task warnings and suggestions 167

Chapter 12: Negotiating Project Constraints **171**

It's about Time 171
Applying contingency reserve 172
Completing a task in less time 174
Getting What You Want for Less 176
The Resource Recourse 176
Checking resource availability 177
Deleting or modifying a resource assignment 178
Beating overallocations with quick-and-dirty rescheduling 179
Finding help 179
Leveling resources 180
Rescheduling the Project 183

Chapter 13: Making the Project Look Good.....................185

Looking Good!...185
Formatting the Gantt Chart..186
 Formatting taskbars..186
 Zeroing in on critical issues...................................189
 Restyling the Gantt chart.......................................190
Formatting Task Boxes..191
Adjusting the Layout..192
Modifying Gridlines...195
Recognizing When a Picture Can Say It All............................197
Creating a Custom Text Field..198

Chapter 14: It All Begins with a Baseline 201

All about Baselines...201
 Saving a baseline..202
 Saving more than one baseline.................................203
 Clearing and resetting a baseline............................205
In the Interim..206
 Saving an interim plan..207
 Clearing and resetting an interim plan.....................208

Part IV: Staying on Track.............................. 211

Chapter 15: On the Right Track 213

Developing a Communications Management Plan.....................213
 Gathering data...214
 Applying a tracking method.....................................215
 Using the tracking tools..216
 For everything, there's a view................................217
Tracking Work for the Record..218
 Specifying the status date.....................................219
 Remaining on track...220
 Determining the percent complete............................220
 Recording start and finish information.......................222
 Knowing what to do when John works three
  hours and Mary works ten....................................222
 Uh-oh — we're in overtime......................................224
 Specifying remaining durations for auto-scheduled tasks...........225
 Entering fixed-cost updates....................................227
Moving a Task..228
Update Project: Sweeping Changes.....................................229
Tracking Materials..231
Tracking More Than One: Consolidated Projects.....................232
 Consolidating projects..232
 Updating consolidated projects................................234
 Changing linking settings.......................................235

Chapter 16: Project Views: Observing Progress................... 237

Seeing Where Tasks Stand.. 238
Baseline versus actual progress 238
Lines of progress.. 239
Delving into the Detail.. 242
Tracking Progress Using Earned Value Management 244
Calculating Behind the Scenes... 246
Earned-value options... 247
An abundance of critical paths 248

Chapter 17: You're Behind — Now What? 251

Using Project with Risk and Issue Logs 251
Printing interim plans and baselines... 252
Printing task notes... 253
What-If Scenarios 254
Sorting tasks 255
Filtering 256
Examining the critical path... 257
Using resource leveling (again) 259
Determining which factors are driving the timing of a task........ 259
How Adding People or Time Affects the Project 260
Hurrying up and making modifications.. 260
Throwing people at the problem 261
Shifting dependencies and task timing 262
When All Else Fails 264
Taking the time you need 264
Finding ways to cut corners 265

Chapter 18: Spreading the News: Reporting 267

Generating Standard Reports... 268
What's available.. 268
Overviewing the dashboard reports 269
Creating New Reports 270
Gaining a new perspective on data with visual reports................ 271
Creating a visual report 272
Fine-Tuning a Report... 273
Dragging, dropping, and sizing 273
Looking good!... 274
Spiffing Things Up.. 276
Call the Printer!.. 278
Working with Page Setup 279
Getting a preview 283
Printing, at last! 284

Working on the Timeline 285
    Adding tasks to the Timeline..............................285
    Customizing the Timeline 287
    Copying the Timeline 288
Enhanced Copy and Paste 288

Chapter 19: Getting Better All the Time 289
Reviewing the Project 289
    Learning from your mistakes 290
    Debriefing the team 291
Comparing Versions of a Project................................292
Building on Success...294
    Creating a template 294
    Mastering the Organizer 296

Part V: The Part of Tens *299*

Chapter 20: Ten Golden Rules of Project Management 301
Roll with It 301
Put Your Ducks in a Row 302
Expect the Unexpected 303
Don't Put Off until Tomorrow 303
Delegate, Delegate, Delegate 304
Document It..305
Keep the Team in the Loop 305
Measure Success 306
Maintain a Flexible Strategy 306
Learn from Your Mistakes 307

Chapter 21: Ten Cool Shortcuts in Project 2016 309
Task Information..309
Resource Information 310
Frequently Used Functions 310
Subtasks...311
Indenting and Outdenting..312
Fill Down 312
Navigation...312
Hours to Years 312
Timeline Shortcuts 313
Quick Find...313

Appendix: Glossary *315*

Index *325*

Introduction

• •

*O*ver the years, project management has evolved from a discipline that began with index cards and yarn to one that now uses sophisticated analyses, techniques, projections, reporting, and time and money tracking. Project management software brings functionality to project management that makes planning and tracking the complex projects we undertake a little more manageable.

About This Book

Microsoft Office Project 2016, the most recent incarnation of the world's most popular project management software, offers a tremendous wealth of functionality to users. In the beginning, however, as with most software, mastering it can seem like a daunting process. It helps to understand how Project's features relate to what you do every day as a project manager.

In *Project 2016 For Dummies,* my goal is to help you explore Project 2016, providing information on relevant project management concepts while also offering specific procedures to build and track a Project schedule. More important, I offer advice on how to make all these features and procedures mesh with what you already know as a project manager to ease the transition to using Project 2016.

Here are some broad topics that I help you explore in this book. You can

- ✔ Start out in Project 2016 by entering tasks and dependencies, estimating durations, and working with views
- ✔ Work with resources, calendars, and costs
- ✔ Negotiate constraints, fine-tune the schedule, and set a baseline
- ✔ Gather data, analyze progress, take corrective actions, and report project status

Within this book, you may note that some web addresses break across two lines of text. If you're reading this book in print and want to visit one of these web pages, simply key in the web address exactly as it's noted in the text, pretending as though the line break doesn't exist. If you're reading this as an e-book, you've got it easy — just click the web address to be taken directly to the web page.

Foolish Assumptions

I've made some assumptions about you, gentle reader. I figure that you're computer-literate and that you know how to use the mouse, the keyboard, software menus, and toolbars. I assume that you know how to use most common Windows functions (such as the Clipboard), as well as many basic software functions, such as selecting text and dragging and dropping items with the mouse.

I also assume that you have experience in managing projects. Whether you manage very large projects that are several years long or you have been a team lead on a project, the information in this book is more accessible if you have a background in project management.

I do *not* assume that you've used Project or any other project management software. If you're new to Project, you'll find what you need to get up to speed, including information on how Project works, finding your way around the Project interface, and building your first Project plan. If you've used an earlier version of Project, you'll find out about Project 2016 and all the new features it provides.

Icons Used in This Book

One picture is worth . . . well, you know. That's why *For Dummies* books use icons to provide visual clues to what's going on. Essentially, icons call your attention to bits of special information that may well make your life easier. The following icons are used in this book.

The Remember icon signals either a pertinent fact that relates to what you're reading at the time (but is also mentioned elsewhere in the book) or a reiteration of a particularly important piece of information that's, well, worth repeating.

Tips are the advice columns of computer books: They offer sage advice, a bit more information about topics under discussion that may be of interest, or ways to do things a bit more efficiently.

Warning icons spell trouble with a capital *T*: When you see a warning, read it. If you're not careful, you might do something at this point that could cause disaster.

Beyond the Book

In addition to the material in the print or e-book you're reading right now, this product also comes with some access-anywhere goodies on the web:

- ✔ **Cheat Sheet:** The cheat sheet has lots of shortcuts and other nifty tips and tricks. You can find the Cheat Sheet at www.dummies.com/cheatsheet/project2016.
- ✔ **Web Extras:** There is a web extra for every part in this book. Just follow the link to the Web Extras at www.dummies.com/extras/project2016.
- ✔ **Companion website:** This book is accompanied by a companion website that includes a project charter example and template, as well as several sample forms to help you plan and manage the schedule. To access this additional material, point your web browser to www.dummies.com/go/project2016fd.

Where to Go from Here

Take what you've learned in the project management school of hard knocks and jump into the world of Project 2016. When you do, you'll be rewarded with a wealth of tools and information that help you manage your projects much more efficiently.

Your first step might be to read the table of contents and find the sections of this book that you need — or simply turn to Chapter 1 and start reading.

Part I

Getting Started with Project 2016

getting started

with

Project 2016

In this part . . .

- ✔ Get familiar with the Ribbons and file tabs in Project 2016.
- ✔ See how to open a new project, enter tasks, and organize a project.
- ✔ Become skilled in working with summary tasks, milestones, and notes.
- ✔ Identify and arrange task dependencies to create a network diagram.
- ✔ Develop duration estimates for tasks.
- ✔ Customize Project views to meet your needs.

Chapter 1

Project Management, Project 2016, and You

In This Chapter

▶ Understanding the elements of a project

▶ Laying out the project manager's role

▶ Benefitting from Project 2016

▶ Exploring the software interface

▶ Finding help in Project

*W*elcome to the world of computerized project management with Microsoft Project. If you've never used project management software, you're entering a brave new world.

Everything you used to do with handwritten to-do lists, word processors, and spreadsheets magically comes together in Project. However, this transition doesn't come in a moment, and you need a basic understanding of what project management software can do to get you up to speed. If you've used previous versions of Project, the overview in this chapter can refresh your memory and ease you into a few of the new Project 2016 features.

Even if you're a seasoned project manager, this chapter provides the foundation for how to work with Project.

Introducing Project Management

You probably handle projects day in and day out. Some are obvious, because your boss named them so that any fool would know that they're projects: Acme Drilling Project or Network Expansion IT Project, for example.

Others are less obvious, such as that presentation you need to put together for your director or that how-to guide on planting a vegetable garden in your backyard.

In this book, a project is defined as a unique venture undertaken to produce distinct deliverables, products, or outcomes. In the context of a project, a *deliverable* is a discrete component or item that meets the requirements of the project, such as a design document or a prototype. Projects have multiple variables; some are straightforward to define, and others aren't.

Using the information about variables in Table 1-1, you can say that *project management* is the practice of organizing, managing, and controlling project variables to meet the project outcomes and mission.

Table 1-1	Project Variables
Variable	*Description*
Defined	
Scope	The work needed to produce the deliverables, products, or outcomes for the project.
Time	The duration required to complete the project work.
Cost	The funds required to complete the project.
Resources	The people, equipment, material, supplies, and facilities needed to accomplish the project.
Undefined	
Change	The type, timing, number, and degree of modifications from a project baseline; can affect the project's scope, time, cost, or resources.
Risk	Uncertainty (associated with the scope, time, cost, resources, stakeholders, or environment) that can threaten the completion of any aspect of the project. Fortunately, risks can also present opportunities to accelerate the schedule or come in under budget.
Stakeholder	A person who can affect, or who is affected by, the project, either positively or negatively.
Environment	The location, culture, or organization in which the project occurs.

Defining project manager

Although understanding the role (let alone the usefulness) of certain managers isn't always easy, you can easily spot the value of a *project manager:*

This person creates the master plan for a project and ensures that it is implemented successfully. Along the way, the project manager uses technical, business, and professional skills to manage the completion of tasks and keep the schedule on track.

A truly professional project manager may have a degree in project management or a professional certification. For example, if you see the initials *PMP* beside a name, that person has been certified as a project management professional by the Project Management Institute, the leading global organization establishing project management standards and credentials, and offering educational and other types of resources in the field.

Identifying what a project manager does

A project manager isn't always the highest authority in a project. Often, that role belongs to whoever manages the project manager — including, possibly, members of senior management. Rather, the project manager is the person who ensures that aspects of the project are integrated and assumes hands-on responsibility for successes as well as failures.

In project management parlance, the person who champions (and funds) a project is the *project sponsor.* Although the project manager may work for the project sponsor, the project often also has a *customer* — outside the project manager's own company or within it — for whom the end product is produced.

The project manager manages these essential pieces of a project:

- ✔ **Scope:** Define and organize all work that needs to be done in order to meet the project mission and create deliverables.
- ✔ **Schedule:** This element, which you create by working with Project, includes the estimated steps and associated timing involved in reaching the project goal.
- ✔ **Resources:** Assign resources and track their activities on the project as well as resolve resource conflicts and build consensus. This part of the job also involves managing nonhuman resources such as materials and equipment.
- ✔ **Cost:** Estimate project costs and apply those estimates across the schedule to create a time-phased budget.
- ✔ **Communication:** Notify appropriate *stakeholders* (everyone who has a legitimate stake in its success) of the project status.

Creating a logical balance of the defined variables of scope, time, cost, and resources is at the core of a good project manager's job throughout the life of a project. Managing a project requires overseeing all its variables to ensure that the project goals are accomplished on time, within the limits of the budget, and using the assigned resources while also addressing risks, managing change, and satisfying stakeholders. Sound easy? Maybe not. However, one thing is certain: Having software to help organize and structure the work makes managing the project less daunting. That's where Project 2016 can help.

Introducing Project 2016

Project 2016, which is a scheduling tool, helps you organize, manage, and control defined variables, as identified in the preceding section. Project can also help you manage the undefined variables as well. In this book, I show you how to use Project to organize and manage your work, create realistic schedules, and optimize your use of resources.

Take a moment to look at some of the wonderful ways in which Project can help you organize, manage, and control your project. Now that you have, or your company has, bought Project (and this book) and you're investing your time to understand how to use it, you can enjoy these benefits:

- ✔ **Use built-in templates to get a head start on your project.** Project *templates* are prebuilt plans for a typical business project, such as commercial construction, an engineering project, a new product rollout, software development, or an office move.

- ✔ **Organize your project by phase, deliverable, geography, or any other method.** The outline format allows you to progressively elaborate the information in greater granularity depending on how detailed you want your plan to be.

- ✔ **Determine costs by your chosen method.** Examples are time period, resource type, deliverable, or cost type.

- ✔ **Organize resources by resource type.** Level your resources to avoid overallocation, or determine the impact on the duration of a task based on a change in resources.

- ✔ **Calculate costs and timing based on your input.** You can quickly calculate what-if scenarios to solve resource conflicts, maintain costs within your budget, or meet a deliverable deadline.

- ✔ **Use views and reports with the click of a button.** A wealth of information is now available to you — and those you report to. You no longer have to manually build a report on total costs to date to meet a last-minute request from your boss.

- ✔ **Manage complex algorithms** (that you couldn't even begin to figure out on your own) to complete such tasks as leveling resource assignments to solve resource conflicts, filtering tasks by various criteria, modeling what-if scenarios, and calculating the dollar value of work performed to date.

No matter how cool the tool, you have to take the time to enter meaningful data. Great software doesn't ensure great outcomes; it only makes them easier to achieve.

Getting to Know You

The file you create in Project is a Project *schedule model.* It's a model because it models what you think will happen given what you know at the time. However, for ease of reference, I just refer to it as a schedule. The schedule has a plethora of data about various aspects of your project as well as graphical representations of that information.

Some people refer to the project schedule as the project plan. In reality, the project plan *contains* the project schedule — plus information such as the budget, work breakdown structure, project life cycle, risk management plan, and many other ingredients necessary to effectively manage a project.

When you first open Project 2016, you see several options for starting a new project, as shown in Figure 1-1.

You can open a blank project, create a new project from an existing project, or create a new project by importing information from Microsoft Excel or SharePoint. You can also take advantage of premade templates for common project types, such as these examples:

- ✔ Agile project management
- ✔ Software development
- ✔ New product launch
- ✔ Residential construction

Figure 1-1:
What you
see when
you open
Project
2016.

If you don't see the template you need, you can search for online templates by entering keywords in the search box at the top of the page. For purposes of this discussion, I assume that you're starting with a new, blank project.

When you open a new project, you see the Quick Access toolbar, a few file tabs, the Ribbon, the Timeline, a pane with a sheet and a chart, and the status bar, as shown in Figure 1-2.

In Figure 1-2, you see Gantt Chart view. (I discuss views in Chapter 6.) For now, here's an overview of the major elements in Project (refer to Figure 1-2):

- ✔ **Quick Access toolbar:** The Quick Access toolbar, above and to the left of the Ribbon, is onscreen at all times and in all views.

- ✔ **File tab:** The file tabs organize commands based on a particular type of activity. For example, if you're working with resources, you'll likely find the command or setting you want on the Resource tab.

- ✔ **Ribbon:** The Ribbon provides easy access to the most commonly used tools and commands. When you change tabs, the available tools on the Ribbon change.

- ✔ **Group:** A *group* is a set of related commands or choices on the Ribbon. For example, to format text in a cell on the sheet, first find the formatting information you need in the Font group on the Task tab of the Ribbon.

Quick Access Toolbar   Tool Group   Timeline

Figure 1-2:
A blank
project.

Sheet   Status Bar   Chart

- ✔ **Timeline:** The Timeline provides an overview of the entire project — a graphical view of the project from start to finish. You have the option of showing the Timeline or hiding it.

- ✔ **Sheet:** Similar to a spreadsheet, the sheet displays the data in the project. The default fields change depending on the file tab you're working in. You can customize the columns and fields in the sheet to meet your needs.

- ✔ **Chart:** The *chart* is a graphical depiction of the information on the sheet. Depending on the view or file tab you see, you might also see a bar chart depicting the duration of a task or a resource histogram showing resource usage.

- ✔ **Status bar:** The status bar, at the bottom of the Project window, has information on views and zoom level on the right, and information on how newly entered tasks are scheduled on the left.

Navigating file tabs and the Ribbon

Each of the seven file tabs in Project shows different options on the Ribbon. In this section, I provide an overview of each file tab and of the Ribbon and the Quick Access toolbar. I elaborate on various functions and commands on the Ribbon in later chapters.

The first tab on the left, the File tab, stands out in bright green. After you click this tab, you see the menu bar down the left side, as shown in Figure 1-3.

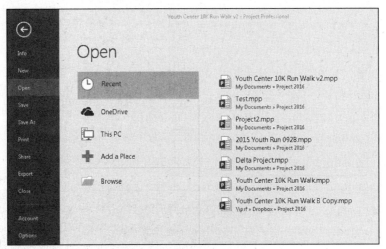

Figure 1-3:
The File tab menu.

The File tab puts you into Backstage view, where you find choices for working with files and changing options. For example, you can create a new project, open an existing project, save your current project, or print your current project. From Backstage view, you can also share, export, or close your current project. If you're feeling adventurous, you can even customize the Ribbon and the Quick Access toolbar.

The Task file tab is where you spend a lot of your time in Project. As you can see in Figure 1-4, on the far left side of the Task file tab is the View. The default view is Gantt Chart view. It shows the task information and the chart that displays a bar chart representing the duration of each task.

Figure 1-4:
The Task file tab.

In addition to Gantt Chart, you can choose these views:

Calendar   Network Diagram
Resource Sheet   Resource Usage
Resource Form   Resource Graph
Task Usage   Task Form
Task Sheet   Team Planner
Timeline   Tracking Gantt

You may recognize some of the groups of commands on the Task file tab. For example, the Clipboard and Font groups are standard in many Windows applications. Other groups, such as Schedule and Tasks, are specific to a particular view — in this case, Gantt Chart view. Look for the deep green Gantt Chart Tools Format tab when you see the Task file tab in Gantt Chart view. In other views, you see different tools above the Format tab.

The Resource file tab, shown in Figure 1-5, helps you organize resources, such as adding, assigning, and leveling resources across tasks. In Project, resources include people, equipment, material, locations, and supplies. You can assign costs and calendars to resources. (I talk more about resources in Chapter 7.)

Figure 1-5:
The
Resource
file tab.

The Report file tab, shown in Figure 1-6, is new in Project 2016. You can create reports on resources, costs, or progress, or put them all together in a dashboard report. You can create a report that compares your current status to previous versions of your project. I tell you all about reports, including how to customize and export your reports, in Chapter 18.

Figure 1-6:
The Report
file tab.

On the Project file tab, you find commands to help you manage your project as a whole, rather than by task or resource. For example, you can enter or change the project start and finish dates and the baseline. If you need to change working time or add a subproject, this is the place to do it. Figure 1-7 shows the Project file tab.

Figure 1-7:
The Project file tab.

The View file tab lets you see some standard views. Examples are Task views, such as Gantt Chart, and Resource views, such as Resource Usage or Team Planner. You can use the View file tab to look at information sorted by date or a specific period. You can see the View file tab in Figure 1-8.

Figure 1-8:
The View file tab.

The Format file tab has commands that help you present your schedule, such as font styles, page breaks, and column settings. You can see the options in Figure 1-9.

Figure 1-9:
The Format file tab.

You can either show or hide the Ribbon to produce more real estate on your screen. The pushpin to the far right of the Ribbon pins it to your display, keeping it open and visible (as shown in Figure 1-10). The upward-facing arrow (^) on the far-right side hides the Ribbon. If your Ribbon is closed, click on any tab, look in the lower-right corner of the Ribbon and you will see a pushpin. Click on the pushpin to keep your Ribbon open. You can also press Ctrl+F1 to show or hide the Ribbon.

Displaying more tools

The Quick Access toolbar, which appears onscreen at all times, initially contains the Save, Undo, and Redo buttons. You can customize the Quick Access toolbar by clicking the down arrow at the right end of the toolbar and clicking the option you want to hide or display. If you don't see the option you want, click More Commands near the bottom of the menu to get a full list of commands you can add. Figure 1-11 shows the list of commands you can choose from.

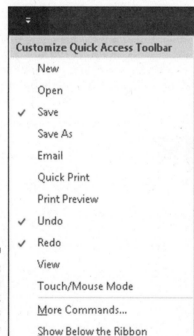

Figure 1-11: Customizing the Quick Access toolbar.

The nifty *Timeline* tool shows the entire scaled time span of the project. To show the Timeline, go to the View file tab, in the Split View group and click the check box that says Timeline. You can add tasks or milestones to the Timeline. You can also copy the Timeline and paste it into reports or other presentations. To hide the Timeline, uncheck the Timeline box. You can also work with the Timeline by right-clicking to insert tasks, copy the Timeline, change the font, or view detailed information.

The *status bar* sits at the bottom of the project, to indicate whether your tasks are manually or automatically scheduled. (Read more on this topic in Chapter 2.) The status bar also lets you move quickly to some of the most popular views, such as Gantt, Task Usage, Team Planner, Resource Sheet, and Reports. You can also adjust the time scale from a high-level, time scaled view to a detailed time-scaled view with the View slider, on the far-right end of the status bar. I talk more about views in Chapter 6.

Tell Me What You Want to Do

In previous versions of Microsoft Office, there was a Help function. That has been replaced by the Tell Me What You Want to Do feature. If you want some coaching on how to do something in Project 2016, just click the light bulb next to the Format tab. Enter a keyword, and you have several options to choose from. I searched on "critical path" and the information in Figure 1-12 came up.

Figure 1-12: A search for "critical path."

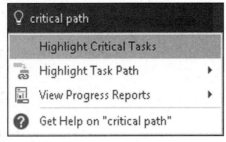

Chapter 2

Starting the Project

In This Chapter

▶ Moving from concept to plan

▶ Creating the project's work breakdown structure (WBS)

▶ Entering project information into Project

▶ Entering the WBS into Project

▶ Entering tasks into Project

▶ Saving the project

Congratulations — you're the proud project manager of a new project! Before you do anything, you need to understand the scope of the project. You must clearly specify, for example, any intended outcomes, expectations for milestones, main deliverables, budgeted amounts, key stakeholders, and what denotes success.

Planning a project isn't as easy as opening a file in Project and entering all the activities you have to complete. Before you can begin to plan, you need to understand the purpose of the project and the high-level information about the project, such as milestone dates and overall budget.

To complete a successful project, you need to plan well. To plan well, you need to understand the project's objectives as well as its success criteria. Therefore, before you enter the first task into Project, you create the project charter (described a little later in this chapter) to initiate the project and develop the work breakdown structure (WBS) to organize project deliverables. Then you can start organizing the project and entering tasks into Project.

This chapter describes how to move from imagining a concept to planning a project so that you know how to enter and work with tasks and how to save the new project.

Creating the Project Charter

Having a high-level understanding of a project is critical to project success. The *project charter* is a document that formally authorizes or recognizes a project; it contains high-level information about the project. The project charter is frequently developed by the project manager, with the project sponsor. The charter functions as an agreement about the purpose and objectives of the project.

The elements of a project charter are

- ✔ Purpose
- ✔ Description
- ✔ Objectives
- ✔ High-level requirements
- ✔ Summary milestone schedule
- ✔ Summary budget
- ✔ Assigned project manager

Other names for the charter are project-initiating document and statement of work.

The high-level information in the charter provides background information to help you plan the project approach and organize the work logically. Using the information from the charter, you can start to define the project's major deliverables and its life cycle — and your approach to accomplishing all the project work.

Throughout this book, I use a sample project to demonstrate key concepts in Project. The project charter for the 10K Run/Walk sample project is shown in Figure 2-1. Project objectives describe the intended outcome to raise $2.5 million for youth recreation facilities in the metro area by November 1.

Summary Milestones	Due Date
Planning begins.	6-1
Call for volunteers opens.	7-1
Finalize course route.	7-15
PR and advertising begin.	8-1
Registration opens.	8-15
All food and beverage contracts are completed.	10-1
Day of event arrives.	11-1
Funds are finalized and turned over to community center board.	11-15
Project is completed.	11-15

Estimated Budget

$10,000

Approvals

Bonnie Rush   *Ida Know*

_____   _____
Project manager signature   Sponsor or originator signature

Figure 2-1:
The 10K
Run/Walk
project
charter.

Introducing the Work Breakdown Structure (WBS)

If you have a small project, you may be able to start entering tasks into Project and organize them on the fly. But for any project with more than 50 tasks, consider how to structure and organize the work before you open Project. One best practice is to create the *work breakdown structure,* or WBS — a hierarchically organized representation of all the project work.

The concept of *project work* includes work that's necessary to *create* the product and work that's necessary to *manage* the project, such as attending meetings, completing training, and creating documentation.

Generally, you approach the WBS from the top down. In other words, you evaluate the entire project and then break it into large chunks, and then break the larger chunks into smaller chunks, and so on, until you have a defined deliverable. That's where the WBS stops and project tasks begin.

The breaking of WBS deliverables into smaller chunks is known as *decomposition.*

The WBS houses all deliverables for the project and product scope. It doesn't include the tasks. Those are strictly for the schedule. Another way of thinking about the WBS is that it's composed of nouns, whereas the schedule is composed of actionable verbs. For example, the Water Stations deliverable might be the lowest-level deliverable you would show on the WBS. Then define these tasks for the schedule using the "verb-noun" naming convention:

1. Identify water companies.

2. Develop request for quote.

3. Receive quotes.

4. Select vendor.

5. Develop contract.

6. Sign contract.

7. Oversee water station setup.

Organizing the Work

Frequently, the most challenging aspect of creating a WBS is figuring out how to organize it. You have several options. For example, if you have multiple locations for a hardware deployment, you can arrange it by geography. Many times, software projects are managed by life-cycle phases, such as Concept, Requirements, Design, Build, Test, and Deploy.

Another common way to organize work is by major deliverable. The needs and deliverables of the project determine how best to organize work. The WBS for the Youth Center Run/Walk is arranged by the type of work. You can see it presented in two different ways. One way looks like an organizational chart, and the other way is via outline. Either way works well; however, when you start decomposing past two levels, the organizational chart method becomes difficult to manage. After you delve into the detail, consider moving to an outline format. Figure 2-2 shows an organizational chart format for the high-level WBS.

Figure 2-2:
High-level
WBS.

Using the high-level WBS, you can further decompose the work into outline format:

1. Registration

   1.1 Database

   1.2 User interface

   1.3 Payment

   1.4 Confirmation

2. PR and advertising

   2.1 Print

   2.2 Television

   2.3 Radio

   2.4 Internet

3. Food and beverage

   3.1 Finish-line food

   3.2 Finish-line beverage

   3.3 Water stations

4. Safety

   4.1 Medical

   4.2 Security

5. Course logistics

   5.1 Route

   5.2 Signage

   5.3 Parking

6. Volunteers

   6.1 Onboard process

   6.2 Management

7. Project management

   7.1 Communication

   7.2 Planning

   7.3 Management

   7.4 Risk management

   7.5 Stakeholder management

After outlining the organization of the work, you can start defining the tasks that comprise the project schedule.

Starting the Project

In Chapter 1, I discuss how to open a blank project. After you open a blank project, you can begin entering basic project information, such as the start or end date.

Entering project information

You can enter project information into Project in two ways:

- ✔ **Choose File ⇨ Info.** In the Project Information section on the right side of the screen, as shown in Figure 2-3, you can enter the start, finish, current, and status dates for the project.

  After choosing File ⇨ Info, you can click the Project Information down arrow, then click advanced properties. Enter the name of the project where it says "Title" and enter your name where it says "Author." You can also enter company name, keywords, and other information. This information is used in many of the automated reports that Project creates.

- ✔ **On the Ribbon, go to the Project tab and click the Project Information icon.** You see the Project Information dialog box, shown in Figure 2-4. It holds the same information as the Project Information section on the File menu.

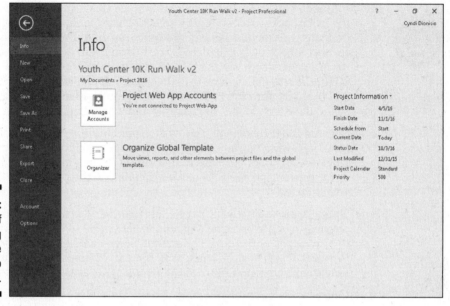

Figure 2-3:
The result of choosing the File ➪ Info command.

Figure 2-4:
The Project Information dialog box.

This list describes the settings within the Project Information dialog box:

- ✔ **Start Date and Finish Date:** For a project scheduled forward from the start date (see the next bullet), enter only the start date. Or if you schedule backward from the finish date, enter a finish date.

- ✔ **Schedule From:** You can choose to have tasks scheduled backward from the finish date or forward from the start date. Most folks move forward from the start date.

Although you can schedule backward, use this feature only to schedule the work backward initially, by selecting the finish date and clicking the OK button. Immediately after doing so, return to this dialog box and revert to the (newly calculated) start date. If you don't, you may encounter problems down the road if you eventually record progress. At that point, the end date will be fixed because you've backward-scheduled, and the start date will be fixed because you've recorded actuals, so the schedule will no longer be dynamic and won't expand or contract.

✔ **Current Date:** By default, this setting matches the computer clock setting. However, you can change it so that it doesn't match the computer clock setting. Changing this date is useful for looking at what-if scenarios or for tracking progress as of a certain date in the past or any date you choose.

✔ **Status Date:** You typically set the current date to track the progress on the project. When tracking, you usually want to see the status of the project as of the current moment, so you can ignore this setting. However, if you want to track as of the end of a fiscal period or another time frame, change it to track the status of tasks as of any other date.

✔ **Calendar:** Select from this drop-down list the Base calendar template to use for the Project calendar. I list this setting first because it's the only one you *have* to deal with when you start a new project. For now, assume you will use the Standard calendar. I describe calendars in Chapter 8.

✔ **Priority:** This field is useful if your organization has many projects and you create links among them. If you use a tool such as resource leveling (see Chapter 12 for more about this topic) to resolve conflicts, it can consider this project priority setting when calculating what to delay and what to keep on track.

Weighing manual scheduling versus automatic scheduling

One of the most valuable aspects offered by Project has traditionally been its ability to recalculate task schedules when you change the project start date or a change to one task's schedule affects one or more dependent *(linked)* tasks. This powerful behavior saves the project manager — *you* — from having to rethink and reenter dates to rescheduled tasks throughout the project.

But flip sides to the benefits of automation always exist, and in the case of project scheduling, automatic scheduling can lead to unwanted schedule changes based on software behavior and not on human expertise.

To retain the helpful aspects of automation that make scheduling less time-consuming while allowing project managers to retain schedule control when needed, Project 2016 allows *user-controlled scheduling*.

In user-controlled scheduling, you can select one of these scheduling modes for each task:

- ✔ **Auto Schedule:** Project calculates task schedules for you based on the project start date and finish date, task dependencies, calendar selections, and resource scheduling.

- ✔ **Manually:** Project enables you to skip entering the duration and dates, and specifying them later. When you enter the duration and dates, Project fixes the schedule for the task and doesn't move it unless you do so manually. The manually scheduled tasks move if you reschedule the entire project, in most cases. The Gantt bars for manually scheduled tasks also differ in appearance from those for automatically scheduled tasks.

The indicator for auto-scheduled and manually scheduled tasks is at the bottom of the Project window. Figure 2-5 shows the Registration tasks are auto-scheduled, as indicated by the time bar and the arrow in the Task Mode column. The User Interface tasks are manually scheduled, as indicated by the pushpin in the Task Mode column. On the time scale, the auto-scheduled tasks show up as blue bars on your screen and the manually scheduled tasks show up as aqua bars with vertical lines on each end.

Figure 2-5: Manually and automatically scheduled tasks.

The project file can have all manually scheduled tasks or all auto-scheduled tasks — or any mix of the two. By default, all tasks that you create use the manually scheduled mode.

You can change the task mode for the overall project in two ways:

✔ To change the mode for all new tasks, select the Task tab, click Mode in the Tasks group, and then choose Auto Schedule or Manually Schedule from the menu, as shown in Figure 2-6.

✔ Another way to change the mode for all new tasks is to click the New Tasks link at the left end of the status bar at the bottom of the project, then select the mode you want.

Figure 2-6: Changing the task mode from the Ribbon.

You can change the task mode for individual tasks in three ways:

✔ Select the task, click the Task tab on the Ribbon, and then click either Manually Schedule or Auto Schedule in the Schedule group.

✔ Select the task, click the Task Mode cell for the task, click the drop-down arrow that appears, and click either Manually Scheduled or Auto Scheduled in the drop-down list.

✔ Go to the Information button (Task tab, Properties group), click the information box, and use the radio buttons to select Manually Scheduled or Auto Scheduled.

You need to balance the desires of your inner control freak versus the need to be an efficient project manager in determining how often to use manual scheduling. Though manual scheduling prevents Project from moving tasks that you want to stay put in the schedule, you may need to edit the schedules for dozens of dependent tasks in a long or complicated project. The best balance — particularly for beginning project managers — may be to use manual scheduling sparingly.

Entering the WBS

The schedule should be set up the same way as the WBS. If you want to continue the outline numbering scheme from the WBS, Project automatically extends to the schedule tasks the outline numbering used for the WBS. You can do this in two ways:

1. **Select the Format tab.**

2. **In the Columns group, click Insert Column.**

3. **Select the Outline Number option.**

4. **Press Enter.**

You can also enter the outline number directly into the task cell by following these steps:

1. **Click to open the Format tab.**

2. **In the Show/Hide group, select the Outline Number check box.**

The first information to enter into the new project is the WBS. Follow these simple steps to enter the WBS in Gantt Chart view:

1. **In the Task Name column, click a blank cell.**

2. **Type the name of the WBS element.**

   Using the example of the Youth Center 10K Run/Walk, the first element is Registration.

3. **Press Enter to move to the next cell in the column and then type the WBS element name.**

4. **Repeat Step 3 until you enter all WBS names.**

   You can edit the text that you type by pressing the Delete or Backspace key to clear characters.

After you enter the WBS, you can use the Indent feature to create the outline format. In Project, you can indent two ways:

✔ Select the Task tab and click the Schedule group's Indent Task or Outdent Task icons.

✔ Select the task you want to indent and press Alt+Shift+right arrow.

Figure 2-7 shows part of the screen display after you enter the WBS outline. This version shows the outline numbering as a separate column. Notice that after you indent a task, its parent task switches from manually scheduled to auto-scheduled because the duration and dependencies of the child tasks determine when the parent task can start and finish. Therefore, you don't fill in the duration or start and finish dates for WBS elements — that information will auto-populate when you enter tasks beneath the WBS elements.

	Task Mode ▾	WBS ▾	Task Name ▾	W	T
1		1	◢ **Registration**		
2		1.1	Database		
3		1.2	User Interface		
4		1.3	Payment		
5		1.4	Confirmation		
6		2	◢ **PR & Advertising**		
7		2.1	Internet		
8		2.2	Print		
9		2.3	Radio		
10		3	◢ **Food & Beverage**		
11		3.1	Finish line food		
12		3.2	Finish line beverage		
13		3.3	Water Stations		

Figure 2-7:
The WBS
for the 10K
run/walk
event.

Entering tasks

After the WBS information is entered, you can start entering tasks. You can create tasks in a few different ways:

- ✔ Type information in the sheet area of the Gantt chart.
- ✔ Enter information in the Task Information dialog box.
- ✔ Import tasks from Outlook.
- ✔ Import tasks from Excel.

You can fill in the details of the task duration and start date when you enter the task, or later.

Entering tasks in Gantt Chart view

Many people who work on lengthy projects find that entering all task names in the sheet pane of Gantt Chart view is the quickest and easiest method. This method is the same one I used to enter the WBS information. You can simply enter a task name in the Task Name column, press the Enter or down-arrow key on the keyboard to move to the next blank row, enter another task, and so on.

Use the Task Mode column to change the task scheduling mode from Manually Schedule to Auto Schedule for any task not using the default method.

Entering tasks via the Task Information dialog box

If dialog boxes provide the kind of centralized information form that fits the way you like to work, consider using the Task Information dialog box to enter, well, task information. The series of tabs in this dialog box contain all the information about a task.

Follow these steps to create a task via the Task Information dialog box:

1. In the Task Name column, double-click a blank cell.

The Task Information dialog box appears, as shown in Figure 2-8.

2. In the Name field, type a task name.

3. Click the OK button to save the new task.

The task name appears in Gantt Chart view in the cell you clicked in Step 1.

4. Press the down-arrow key to move to the next cell.

5. Repeat Steps 1–4 to add as many tasks as you like.

As you name tasks, make task names in the project both descriptive and unique. However, if you can't make all names unique (for example, you have three tasks named Hire Staff), you can use the automatically assigned task number or the outline number to identify tasks; these numbers are always unique for each task.

Naming tasks is a trade-off between giving a full description (which is much too long for a Task Name field) and being too brief (which can lead to misunderstandings and uncertainty). When in doubt, be brief in the Task Name and elaborate with a Task Note. I cover Task Notes in Chapter 3.

To insert a task anywhere within the list of tasks in Project, from the Task tab, Insert group, click a task name cell where you want the new task to appear, and click the Insert Task icon. The new task is inserted in the row above. You can also press the Insert key on the keyboard.

Importing tasks from Outlook

After you start thinking about what has to be accomplished in a project, tasks start resembling breeding rabbits; what might start as a series of simple to-do tasks in Outlook often becomes a full-fledged project. When that happens, you'll be glad to know that Microsoft provides an easy-to-use import feature that transfers the tasks you create in Outlook to Project.

The Import Outlook Tasks feature is essentially an import map that's preset to work with Outlook task fields. Follow these steps to import Outlook tasks into Project:

1. **Open the plan that you want to insert tasks into, or open a new project (choose File ⇨ New, click Blank Project, and click Create).**

2. **Click the Task tab on the Ribbon, click the bottom part (with the down arrow) of the Task button in the Insert group, and click Import Outlook Tasks.**

3. **If a Microsoft Outlook warning message appears, click Allow.**

   The Import Outlook Tasks dialog box appears, as shown in Figure 2-9.

Figure 2-9: Importing task information into Project.

4. Select the check box beside each task you want to import, or click the Select All button to import all Outlook tasks.

By default, Outlook stores tasks in the Tasks folder. Selecting the Folder: Tasks check box is another way to select all tasks in Outlook.

5. Click the OK button.

The tasks are imported and then appear at the end of the list of tasks with change highlighting applied.

When you import a task from Outlook, its name, duration, and notes (if any) are also imported. If a task in Outlook has no duration, and you've set Auto Schedule as the project task mode, Project creates the task with an estimated one-day time frame.

Inserting hyperlinks

You can insert hyperlinks in a project outline, which provides a handy way to quickly open another project, another file of any type, or a web page.

To insert a hyperlink to a project document, follow these steps:

1. Right-click the cell where you want the hyperlinked task to appear.

2. Choose Hyperlink.

The Insert Hyperlink dialog box appears, as shown in Figure 2-10.

Figure 2-10:
Linking
a file.

3. In the Text to Display box, type the text that you want to appear for the hyperlink.

Ensure that this text clearly states what information is being summarized. In this case, I'm linking the Safety Plan to a task in the project.

4. In the Link To area, click the Existing File or Web Page icon.

You can link to a document of any type or to a web page.

5. In the Look In list, locate and select the file to which you want to insert a hyperlink.

In my example, I'm keeping the supporting documentation in a file called Project 2016.

6. Click the OK button.

The link text is inserted, and a hyperlink symbol appears in the Indicator field. You can simply click that link symbol to open the linked file.

Inserting one project into another

You can also insert tasks from one project into another. You do this by inserting an entire, existing project into another project. The project that's inserted is called a *subproject*. This method is useful when various project team members manage different phases of a larger project. The capability to assemble subprojects in one place allows you to create a master schedule from which you can view, all in one place, all the pieces of a larger, more complex project.

Follow these steps to insert another Project file into the schedule:

1. In Gantt Chart view, select the task in the task list above which you want the other project to be inserted.

2. Choose Project ⇨ Subproject.

The Subproject command is in the Insert group. The Insert Project dialog box appears, as shown in Figure 2-11.

Figure 2-11: Inserting a link to another project.

3. **Using the navigation pane and file list, locate the file that you want to insert, and click it to select it.**

4. **If you want to link to the other file so that any updates to it are reflected in the copy of the project you're inserting, make sure that the Link to Project check box is selected.**

5. **Click the Insert button to insert the file.**

   The inserted project appears above the task you selected when you began the insert process.

The inserted project's highest-level task appears at the level of the task you selected when you inserted the project, with all other tasks below it in outline order. If you need to, use the Outdent and Indent tools (described in the following section) on the Formatting toolbar to place the inserted tasks at the appropriate level in the project.

Promoting and demoting: The outdent-and-indent shuffle

Outdenting and indenting are the functions you use to move tasks to higher or lower levels of detail in the WBS and the task list. In several software programs, these terms are *promoting* and *demoting,* respectively:

- ✔ **Outdenting** a task moves it up a level in the outline (literally shifting it to the left in the outline).

- ✔ **Indenting** a task moves it down a level in the outline (literally indenting the task to the right in the outline). Whenever you indent one or more tasks, the task above becomes the summary task. You can read more about summary tasks in Chapter 3.

You use tools from the Schedule group on the Task tab of the Ribbon, shown in Figure 2-12, to outdent and indent tasks in a project outline. The Outdent Task tool has a left-facing arrow; the Indent Task tool has a right-facing arrow.

To outdent or indent a task, follow these steps:

1. **Click a task to select it.**

2. **Click the Indent Task or Outdent Task button, according to the action you want to take.**

   When you indent a task, the task above it becomes a summary task. The summary task is in bold on the sheet. On the chart, a summary task has a bracket that stretches from the beginning of the earliest task to the end of the latest task.

Indent and Outdent Tools   Summary Task Indicators

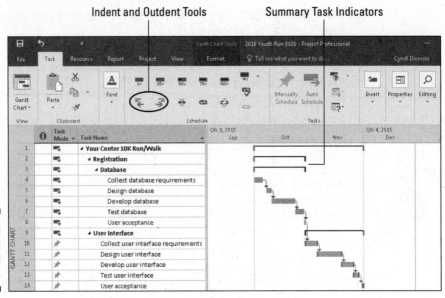

Figure 2-12:
Outdenting
and
indenting.

You can build the outline even faster by indenting multiple tasks at a time. Drag to select multiple task IDs and then indent them. You can also use the standard Shift+click and Ctrl+click selection methods to select multiple tasks in a Project outline. Shift+click the task IDs to select contiguous tasks, and Ctrl+click to select discrete tasks.

You can indent using keystrokes by pressing Alt+Shift+right arrow. You can outdent using keystrokes by pressing Alt+Shift+left arrow.

Saving the Project

Saving Project files works just as saving does in other Microsoft software. Here's a reminder.

To save a Project file that you haven't yet saved, follow these steps:

1. Choose File ⇨ Save As.

You can choose Save instead if you created the project from scratch rather than from a template.

2. **Use the navigation pane at the left to locate the folder where you want to save the file; then double-click to select it.**

3. **The Save As window will open. In the File Name text box, type a name for the project.**

4. **Click the Save button.**

Good organizational practice suggests that you create a folder for your project where you save — in one spot — your Project file and its supporting documents, such as email messages and other items. You can create a new folder from within the Save As dialog box by clicking the New Folder button.

Chapter 3

Becoming a Task Master

In This Chapter

▶ Creating summary tasks and subtasks

▶ Moving tasks

▶ Collapsing and expanding tasks

▶ Creating milestones

▶ Deleting tasks and inactive tasks

▶ Entering a task note

*T*he foundational unit in a project schedule is the project task; everything starts with it. After you identify and document your tasks, you can work with resources, dependencies, costs, durations, and other elements.

To be an effective task master, you need to be nimble in managing your tasks: Determine how to summarize work with a summary task, move work around, start and stop work in the middle of a task, and do all kinds of other tricks that help your schedule reflect what you want to happen on your project.

Creating Summary Tasks and Subtasks

When you look at a project work breakdown structure, also known as WBS (refer to Chapter 2), or a project task list, such as the one shown in Figure 3-1, you see that it organizes tasks into levels. The upper levels are from the WBS. The lower level consists of tasks that have been decomposed from the WBS. A task that has other tasks indented below it in this outline structure is a *summary task,* or *parent task.* The tasks indented below the summary task are *subtasks,* or *child tasks.* Summary tasks are indicated in bold in the Project outline. You can tell when a summary task has a family of subtasks clinging to its skirts: When a subtask is hidden, a little clear triangle is displayed to the left of the summary task. When you click the triangle with the tip of the pointer, the task expands to show its whole clan of subtasks, and the summary task adds a black triangle to its left.

WBS ▾	Task Name ▾
4	◢ **Registration**
4.1	▷ **Database**
4.2	▷ **User Interface**
4.3	◢ **Payment**
4.3.1	Collect payment requirements
4.3.2	Design payment function
4.3.3	Develop payment function
4.3.4	Test payment function
4.3.5	User acceptance
4.4	◢ **Confirmation**
4.4.1	Collect confirmation requirements
4.4.2	Design confirmation function
4.4.3	Develop confirmation function
4.4.4	Test confirmation function
4.4.5	User acceptance
4.4.6	Registration Available

Figure 3-1:
Project
outline,
showing
summary
tasks and
subtasks.

In Figure 3-1 you can see that the summary tasks of Database and User Interface have hidden subtasks. The Payment and Confirmation summary tasks show all their subtasks.

All information about a family of tasks is rolled up into its highest-level summary task. Therefore, any task with subtasks has no timing or cost information of its own: It gathers its total duration and cost from the sum of its parts.

This roll-up functionality is cumulative: The lowest-level task rolls up to its parent, which might roll up into another summary task, which rolls up (for example) into a project summary task. Any task with tasks below it gets its duration and cost information from a roll-up of its subtasks, no matter how deeply nested it may be in the hierarchy.

The structure of families in an outline is also useful when you need to reorganize an outline: When you move a summary task, all its subtasks come right along for the ride, regardless of whether it's expanded!

If a summary task is manually scheduled, the roll-up functionality doesn't work, and Project displays warnings telling you so. The Gantt bar for the summary task has a red warning bar that shows you the calculated duration of the subtasks when they don't match up with the summary task's duration. The summary task's Finish field entry also has a red, squiggly underline to indicate a potential scheduling problem. To deal with this situation, you can change the summary task to use auto-scheduling, in which case it calculates roll-up data correctly. If you want the summary task to continue to be manually scheduled, you can edit its finish date or use the Task Inspector as described in Chapter 11 to fix the summary task schedule.

How many levels can you go?

You have no practical limit on how many levels of tasks you can create in an outline. Project enables you to indent to more levels of detail than you'll need for all but the most complex schedules. Remember, though: At some point, you have to deal with assigning timing and resources to each of these tasks and then track their progress. Too much detail can make your project plan difficult to manage. For example, if your project is a few months long, you don't want to track to a level where activities last only a few hours. Best practices suggest that you always set up your schedule to the level to which you want to manage your team — typically, business (working) days or weeks.

For longer projects, you can schedule by using *rolling wave planning*, a method of progressively elaborating the amount of detail for near-term work and keep at a higher level any work that's further out. For example, if you have a two-year project, you may have the first three months planned out in detail, the next three months at a higher level, and the remainder of the project schedule showing only milestones and key deliverables. As you progress through the project, you start to add more detail for six months and beyond. A good rule of thumb is to keep a good amount of detail for 90 days out.

Rolling wave planning isn't an excuse to add scope; it's only the elaboration of existing scope.

The project summary task

Just as a ship has only one captain, only one task summarizes all other tasks in a project. I strongly suggest that you display the *project summary task*, which represents the highest (least detailed) level of information and is often simply the title of the project, such as New Product Rollout. When you tell Project to display the project summary task, every task in the project falls under it in the outline, as shown in Figure 3-2.

As you build your project, you can easily create a project summary task yourself (indent other tasks beneath it) or use a Project feature to generate one automatically at any time — even after you build all the phases of your project. To have Project automatically display a project summary task, follow these steps:

1. **In the Gantt Chart view, select the Gantt Chart Tools Format context tab.**

2. **In the Show/Hide group, select the Project Summary Task check box.**

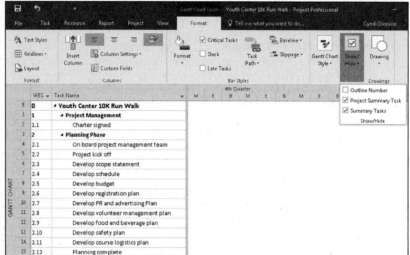

Figure 3-2:
The project
summary
task.

As you can see in Figure 3-2, Task 0, Youth Center 10K Run/Walk, is the project summary task. Notice that the bar for the project summary task on the chart is gray and that the bars for other summary tasks are black.

When you think about it, an upper-level headline in an outline is the sum of its parts: The headline reflects the overall topic for all items below it. The project summary task advances this concept a step further: This task rolls up all actual data from other tasks into one line item. Thus, the project summary task's duration reflects the duration of the entire project. From a monetary angle, the project summary task's total cost reflects the total costs for the entire project. Figures such as these can be handy to have at your fingertips — and that's one value of a summary task.

If you're confused about the length of your summary task, remember that the *summary task duration* is the difference between the earliest task start date and latest task end date. However, nonworking days aren't counted in the summary task duration. The length of the summary task, therefore, equals the number of days of work over the course of the subtasks, not the number of calendar days between the start of the first task and end of the last.

Not everyone uses project summary tasks. You can simply create, at the highest level of your outline, tasks that represent major project deliverables or phases — with subphases and subtasks below them — and not create one task that's higher in the order than all others. However, having a project summary task has certain benefits:

> ✔ **You can quickly view totals for the project at a glance in the columns of data in Gantt Chart view and other views.**
>
> ✔ **You can place a link to your project summary task in another project so that all data for one project is reflected in another.** For example, if you create five schedules for new product launches in your company, you can easily create a master schedule for all company product launches by linking to the project summary tasks in each of the projects.

Moving Tasks Up, Down, and All Around

In Chapter 2, I show you how to outdent and indent tasks to create the WBS and the project outline. In this section, I show you additional ways to move tasks, collapse and expand tasks, and set up recurring tasks.

A maxim of project management says that things change: Tasks that you thought you could complete early can't happen yet because money, people, or materials are in short supply. Or a task that you thought you couldn't start until next July gets bumped up in priority when your customer changes his mind (again) about deliverables. Because of this changeability, when you enter tasks in a project outline, odds are that you'll need to move those tasks around at some point.

You should understand that moving a task can change its outline level. A task retains its level in the outline only when you move the task to follow a task at the same level. (Okay, there's an exception, which I get to in a minute.) Comparatively, if you move a lower-level task to a section of tasks at a higher level — for example, move a third-level task to a section of second-level tasks — the moved task takes on the level of the task preceding it. And the converse is true when you move a higher-level task to follow a lower-level task. The point is that you'll need to check your outline level for the tasks you move and adjust it using the indent and outdent features.

The exception I hinted at happens when you move a lower-level task to follow a summary task. For example, a second-level task that you move to immediately follow a summary task stays at the second level rather than taking on the summary task level of the task that now precedes it, because there's only one summary task.

Moving tasks with the drag-and-drop method

If you ask me, drag-and-drop is to computing what the remote control is to television. It's a quick, no-brainer method of moving stuff around in software that just makes life simpler. Here's an example:

To move a task up and down with the drag-and-drop method, follow these steps:

1. **Display a column view, such as Gantt Chart view.**

2. **Select a task by clicking its task ID number.**

   Simply click and release; don't hold down the mouse button.

3. **Click and drag the task to wherever you want it to appear in the outline.**

   A gray "T-bar" line appears, indicating the new task position.

4. **When the gray line is located where you want to insert the task, release the mouse button.**

   The task appears in its new location. If you want the task to be at a different level of the outline, you can now indent or outdent it as needed.

Moving tasks with the cut-and-paste (or copy-and-paste) method

Dragging and dropping works fine in most cases, but in very large projects — with a few hundred tasks or more, for example — it's easier to cut and paste.

In a larger outline, use the cut-and-paste method to move tasks:

1. **Select a task by clicking its task ID number.**

2. **Click the Cut button in the Clipboard group on the Task tab.**

   The task is removed from its current location and placed on the Windows Clipboard.

3. **Scroll to display the location where you want the task to appear.**

4. **Click the task after which you want to insert the task.**

5. **Click the top part of the Paste button, also on the Task tab.**

If you want to insert a copy of a task in a project outline, you can follow the preceding steps and click Copy rather than Cut.

If you're cutting and copying only a single cell and not a whole task, click in the cell rather than click the task ID number.

You can use the standard Microsoft shortcuts Ctrl+C to copy, Ctrl+X to cut, and Ctrl+V to paste.

Now You See It, Now You Don't: Collapsing and Expanding the Task Outline

Since the caveman days (or whenever the first fourth-grade teacher taught the first set of kids how to outline their book reports), outlines have allowed you to focus on different levels of detail. Outlines do this on paper by essentially ordering information so that you can more easily focus on the level of information you need and ignore the rest.

With the invention of computer outlining, the capability to focus on only certain portions of an outline comes into its own, because you can easily open and close an outline to show or hide different levels of information — or entire sections of your outline. The black triangle symbol next to the Database summary (refer to Figure 3-1) indicates that all subtasks below it are displayed. The clear triangle next to the User Interface label indicates that the subtasks aren't displayed. Remember that all summary tasks are in bold in the project outline.

This capability means that you can hide all but the upper level of tasks in a project to give your manager an overview of progress. Or you can close every phase of your project except the one in progress so that your team can focus on only those tasks in a status meeting. Or you can close most of your outline to make it easy to move to a late phase of a very large schedule.

If you want to hide all the summary tasks and just see the child tasks, you can go to the Gantt Chart Tools context tab and uncheck the Summary Tasks box. Another nifty feature in Project is the ability to choose which level of detail you want to see in your outline. To wrangle the tasks to the level you want them, it's best to work with the View tab. In the View tab under the Data group, there is a drop-down option called Outline. Figure 3-3 shows you the options you have for looking at your outline.

The options that say Show Subtasks and Hide Subtasks can be done at any level of summary tasks. Just select the summary task you want — regardless of whether it's at Level 1 or Level 5 — and click Show Subtasks to see everything underneath, or click Hide Subtasks to just see the summary task.

When you want an overview of your project, it's helpful to look at it from Level 1 or Level 2. You can see our 10K Run at Level 1 in Figure 3-4. Notice the duration for each of the summary level tasks and you can see how they nest within the Project Summary Task.

Level 2, shown in Figure 3-5, shows all the subtasks and the two milestones of Charter Signed and Race. This level gives you a good overview of the project with a bit more detail than Level 1. Level 2 is the view I like to show management or other high-level stakeholders to give them an overall understanding of the project.

To quickly reveal all subtasks in a project, click the Show Outline button and then click All Subtasks.

Figure 3-4:
Level 1
Outline for
10K Run.

Figure 3-5:
Level 2
Outline for
10K Run.

To show subtasks from the keyboard, you can press Alt+Shift+* (asterisk). To hide subtasks, you can press Alt+Shift+– (hyphen) or Alt+Shift+– (minus sign) if you're using the numeric keypad.

Showing Up Again and Again: Recurring Tasks

Some tasks occur repeatedly in projects. For example, attending a monthly project debriefing or generating a quarterly project report is considered a recurring task.

No one wants to create all the tasks for the monthly debriefing in a project that will take a year to complete. Instead, you can designate the recurrence, and Project automatically creates the 12 tasks for you.

Here's how to create a recurring task:

1. **Click the Task tab on the Ribbon, click the bottom part of the Task button (with the down arrow) in the Insert group, and then click Recurring Task.**

   Figure 3-6 shows the Recurring Task Information dialog box that will insert a recurring task for a monthly meeting on the 11th of every month. The meeting is scheduled to occur every month for eight months.

Figure 3-6:
The Recur-
ring Task
Information
dialog box.

Recurring Task Information	
Task Name:	Duration: 1d
Recurrence pattern	
○ Daily Recur every 1 week(s) on:	
● Weekly	
○ Monthly ☐ Sunday ☐ Monday ☐ Tuesday ☐ Wednesday	
○ Yearly ☐ Thursday ☐ Friday ☐ Saturday	
Range of recurrence	
Start: T 4/5/16 ○ End after: 0 occurrences	
● End by: T 11/1/16	
Calendar for scheduling this task	
Calendar: None ☐ Scheduling ignores resource calendars	
Help OK Cancel	

2. **In the Task Name box, type a name for the task.**

3. **In the Duration box, click the spinner arrows to set a duration, or type a duration, such as** 10d **for 10 days.**

Edit the abbreviation to specify a different time unit, if needed.

You can read about the abbreviations that you can use for units of duration — such as *h* for hours — in Chapter 5.

4. **Select a recurrence pattern by selecting the Daily, Weekly, Monthly, or Yearly option.**

   The option you select provides different choices for the rest of the recurrence pattern.

5. **Depending on the selections offered to you, make choices for the rest of the pattern.**

   For example, if you select the Weekly option, you must choose a Recur Every *x* Week(s) On setting and then choose a day such as Friday. Or, if you select Monthly, you must specify which day of every month the task is to recur.

6. **In the Range of Recurrence area, type a date in the Start box; then select and fill in either the End After or End By option.**

   For example, you might start on January 1 and end after 12 occurrences to create a task that occurs every month for a year.

7. **Click the OK button to save the recurring task.**

If your settings cause a task to fall on a nonworking day (for example, if you choose to meet on the eighth day of every month and the eighth day is a Sunday in one of those months), a dialog box appears, asking you how to handle this situation. You can choose not to create the task, or you can let Project adjust the day to the next working day in that period.

To assign resources to a recurring task, you have to assign the resources to the individual recurrences, not to the "summary" recurring task. If you assign resources to the summary recurring task, Project doesn't calculate the hours of work correctly. I talk about assigning resources to tasks in Chapter 9.

Setting Milestones

Milestones are signposts that mark significant events. Examples of milestones are the approval of a prototype (although the deliberations to make that decision might have taken months), the completion of a key deliverable, or the start or end of a project phase.

Some people include tasks such as Design Completed or Testing Completed at the end of each phase of their projects. They can then create timing relationships to the moment of completion — for example, allowing the production of a drug to proceed after the testing and approval is complete. Such milestones also alert you and your team members to a moment of progress in your project that can help keep the team motivated.

Project creates new tasks with an estimated duration of one day unless you enter a duration. To create a milestone, you indicate that the task has zero duration. An easy way to do this is to simply type **0** in the Duration column in Gantt Chart view. When you do, the milestone is designated in Gantt Chart view with a diamond shape rather than a taskbar. You can also click Milestone in the Insert Group of the Task Ribbon. As shown in Figure 3-7, a new task will show up that says <New Milestone>. Finally, you can click the Advanced tab in the Task Information dialog box and select the Mark Task As Milestone check box. Use this latter method for any milestone that has a duration other than zero but that you want to mark as a milestone anyway; its milestone marker is charted at the end of the duration period on the Gantt chart.

Figure 3-7: Creating a new milestone.

Deleting Tasks and Using Inactive Tasks

If your style is to delve into a lot of planning detail for everything you do, you may tend to overanalyze and add more tasks than you need to track in a project plan. In such cases, when you're refining the project plan, you may decide that you need to delete a task or two to tighten up the plan. After all, the process of planning includes not only decomposing the work, but also consolidating tasks when they become too detailed. To delete a task, click its row (Task ID) number at the left side of the sheet and press the Delete key.

Project doesn't display a warning or ask you to confirm deleting a task, so make sure that you *really* mean it when you press Delete. If you screw up, click the undo arrow in your Quick Access toolbar or press Ctrl+Z immediately to restore the deleted task. Also, be sure to check that any task dependencies (links) adjust as needed after you delete the task.

Another approach is to mark a task as *inactive.* Doing this leaves the task visible in the plan but strikes it out in the task sheet and on the Gantt chart, as shown in Figure 3-8. If any automatically scheduled tasks were dependent on the inactive task, Project ignores the now-inactive task when calculating the schedules for those other tasks. Leaving an inactive task in the schedule provides another opportunity to track and document what happened. For example, you can add a note explaining why the task was removed, such as not having a budget that's sufficient for television advertising.

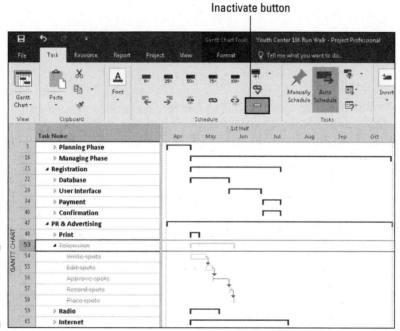

Figure 3-8: Marking a task as Inactive.

Follow these steps to mark a task as inactive:

1. **In Gantt Chart view, select the task to make inactive.**

2. **Click the Inactivate button in the Schedule group on the Task tab of the Ribbon.**

   Project immediately reformats the task as inactive.

Making a Task Note

Despite the wealth of information that you can enter about a task and its timing, not everything can be said with settings. That's why every task includes an area to enter notes. You may use this feature, for example, to enter background information about constraints, detail a step-by-step process that's summarized by the task duration, change the timing, or list vendor contact information that's relevant to the task.

To enter task notes, follow these steps:

1. **Double-click a task.**

   The Task Information dialog box appears.

2. **Select the Notes tab, as shown in Figure 3-9.**

Figure 3-9:
Task note.

3. **In the Notes area, type any information you like.**

   You can enter contact information, notes about resources, or other useful information about the task.

4. **Format the note.**

   Click the buttons at the top of the Notes area to change the font. You can also

   • Left-align, center, or right-align text.

   • Format text as a bulleted list.

   • Insert an object.

5. **Click the OK button to save the note.**

   You will notice that a note icon appears in the information column indicating there is now a note there.

Chapter 4

The Codependent Nature of Tasks

In This Chapter

▶ Identifying the different kinds of dependency relationships

▶ Creating dependency links

▶ Discovering how dependency links affect timing

▶ Allowing for lag and lead time

▶ Reflecting the timing of external tasks in your project

*I*magine this: If you create a hundred tasks and leave their default constraints so that they start as soon as possible and have no dependencies, all those tasks start on the project start date and occur simultaneously. The project consisting of a hundred tasks takes exactly as long to complete as the longest task.

Wander back over here to reality for a moment. When did you ever have a set of tasks in which not a single task had to be completed before another one could start? Imagine what would happen if you tried to train your employees to use a new piece of equipment before the equipment even arrived.

The reality is that not all tasks in a project start at the same time. To reflect this reality in a Project plan, you have to set dependency links between tasks. *Dependencies* are timing relationships between tasks — for example, when one task depends on the completion of another. Dependencies are caused by one of these factors:

✓ **The nature of the tasks:** You can't frame a house, for example, until its concrete foundation is dry; otherwise, the building will sink. This concept is sometimes referred to as a *mandatory dependency* or *hard logic*.

✓ **A best practice or preference:** You should document all requirements before you start designing, however — you can start *some* of the high-level design work before documenting every requirement; it just isn't a good practice to do so. This concept is sometimes referred to as a *discretionary dependency* or *soft logic*.

✓ **Resource availability:** When your operations manager can't attend two plant inspections simultaneously, the situation is known as a *resource dependency*.

> ✔ **Reliance on a resource or an action outside the project:** When you need a deliverable from another project before you can start your work, or you're waiting on someone from an external agency to sign off on it, you have an *external dependency.*

How Tasks Become Dependent

In Chapter 1, I talk about manually scheduled tasks versus auto-scheduled tasks. If you allow the auto-scheduling and your network logic (dependencies) to build your schedule instead of manually assigning specific dates to tasks, Project can reflect changes to your schedule and adjust the dates and timing automatically.

For example, if the task of receiving materials in-house is delayed by a week, the dependent task of starting the manufacturing process moves out a week automatically. You can note the change when you're tracking activity in your plan, and Project makes adjustments accordingly. The alternative is to change the start date of just about every task in your schedule *every time a task is running late;* you don't even want to think about doing that!

Dependent tasks: Which comes first?

When we talk about task relationships, we talk about a task having a predecessor and successor. The predecessor task comes first and impacts when the *successor* (following) task is scheduled, particularly under the auto-scheduling method.

Figure 4-1 shows you how the taskbars in Gantt Chart view graphically depict the predecessors and successors in dependency relationships between tasks. Notice how taskbars represent the relationship when a task starts after another task. Also notice the lines drawn between tasks: These lines indicate *dependency links.*

Here's some important advice about dependencies: You can have more than one dependency link to a task, but don't overdo it. Many people who are new to Project make the mistake of building every logical timing relationship that can exist. If the situation changes and the dependencies have to be deleted or changed (for example, to shorten a schedule), the web of dependencies starts to get convoluted — and can easily create a nightmare.

For example, you must complete the tasks of obtaining a permit and pouring a foundation for a building before you can start framing it. However, if you set up a dependency between obtaining the permit and pouring the foundation, setting a dependency from foundation to framing is sufficient to establish the correct timing. Because you can't start pouring the foundation until you have a permit, and you can't frame until you pour the foundation, framing can't start before you have a permit. This common mistake is known as having a *redundant predecessor.*

Figure 4-1:
Dependency
relationships.

You don't have to use dependencies to prevent resources from working on two tasks simultaneously. When you set the availability of resources and assign them to two tasks happening at the same time, you can use tools such as Team Planner view (see Chapter 9) and resource leveling (discussed in Chapter 12) rather than establish a dependency that forces one task to happen after another. This feature delays tasks when scheduling causes a resource overallocation. See Chapters 9 and 12 for more about how resource assignments affect task timing.

Dependency types

There are four types of dependency links: finish-to-start, start-to-start, finish-to-finish, and start-to-finish. Using these types efficiently can mean the difference between a project that finishes on time and one that's still limping along long after you retire.

Here's how the four dependency types work:

✔ **Finish-to-start:** This most common type of dependency link should account for about 90 percent of the dependencies you create. In this relationship, the predecessor task must be completed before the successor task can start. When you create a dependency, the default setting is finish-to-start.

An example of a finish-to-start dependency is when you must complete the Develop Database task before you can begin the Test Database task. All the dependencies shown in Figure 4-1 are finish-to-start. The relationship is indicated by a successor taskbar that starts where the predecessor taskbar leaves off. You see the finish-to-start type abbreviated as FS.

✔ **Start-to-start:** The start of one task is dependent on the start of another. In this dependency type, two tasks can start simultaneously, or one task might have to start before another task can start. For example, assuming that you have the resources, you can start collecting requirements for payment and confirmation at the same time. A start-to-start relationship is abbreviated as SS.

Figure 4-2 shows, accordingly, the start-to-start relationship between the Collect Payment Requirements and Collect Confirmation Requirements tasks.

Figure 4-2:
The start-to-start relationship.

✔ **Finish-to-finish:** In a finish-to-finish relationship, one task (you guessed it) must finish before or at the same time as another task.

Suppose that you're developing copy for print advertising. You know that the copy will require several rounds of writing and editing. Rather than show a Write ⇨ Edit ⇨ Write ⇨ Edit ⇨ Write ⇨ Edit set of tasks, you can show Write and Edit in a finish-to-finish relationship in which editing finishes at the same time as, or after, writing is done. Figure 4-3 shows a finish-to-finish relationship between Write Copy and Edit Copy. Finish-to-finish is abbreviated as FF.

Finish-to-Finish

Figure 4-3:
The finish-
to-finish
relationship.

Task Name		4/24	5/1	5/8
◢ Print				
Write copy				
Edit copy				
Approve copy				
Place print ads				

✔ **Start-to-finish:** In a start-to-finish dependency, the predecessor task can finish only after the successor task has started. If the successor is delayed, the predecessor task can't finish. Of course, this type of relationship is abbreviated as SF.

Suppose that you're bringing online a new accounting application. The predecessor task of Turn-Off Old Application can't be completed before the successor task of Start Up New Application has started. You need to make sure the new application works as expected, even though you have tested it — run both for a month or so. Therefore, the demise of the old application is dependent on when the new application starts up.

The start-to-finish dependency type is tricky. Leave this type of logic to the professional schedulers and try to find a different way to indicate the relationship between tasks. Often, simply breaking down the tasks and resequencing them accomplishes the same goal.

Allowing for Murphy's Law: Lag and lead time

Dependencies can become a little more complex than simply applying the four types of dependency links that I describe in the preceding section. You can use lag time or lead time to fine-tune your timing relationships:

✔ **Lag time** occurs when you add time to the start or finish of a predecessor task; lag time causes a gap in timing, which delays the start of the successor task. For example, a period almost always exists between sending out a Request for Quote for a service and receiving the quotes. Figure 4-4 shows the lag time that's scheduled between the Send Out RFQ and Review Quotes tasks. When you show a lag, you show the plus (+) sign and then the amount of lag. For example, a lag of one week is shown as +1wk (*wk* is the abbreviation for *week*). Therefore, the relationship between Send Out RFQ and Review Quotes is FS+1wk.

Figure 4-4:
Lag time
between
tasks.

✔ **Lead time** is created when you accelerate time between the start or finish of the predecessor. In Figure 4-5, you see that the call for volunteers is set to start eight weeks before the race day — this gives us a start-to-start with an eight-week lead. We also don't have to wait for all the volunteers to be onboard before we start assigning roles. In this case, we're overlapping the call for volunteers and assigning the roles by a week. This is called *fast tracking*. Finally, we want the Train volunteers task to be done two days prior to the race, so we set a finish-to-finish with a two-day lead (FF-2d). A lead is sometimes considered negative lag.

Figure 4-5:
Lead time
between
tasks.

Setting the Dependency Connection

Setting dependency relationships is simple: You create a dependency, select the dependency type, and build in any lag time or lead time. The tricky part lies in understanding how each type of dependency affects your plan when your project goes live and you start to record actual work that resources perform on tasks.

Adding the dependency link

When you create a dependency, it's a finish-to-start relationship by default: One task must finish before another can start. If that's just the kind of dependency you want, that's all there is to it. If it isn't the kind you want, after you create this link, you can edit it to change the dependency type or to build in lag or lead time.

To establish a simple finish-to-start link, follow these steps:

1. **Display Gantt Chart view and ensure that the two tasks you want to link are visible.**

   You may have to collapse some tasks in your project or use the Zoom button on the View tab to fit more tasks on the screen.

2. **Click the predecessor task and Ctrl+click the successor task, and when both tasks are highlighted, click the Chain Link icon (see Figure 4-6) on the Task file tab in the Schedule Group.**

   You can continue holding down the Ctrl key and highlighting as many tasks as you want to link. Figure 4-6 outlines the Link button and Unlink buttons.

Figure 4-6:
Linking and
unlinking
tasks.

You can link multiple tasks in a row in a finish-to-start relationship by clicking the first task and dragging to the last task. When you release the mouse button, click the Chain Link icon to link all the tasks in order.

Best practice is to link only subtasks, which represent the actual work performed, not the summary tasks. The Ctrl+click method is helpful for skipping over summary tasks when selecting tasks for linking. Also, whether you use the mouse or the Link Tasks button to drag between tasks, the task that's selected first always becomes the predecessor. Therefore, if you're not careful in how you select the tasks, the dependency arrow could move backward in the schedule.

To establish a link in the Task Information dialog box or to modify an existing relationship, make note of the task ID number of the predecessor task and then follow these steps:

1. **Double-click the successor task.**

   The Task Information dialog box opens for the selected task.

2. **Click the Predecessors tab, as shown in Figure 4-7.**

   On this tab, you can build as many dependency relationships as you like.

Figure 4-7:
Setting
dependency
relationships.

3. **In the ID field, type a task ID number for the predecessor task.**

   Alternatively, you can select the task from the Task Name drop-down list. All the tasks you've already entered into the project appear. To display this list, click the next blank Task Name cell and then click the drop-down list arrow that appears.

4. **Press Tab.**

   The task name and the default finish-to-start dependency type showing 0d (no days, which is the default unit of time) of lag time are entered automatically.

5. **Click the Type column and click the arrow that appears to display the dependency types, and then click the appropriate dependency for your situation (refer to Figure 4-6).**

6. **If you want to add lag or lead time, click the Lag field and use the spinner arrows that appear to set the amount of time.**

   Click up to a positive number for lag time, or click down to a negative number for lead time.

7. **Repeat Steps 3 through 6 to establish additional dependency relationships.**

8. **When you're finished, click the OK button to save the dependencies.**

To "keystroke" a link between tasks, select both tasks and then press Ctrl+F2. To unlink, press Ctrl+Shift+F2.

Another way to enter dependencies is to expand the Task Sheet pane until you see the Predecessors column. You can enter the task number of the predecessor task directly into that column, as shown in Figures 4-4 and 4-5.

Extending your reach with external dependencies

Unfortunately, no project exists in isolation. Many times, another project you're managing or another project going on somewhere else in your organization affects your project. Perhaps resources or facilities are shared, or perhaps the timing of tasks in other projects affects the timing of tasks in yours. For example, if your project is to plan the opening of a new store, you may have to create a dependency from your Begin Move-In task to the Final Building Inspection Complete task in someone else's construction project.

To deal with this balancing act, you can create a linked task that represents the timing of the other project (or of a particular task in it). This is also called creating a *cross-project link*. Make sure that both the file with the predecessor task and the file with the successor task are open. Identify the filename and task ID (row) number for the predecessor task. Then switch to the file with the successor task and open the Task Information dialog box for the successor task, as just described. Click in the ID column on a blank row. Type the predecessor filename, a backslash, and then the predecessor task ID number, as in Delta Project/2. Then press Tab to complete the entry. The linked task from the other file appears in the list, as shown in Figure 4-8. In the Gantt chart, that external successor appears in gray so you know that it doesn't really "live" in the current schedule file.

You can also insert an entire project and add a link to it so that updates to the other file are reflected in your plan automatically.

Figure 4-8: The task ID refers to an external task.

Words to the wise

I can't stress enough how important it is to understand the nature of your dependencies. Assuming that you have identified the project work correctly — the way tasks are linked, coupled with your duration estimates (described in Chapter 5) — is the key driver to developing an accurate schedule for your project. If you don't enter the correct relationship between tasks, or if you leave out a linkage, your schedule will be incorrect.

When all your tasks are logically linked, the result is a *network diagram,* or *precedence diagram* — a visual display of how all the tasks relate to one another. This diagram shows the flow of work through the project. If you're missing a relationship or dependency, the flow isn't right, and you're likely to be late or to have to scurry to try to make up for your oversight.

Every task except the first and last tasks has a predecessor and a successor. If one of these elements is missing, the *hanger* task is left dangling. If a task has no predecessor, connect the task to the start milestone of the project. If the task has no successor, connect the task to the end of the phase or the finish milestone of the project.

In addition to making sure you understand the predecessor and successors of each task, you should make sure that the type of relationship is correct. If you try to save time by overlapping tasks, you should understand whether a FS relationship with a lead is a better option than an FF or SS with a lag. To help you determine the better option, ask yourself these questions:

- ✔ If the start of the predecessor is delayed, will it cause the successor to be delayed?
- ✔ If the finish of the predecessor is delayed, will it cause the successor to be delayed?

The answer to these questions will help you understand how the predecessor task affects the scheduling of the successor task.

Understanding that things change: Deleting dependencies

Just like the latest trend in fashion, dependencies in a project can suddenly change. For example, sometimes they're no longer needed because of a shift in priorities or overall project timing. When you need to get rid of a dependency, you can undo what you did in either the Gantt Chart or the Task Information dialog box.

Leading practices in project management suggest that dependencies should not be built based on resource availability when first creating the schedule. Rather, you should concern yourself with the logical order of the work regardless of who does it at this point in creating your schedule. *Resource leveling,* or the smoothing out of the peaks and valleys of resource usage, is always a factor in scheduling, of course, but it is a factor that will be addressed in later steps in project planning.

With Gantt Chart view displayed, follow these steps:

1. **Select the two tasks whose dependency you want to delete.**

   - *For two adjacent tasks:* Drag to select their ID numbers.

   - *For nonadjacent tasks:* Click one task, press and hold Ctrl, and then click a nonadjacent task.

2. **Click the Unlink Tasks button in the Schedule group on the Task tab (refer to Figure 4-6).**

Use the above method carefully. If you click only one task and then click the Unlink Tasks button, the result is somewhat drastic: *All* dependency relationships for that task are removed.

To remove dependency relationships in the Task Information dialog box, here's the drill:

1. **Double-click a successor task name.**

   The Task Information dialog box appears.

2. **Click the Predecessors tab to display it.**

3. **Click the Type box for the dependency you want to delete.**

   A list of dependency types appears, as shown in Figure 4-9.

Figure 4-9: You can use the Predecessors tab to create and delete dependency links.

4. **Choose None.**

5. **Click the OK button to save the change.**

   The dependency line on the Gantt chart is gone. The next time you open that Task Information dialog box, the dependency is gone, too.

Chapter 5

Estimating Task Time

• •

In This Chapter

▶ Determining task types

▶ Effort-driven tasks

▶ Estimating effort and duration

▶ Using constraints

▶ Entering the start date

▶ Splitting tasks

• •

*O*ne of the most challenging aspects of managing a project is estimating how long a task will take to complete. Your team members usually make a good guess on task duration and hope for the best. But the estimate is where the concept of "garbage in, garbage out" (or, scarier, "garbage in, gospel out") truly applies. After all, the duration of individual tasks combined with network logic and the applied calendars determines the overall duration of the project — at least on paper.

An accurate estimate accommodates the nature of the task and employs the most applicable technique for estimating. Sometimes you estimate the effort involved, and sometimes you estimate the duration (the number of business days); it all depends on the nature of the task and the level of accuracy you need.

An accurate estimate isn't the only aspect of making a schedule realistic. Project helps your schedule reflect reality by allowing you to enter constraints, pause tasks, and split tasks.

The schedule you build in Project is a model. It reflects what you think will happen — or what you plan for — given the information you enter. The more realistic the information you enter, the more realistic your schedule. However, ultimately, the schedule is a tool to help you and your team; it isn't reality. Do the best you can to acquire accurate data, but don't forget that you manage the schedule; it doesn't manage you.

You're in It for the Duration

In projects, as in life, timing is everything. Timing in your projects starts with the durations that you assign to tasks. Although Project helps you see the effect of the timing of your tasks on the overall length of your plan, it can't tell you how much time each task will take. That's up to you.

Estimating the duration of tasks isn't always easy. Your estimate has to be based on your experience with similar tasks and your knowledge of the specifics of your project.

If your projects often share similar tasks, consider saving a copy of your schedule as a template that you can use in the future, thereby saving yourself the effort of reestimating durations every time you start a similar project. Find out about saving templates in Chapter 19.

Tasks come in all flavors: Identifying task types

Before you begin to enter task durations, be aware of task types in Project; they have an effect on how Project schedules the work of a task using the automatic scheduling mode after you begin assigning resources.

Essentially, your choice of task type determines which element of the task remains constant (doesn't vary) when you make changes to the task:

- ✓ **Fixed Units:** When you assign resources (Project considers them fixed units) to a task, they continue to work on that task even if the duration changes. (This type is the default.) For example, if you assign someone full time to build a presentation for senior management and you set the duration for three days, and then you realize that five days is more realistic, the number of units stays the same. In other words, the same person is still working on the task full time, but for five days rather than three days.

- ✓ **Fixed Duration:** The task takes a set amount of time to complete, no matter how many resources you add to the mix. For example, a test on a substance that requires leaving the test running for 24 hours has a fixed duration, even if you add 20 scientists to oversee the test.

- ✓ **Fixed Work:** The number of resource hours assigned to the task determines its length. If you set the duration of a Fixed Work task at 40 hours, for example, and you assign two resources to work 20 hours each (simultaneously) at units of 100 percent, the task will be completed in 20 hours. If you remove one resource, the single resource must spend 40 hours at units of 100 percent to complete the task.

You can see how understanding the various task types (along with how each one causes the task timing or resource assignments to fluctuate) is an important part of creating an efficient project.

Follow these steps to set the task type:

1. **Double-click a task.**

   The Task Information dialog box appears.

2. **Click the Advanced tab, as shown in Figure 5-1.**

Figure 5-1: Setting the task type.

3. **Choose one of the three options from the Task Type list.**

4. **Click the OK button.**

You can also display the Type column on a Gantt Chart sheet and set the task type there.

Effort-driven tasks: 1 + 1 = ½

When you hear the word *effort* in Project, think *work*. For a task that's automatically scheduled, you can also set it up to be *effort driven:* If you adjust resource assignments, the duration might change, but the number of hours of effort (work) resources needed to complete the task stays the same. (Effort-driven scheduling isn't available for manually scheduled tasks.) When you add or delete a resource assignment on an effort-driven task, work is distributed equally among resources. (Refer to the description of fixed-work tasks in the preceding section.) In fact, all fixed-work tasks are effort driven. The more people you add, or the more hours they work, the shorter the duration, and vice versa.

A task type example

Because the task type is a complex concept, the example in this sidebar starts with a fixed-unit task that has a duration of 80 hours and two people assigned to the task full time for five days.

Change	Impact
Remove a resource.	The duration is recalculated to ten days. The work stays the same at 80 hours.
Increase the duration.	The work increases to be consistent with the new duration. If you increase the duration from five days to seven days, you add 32 hours of work (two units x two 8-hour days).
Increase the work.	The duration increases to accommodate the extra work. If the work changes from 80 hours to 96 hours, for example, the duration increases from five days to six.

Assume that the task type for the same task is Fixed Work. Thus, the work is set at 80 hours — no more, no less.

Change	Impact
Remove a resource.	The duration is recalculated to take ten days. The work stays the same at 80 hours.
Increase the duration.	The units increase to be consistent with the new duration. If you increase the duration from five days to seven, your resources are now only allocated. When Project divides the 80 hours by seven days, the result is 11.43 hours of work per day. You have two resources, so each resource works 5.7 hours per day.
Increase the work.	The duration increases to account for the extra work. If the work changes from 80 hours to 96 hours, the duration increases from five days to six.

Finally, assume that the same task has a fixed duration: The work must be done in five days.

Change	Impact
Remove a resource.	The remaining resource is overallocated by 100 percent. In other words, to complete the task, the person would have to work 16 hours per day (which is unlikely, of course).
Increase the duration.	The work increases to be consistent with the new duration. If you increase the duration from five days to seven, you add 32 hours of work (two units x two 8-hour days).
Increase the work.	The resources are either overallocated or you need to acquire an additional resource. If you have five days to accomplish 80 hours of work and you increase the work to 96 hours, your resources are 20 percent overallocated (96/80 = 1.2).

Suppose that you need to set up a computer network in a new office in two days. You assign to this task one resource who works 8 hours per day, so the work will take 16 hours to complete (two 8-hour days). If you then assign a second resource, this effort-driven task no longer takes two days, because the hours of effort required will be completed more quickly by the two people working simultaneously — in this case, in one 8-hour period.

Behind the scenes, effort-driven scheduling uses this formula to work this "magic":

```
Duration = Work ÷ Units
```

After you make the first assignment, any time you add or remove more units (people), Project recalculates the duration accordingly.

Adding resources doesn't cause a task to be completed sooner — in fact, the behavior changes from fixed work to fixed duration. Select the Effort Driven check box on the Advanced tab in the Task Information dialog box to enable or disable the Effort Driven setting; it isn't selected by default (refer to Figure 5-1). When you clear this check box, the same task that you set to run two days takes two days, no matter how much effort your resources contribute.

Table 5-1 describes limiting behaviors in working with Project on effort-driven tasks.

Table 5-1	Limiting Behaviors
Behavior	*What Happens*
First Assignment	When you first enter resources for an effort-driven task, the duration remains the same. If you add or delete resources after the task has been fully entered, the duration changes.
Fixed Work	Assigning additional resources reduces the task duration; reducing resources increases the duration. Fixed work is essentially effort-driven work, so you can't deselect the Effort Driven check box in fixed-work tasks.
Fixed Units	Assigning additional resources reduces the task duration; reducing resources increases the duration.
Fixed Duration	Assigning additional resources decreases the unit value of each resource; reducing resources increases the unit value of each resource.
Summary Tasks	Summary tasks can't be set to Effort Driven.
Inserted Projects	Inserted projects can't be set to Effort Driven.

Estimating Effort and Duration

Developing accurate estimates — whether for resources, durations, or costs — is one of the most challenging and contentious parts of managing a project. You should understand the nature of estimating and the difference between the effort needed to accomplish the work and the duration, which indicates the number of required work periods (task duration). Several techniques are available to help you develop estimates, depending on the nature of the work. You can start by looking at the difference between effort and duration and then at the skills you need to develop accurate estimates.

Effort is number of labor units required to complete a task. Effort is usually expressed as staff hours, staff days, or staff weeks.

Duration is the total number of work periods (not including holidays or other nonworking periods) required to complete a task. Duration is usually expressed as workdays or workweeks.

Estimating techniques

Sometimes, people seem to estimate durations by snatching them out of the air or consulting a Magic 8 Ball. Estimating is undoubtedly an art and a science. The art stems from the expert judgment that team members and estimators bring to the process. Their experience and wisdom from past projects are invaluable in developing estimates, determining the best estimating method, and evaluating estimates (or the assumptions behind them) to assess their validity. In addition to the artful contribution of experts, team members, and estimators, a number of methods comprise the science of estimating.

Analogous estimating

Analogous estimating is the most common method of estimating. The aforementioned experts normally conduct this form of estimating. In its most basic form, this method compares past projects with the current project, determines their areas of similarity and areas of difference, and then develops an estimate accordingly.

A more robust application determines the duration drivers and analyzes the relationship between past similar projects with the current project. Duration drivers can include size, complexity, risk, number of resources, weight, or whatever other aspects of the project influence duration.

If you want to use analogous estimating effectively, your projects must be similar in fact, not simply similar in appearance. A software upgrade may sound similar to someone who is not familiar with software, but there are vast differences in what a software upgrade entails, so one software upgrade is not necessarily similar to others. The difference between moving from Windows 7 to Windows 10, for example, is much different from moving from Project 2013 to Project 2016; the magnitude of the work, and thus the time is different!

Parametric estimating

Parametric estimating uses a mathematical model to determine project duration. Though not all work can be estimated using this method, it's quick and simple: Multiply the quantity of work by the number of hours required to accomplish it. For example, if a painter can paint 100 square feet per hour and you have 6,000 square feet to paint, you can assume 60 hours of effort. If three people are painting (60 ÷ 3), the task should take 20 hours, or the equivalent of 2.5 days.

Three-point estimating

When a lot of uncertainty, risk, or unknown factors surround an activity or a work package, you can use *three-point estimating* to produce a range and an expected duration. In this method, you collect three estimates based on these types of scenarios:

- ✔ **Best case:** In this optimistic (represented by the letter *O*) scenario, all required resources are available, nothing goes wrong, and everything works correctly the first time. You might see this type represented instead as t_o (for *time* optimistic).

- ✔ **Most likely:** The realities of project life are factored into the estimate, such as the extended unavailability of a resource, a work interruption, or an error that causes a delay. The *most-likely* (or M) scenario can also be represented by t_m (*time* most likely).

- ✔ **Worst case:** This *pessimistic* (P) estimate assumes unskilled resources, or insufficient resources, a great deal of rework, and delays. It's represented by t_p (for *time* pessimistic).

The simplest way to develop the expected duration, or t_e (*time* expected) is to sum the three estimates and divide by 3. However, this technique isn't the most accurate one because it assumes — unrealistically — an equal probability that the best-case, most-likely, and worst-case scenarios would occur. In reality, the most-likely estimate has a greater chance of occurring than either the best-case or worst-case scenarios. Therefore, weight the most-likely scenario and determine the weighted average.

The most common way to calculate the weighted average is

$$t_e = (t_o + 4t_m + t_p) / 6$$

Setting the task duration

Most tasks in a project (except milestones) have a duration, whether it's ten minutes or a year or another span of time. The needs of your project and the degree of control you require determine how finely you break down your tasks.

If your project is to launch a satellite, for example, tracking the task duration by minutes on launch day makes sense. In most other circumstances, tracking the duration by days (or weeks, sometimes) is sufficient.

As with all task information, you can enter the duration in a Gantt Chart sheet or in the Task Information dialog box. Follow these steps to enter the duration in the dialog box:

1. **Double-click a task to display the Task Information dialog box.**

2. **If necessary, click the General tab to display it.**

3. **In the Duration box, use the spinner arrows to increase or decrease the duration, as shown in Figure 5-2.**

Figure 5-2:
Setting the duration.

4. **If the current duration units aren't appropriate (for example, days when you want hours), type a new duration in the Duration box.**

   A new task is created with an estimated duration of one day unless you change the duration. You can use these abbreviations for various time units:

   - *m:* Minute
   - *h:* Hour
   - *d:* Day
   - *w:* Week
   - *mo:* Month

Don't assume that changing the start and finish dates of a task changes its duration; it doesn't. You have to manually change the duration. If you don't, your project plan won't be what you intended.

5. **Click the OK button to accept the duration setting.**

If you're unsure about the timing of a particular task, select the Estimated check box (on the General tab) when you enter the duration. This strategy alerts people to your lack of certainty. You can always go back and uncheck the box when you have better information.

Controlling Timing with Constraints

In Project, *constraints* are timing conditions that control an automatically scheduled task. You tell Project which (if any) constraints are required for each task. Because manually scheduled tasks must follow the start and finish dates you specify for them, they already have de facto constraints.

Understanding how constraints work

When you create a task and set it to be automatically scheduled, the As Soon As Possible constraint is selected by default. In other words, the task starts as soon as the project starts, assuming that no dependencies with other tasks exist that would delay it.

A task's start and finish dates, task dependencies, task type, Effort Driven setting, and constraints all work together to set the timing of each task. However, when Project performs calculations to save you time in a project that's running late, constraint settings are considered sacred (untouchable).

For example, if you set a constraint that a task must finish on a certain date, Project shifts almost any other scheduled task to recalculate the timing before suggesting that the task might finish on another date.

The excessive use of constraints limits your scheduling flexibility. Use constraints only when you absolutely need to force a task's timing.

Table 5-2 describes the effects of constraints on a task's timing.

Table 5-2	Task Constraints
Constraint	*What Happens When You Apply It*
As Soon As Possible	The task starts as early in the schedule as possible based on dependencies, calendars, and the project start date. (It's the default setting.)
As Late As Possible	The task occurs as late as possible in the schedule, based on dependencies, calendars, and the project's finish date.
Finish No Earlier Than	The end of the task can occur no earlier than the date you specify.
Finish No Later Than	The end of the task can occur no later than the date you specify.
Must Start On	The task must start on an absolute date.
Must Finish On	The task must finish on an absolute date.
Start No Earlier Than	The task can start no earlier than the date you specify.
Start No Later Than	The task can start no later than the date you specify.

Establishing constraints

To set a constraint, you select the type of constraint you want in the Task Information dialog box. Though you can set only one constraint for a task, some constraints work together with a date you choose. For example, if you want a task to start no later than a certain date, you select a date by which the task must start. Other settings, such as As Soon As Possible, work from a different date — in this case, the start date you set for the whole project or any dependency relationships you set up with other tasks. (See Chapter 4 for more about dependency relationships.)

To set a task constraint, follow these steps:

1. **Double-click a task.**

   The Task Information dialog box appears.

2. **Click the Advanced tab.**

3. **Select a constraint from the Constraint Type list (see Figure 5-3).**

4. **If the constraint requires a date, select one from the Constraint Date list.**

5. **Click the OK button to save the settings.**

Figure 5-3:
Setting a
constraint.

The default constraint, As Soon As Possible, is already set, so you usually don't need to modify it.

Setting a deadline

Sometimes I think that deadlines were made to be overlooked. Project agrees because, strictly speaking, deadlines aren't constraints (though the setting for the deadline is in the Constraint Task area of the Task Information dialog box, on the Advanced tab). Deadlines, which aren't the same as constraints, don't force the timing of task schedules. If you set a deadline and the task exceeds it, Project simply displays a symbol in the Indicator column to alert you so that you can panic — I mean, *take action* — appropriately.

To set a deadline, follow these steps:

1. **Double-click a task.**

   The Task Information dialog box appears.

2. **Click the Advanced tab.**

3. **Click the drop-down arrow in the Deadline field (shown in Figure 5-4) to display a calendar and then select a date.**

   If necessary, click the forward- or backward-facing arrow to move to a different month.

4. **Click the OK button to save the deadline setting.**

Figure 5-4: Setting a deadline.

Display a Deadline column in the Gantt Chart sheet pane to enter the deadline or to show yourself and others your targeted deadline date.

Starting and Pausing Tasks

When most people start using Project, they initially try to enter a start date for every task in the project. After all, you include dates when you create to-do lists, right? You're jumping the gun, though, and missing out on one of the great strengths of project management software: the capability to schedule tasks according to sometimes-complex combinations of factors, such as dependencies between tasks and task constraints. By allowing Project to determine the start date of a task, you allow it to make adjustments automatically when changes occur.

If you enter a task duration but not a start date for an automatically sched-uled task, that task starts by default as soon as possible after the project start date that you specified in the Project Information dialog box, based on any dependencies you set up between tasks. For manually scheduled tasks, you eventually have to specify a start date to set the beginning schedule for the task.

Certain tasks, however, must start on a specific date. Examples are holidays, annual meetings, and the first day of the fishing season.

Project sets the finish date of a task based on when the task starts and on the task duration — along with any calendar that has been set up. If a task must finish on a certain date, however, you can set a finish date and let Project determine the start date.

Entering the task's start date

Setting a start date or a finish date for a task applies a kind of constraint on it that can override dependency relationships or other timing factors. A task constraint is the preferred way to force a task to start or end on a certain day. If you determine, however, that a particular task must begin or end on a set date no matter what, you can enter a specific start or finish date. Setting the start or finish date is simple.

To enter a start or finish date for a task, simply follow these steps:

1. **Double-click a task.**

   The Task Information dialog box appears.

2. **Click the General tab, if it's not already displayed.**

3. **Click the drop-down arrow at the end of the Start box or the Finish box.**

   A calendar appears.

4. **Click a date to select it, or click the forward- or backward-facing arrow to move to a different month and select a date.**

   If the current date is the date you want, take a shortcut and click the Today button on the drop-down calendar.

5. **Click the OK button.**

When Project determines timing, a Must Start On constraint overrides the start date that is calculated based on start dates and durations.

Taking a break: Splitting tasks

Did you ever start a task — filing your taxes, for example — and find that you simply had to drop everything before you were done and go do something else? (In the case of filing my taxes, I usually need a break for a good cry.)

Projects work the same way. Sometimes, tasks start and then have to be placed on hold before they can start again later — for example, if you experience a work shutdown caused by labor negotiations. Or perhaps you can anticipate a delay in the course of a task and you want to structure it that way when you create it. In this case, you can use a Project feature to split a task so that a second or third portion starts at a later date, with no activity in the interim. You can place as many splits in a task as you like.

Follow these steps to split a task:

1. **On the Task tab of the Ribbon, click the Split Task button in the Schedule group.**

   A readout appears and guides you as you set the start date for the continuation of the task.

2. **Move the mouse pointer over the taskbar on the Gantt chart, and adjust the pointer's position until the box displays the date on which you want to start the task split; then drag to the right until the box contains the date on which you want the task to begin again.**

3. **Release the mouse button.**

   The split task shows up as a short task, a series of dots, and then the rest of the task, as shown in Figure 5-5.

Split task button

Figure 5-5:
Splitting a task.

To rejoin a split task, place the mouse cursor over the taskbar until the move cursor appears, and then drag the split taskbar backward to join with the other portion of the taskbar.

Don't use the split-task approach to place an artificial hold on a task until another task is complete. Suppose that you start testing a product and then have to wait for approval before finalizing the test results. In this case, create a Testing task, a Final Approval milestone, and a Finalize Test Results task — and then create dependency relationships among them. This way, if a task runs late, your final task shifts along with it instead of being set in stone (as a split task can be).

Chapter 6

Check Out This View!

In This Chapter

▶ Finding your way around Project

▶ Exploring Project views

▶ Personalizing views for your needs

*I*n Project, a *view* is a way to display task and resource information. It's essentially a template with a predetermined set of columns in the worksheet, a way to enter data in a pane, or a way to view data in a chart. Though earlier chapters in this book describe how to enter task information into a worksheet in Gantt Chart view (the default view and the most common view), it is by no means the *only* way to look at data in Project. Project has 27 different views that you can use to look at and analyze your project data.

After you know how to enter basic task information into Project, you can begin to display the information in different ways. First, I give you a high-level explanation of views and then dip into more detail about the more common views. Though I can't possibly cover every combination of data that you might want to see, I show you how to customize the views in Project to look at data in the way that best suits your needs at the time.

A Project with a View

Views organize data so that you can see information in logical ways. Because of the complexity of information in a typical Project schedule, Project offers many views for slicing and dicing (organizing) the information. If an average word processing document is as complex as a cookie, your average Project file is more like a five-tier wedding cake adorned with intricate flowers and garlands in delicate swirls of sugary icing.

A Project file holds information about these elements:

- ✔ **Tasks:** Task name, duration, start and finish dates, assigned resources, costs, constraints, and dependencies, for example

- ✔ **Resources:** Resource name, resource type, rate per hour, overtime rate, department, cost per use, and others

- ✔ **Assignments:** Information about which resources will complete which tasks, including hours of work, units of effort, and remaining work

- ✔ **Timing and progress:** Several types of calendars, project start and finish dates, percentage of tasks completed, resource hours spent, baseline information, critical path information, and more

- ✔ **Financial information:** Earned value, time-and-cost variance, and projected costs for work not completed, for example

Navigating tabs and views

For each project schedule file you create, Project essentially builds an extensive database of information. The different views in Project enable you to zero in on different combinations of the data you need. Having several views from which to observe your project information is helpful, but having all those views does you no good if you don't know how to move around in a view after you find it or how to move from one to another.

One way to move from one view to another is by using the Task tab on the Ribbon. Clicking the bottom section (with the down arrow) of the Gantt Chart button to the left of the Task tab displays a menu of Project's most-often-used views, as shown in Figure 6-1, as well as any custom views you create. Simply click any listed view to display it. In case it isn't obvious, clicking the top section of the Gantt Chart button redisplays Gantt Chart view.

You can see the same list of views by going to the Resource tab and clicking the View group's Team Planner drop-down menu.

Clicking the View tab on the Ribbon gives you all kinds of options for selecting a view. Using the Task Views group on the far left end, you can select the Gantt Chart, Task Usage, Network Diagram, Calendar, Task Sheet, Task Form, or Timeline view. The Resource Views group enables you to select the Team Planner, Resource Usage, Resource Sheet, Resource Graph, or Resource Form view. Other groups on the View tab offer choices for sorting data, changing the timescale, and zooming a view to see it better. You can also split the view by adding the timescale to whichever view is active, or you can add details to a specific view. Check out Chapter 1 for more on navigating around Project 2016.

Figure 6-1:
View
choices.

The lower-right corner of the Project window has buttons for jumping directly to the Gantt Chart, Task Usage, Team Planner, Resource Sheet, and Report views.

In addition to the views you can display via the Task tab or the View tab, you may need to use one of the dozen or so other views as you work on your project. To display views not directly available via the Ribbon, follow these steps:

1. **Select either the Task tab or Resource tab on the Ribbon.**

2. **Click the down arrow on the Gantt Chart button.**

3. **Click More Views at the bottom of the menu.**

   The More Views box appears, as shown in Figure 6-2.

4. **Use the scroll bar to locate the view you want.**

5. **Select the view you want and click the Apply button.**

If you liked the View bar that was available in earlier versions of Project, you can still use it: Right-click the gray bar on the left side of Project, and choose View Bar to display the View bar. To hide it again, right-click the View bar and choose View Bar.

Figure 6-2:
More than
two dozen
views are
available for
display in
Project.

Scrolling around

The simplest views, such as Calendar view, have a single pane, with horizontal and vertical scroll bars. Other views, such as Resource Usage view (shown in Figure 6-3), have two panes: Each pane has its own horizontal scroll bar, and because the panes share the vertical scroll bar, the panes move up and down together.

Figure 6-3:
Multiple
panes of
information
maximize
space in
many views.

In most views with two panes, the pane to the left is the *sheet* — a spreadsheet-like interface that displays columns of information. To the right of this view is the *chart;* it uses bars, symbols, and lines to represent each task in your project and the dependency relationships among them.

At the top of the chart area is the *timescale.* This tool is used as a scale against which you can interpret the timing of the taskbars. To see your plan in greater or lesser timing detail, you modify the time units used in the timescale. For example, you can look at your tasks in detail over days or in a broader overview in months.

See the "Changing the timescale" section, later in this chapter, to find out how to change the time increments displayed in the timescale.

By using the horizontal scroll bars in each pane, you can view additional columns or additional periods in any pane with a timescale. Timescale panes cover the life of the project.

Use these methods to work with scroll bars:

- ✓ **Drag the scroll box on a scroll bar until you reach the location in the pane that you want to look at.** When you drag the scroll box to move in a timescale display, the date display indicates where you are at any time in the scrolling calendar. Release the mouse button when the date display matches the date you want to view.

- ✓ **Click to the left or right of the horizontal scroll box to move one page at a time.** Note that a page in this instance is controlled to some extent by how you resize a given pane. For example, with a timescale pane and a timescale set to weeks, you move one week at a time. In a sheet pane that displays three columns, you move to the next (or preceding) column.

- ✓ **Click the right or left arrow at either end of a scroll bar to move in smaller increments.** On a sheet pane, you move about one half column per click. In a timescale view with weeks displayed, you move about a day at a time.

Reaching a specific spot in your plan

To reach a particular area of your Project plan, you can also press the F5 key to use the Go To feature. Simply enter either of two items in the Go To dialog box when you want to find a task:

- ✓ A date from a drop-down calendar
- ✓ A task ID

You can also click the Scroll to Task button on the far right of the Task tab of the Ribbon (or press Ctrl+Shift+F5) to scroll the chart pane of the view to show the taskbar for a selected task in the sheet pane.

The task ID, which is a number that's assigned automatically whenever you create a task, provides a unique identifier for every task in the plan.

To see more or less detail in your schedule, use the Zoom command on the View tab — in every view. Read more about using the Zoom button in the sidebar "Zooming in and out," later in this chapter.

For more about modifying the format of elements displayed in a view, see Chapter 13.

More Detail about Views

Finding out how to use Project views to enter, edit, review, and analyze Project data can help you focus your attention on the aspects of the project you are interested in, whether it's resources, budget, task sequencing, or some other aspect. Don't worry that you'll be overwhelmed by the number of views you can use: After a while, using them will become second nature.

This section describes the most common views: Gantt Chart, Resource Sheet, Team Planner, Network Diagram, Timeline, and Calendar.

Home base: Gantt Chart view

Gantt Chart view is similar to a favorite room in your house — the place where your family members most often hang out. It's the view that appears first whenever you open a new project. Gantt Chart view, shown in Figure 6-4, is a combination of spreadsheet data and a chart with a graphical representation of tasks; it offers a wealth of information in one place. The spreadsheet can display any combination of columns of data that you want.

Gantt Chart view has two major sections: the sheet pane on the left and the chart pane on the right. In Gantt Chart view (or in any view with a sheet pane), you can use tables to specify which information is shown in the sheet. A *table* is a preset combination of columns (fields) of data that you can easily display by going to the View Tab, and then clicking the Table button in the Data Group. From there you can choose one of nine preset tables:

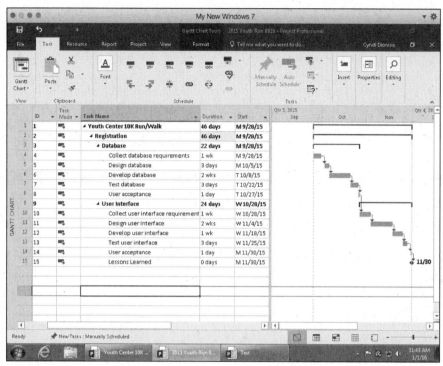

Figure 6-4:
Gantt Chart
view.

✔ Cost

✔ Entry (the default table)

✔ Hyperlink

✔ Schedule

✔ Tracking

✔ Variance

✔ Work

✔ Summary

✔ Usage

You can also customize the column display of any table by displaying or hiding individual columns of data, one at a time. (See the section "Displaying different columns," later in this chapter, for information about this procedure.)

Resourceful views: Resource Sheet and Team Planner

In Resource Sheet view, shown in Figure 6-5, you add the resources that will handle the work in your project. You can type entries in cells and press the Tab and arrow keys to move around. Chapter 7 describes the purpose of each field in this view and tells you how to set up your resource information correctly.

Team Planner view, shown in Figure 6-6, shows you what each team member is scheduled to work on, and when. You can change an assignment by simply dragging it from one resource to another. Voilà — assignment problems solved! You can find out more about this view in Chapter 9.

Getting your timing down with the Timeline

Your sponsor and the project's client may not want to see every detail in your grand plan. If you need to share project information with a person whose eyes glaze over easily, meet your new best friend: the Project Timeline. Appearing in its own, small pane (by default) with certain other views, it presents a simplified picture of the entire schedule. As shown in Figure 6-7, you can also display individual tasks, parent tasks, or milestones on the Timeline. To display the Timeline go to the View Tab, Split View, and click Timeline. Chapter 18 delves into how to work with the Timeline and use it as a communication tool.

Figure 6-6:
Team
Planner
view.

Figure 6-7:
Timeline
view covers
the whole
schedule.

Going with the flow:
Network Diagram view

The organization of information in Network Diagram view, as shown in
Figure 6-8, represents the workflow in your project in a series of task boxes.
The boxes include dependency lines that connect them to reflect the sequence
of tasks. (See Chapter 4 for more about dependency relationships.) You read
this view from left to right; earlier tasks on the left flow into later tasks and
subtasks to the right. Tasks that happen in the same time frame are aligned
vertically above each other. Tasks with an X through them have been marked
as complete. Tasks with only one line through them have some progress but
are less than 100 percent complete.

Traditionally known as a *PERT chart,* the network diagram method was
developed by the U.S. Navy in the 1950s for use in building the Polaris mis-
sile program.

Figure 6-8:
Network
Diagram
view.

Network Diagram view has no timescale; the view isn't used to see specific timing, but to see the general logical order of tasks in a plan. However, each task box, or *node,* holds specific timing information about each task, such as its start date, finish date, and duration. (You can customize the information in the task boxes, as described in the later section "Customizing Views.") Timeline view appears by default along the top of this view.

Calling up Calendar view

Who can conceive of creating a schedule without opening a calendar? This familiar view of time is one of the many views offered in Project. Calendar view, as shown in Figure 6-9, looks like a monthly wall calendar, with boxes that represent days on a calendar in rows that represent the days in a week. Using this view, you can see all tasks that are scheduled to happen in any given day, week, or month.

You can modify Calendar view to display as many weeks as you need by clicking the Custom button located directly along the upper-left side of the calendar and changing the Number of Weeks setting in the Zoom dialog box.

More than two dozen views are built into Project. You encounter many more as you work on specific elements of Project in this book.

Figure 6-9:
Calendar
view.

Customizing Views

Just when you thought you were starting to get a handle on the two dozen or so views available in Project, I dazzle you with even more possibilities: Every one of those views can be customized to show a different type of information.

You can customize every view in Project to show specific types of information. For example, you can choose to show columns of information in spreadsheets, labels in Network Diagram boxes or taskbars, and sets of data in graph views. You can also modify the size of panes of information and adjust the timescale.

Why all this flexibility with the information you see onscreen? At various times in a project, you need to focus on different aspects of your tasks. If you're having a problem with costs, take a look at Resource Usage view and insert various columns of cost information, such as resource rates and total actual costs. If your plan is taking longer than the Hundred Years' War, consider displaying Tracking Gantt view and looking at a bunch of baseline columns with timing and dependency data or examining the project's critical path in the chart pane. If you need to display more of the sheet area so that you can read those columns without having to scroll, you can do that, too. In the following sections, you find out how to do all the things you need to do to show a variety of information in each view.

Working with view panes

In addition to Gantt Chart view, several views have two panes, such as Task Usage, Tracking Gantt, and Resource Usage. When the Timeline appears with a view, it appears in a third, horizontal pane at the top. You can modify the information you see in the sheet pane as well as the scale for timing in the chart pane. You can also display information near taskbars in the chart pane.

Resizing a pane

In views that show more than one pane, you can reduce or enlarge each pane. This capability helps you see more information in one area, depending on your focus at the time.

The overall area occupied by the panes is constant, so when you enlarge one pane, you reduce the other.

Follow these steps to change the size of a pane in a view:

1. **Place the mouse pointer over the edge of a pane.**

2. **When you see a pointer composed of a line and two arrows pointing in opposite directions, you can drag the pointer to resize the pane:**

   • *Drag to the left:* Enlarge the pane on the right.

   • *Drag to the right:* Enlarge the pane on the left.

   • *Drag up or down:* Change the size of the Timeline pane versus the area that's available for the rest of the view.

3. **Release the mouse button.**

   The panes are resized.

Changing the timescale

I wish I could tell you that Project lets you control time and bestow lots more of it on your project, but it doesn't. What it does allow you to do is modify the timescale to display your plan in larger or smaller time increments.

A *timescale* consists of a possible total of three tiers that you can use to display different time increments. For example, the top tier can mark months; the middle tier, weeks; and the bottom tier, days. This variety of detail lets you easily observe the overall task length and points in time during the life of the task. You can use all three tiers, only the middle tier, or the middle and bottom tiers (as shown in Figure 6-10). This feature is especially helpful because projects can span several weeks to several years, such as construction or pharmaceutical projects. This scaling feature is the only way to view such large-scale efforts.

Figure 6-10:
The three-tiered Timescale dialog box.

You can modify the units of time and the alignment of each tier and also add tick lines to mark the beginning of each increment on the timescale. You also decide whether to include nonworking time on the timescale. For example, if you add an indication of nonworking time on a project for which weekends are nonworking, Saturdays and Sundays are indicated by a shaded area in the display, which can make a useful visual divider between weeks.

You can also display text labels near taskbars and specify which data is included. Labels can be placed above, below, inside, or to the left or right of the taskbars. Especially in projects where you display many columns of data and a lengthy schedule, a taskbar can be placed far to the right of the sheet pane data. You can then include information such as task name or start date alongside the taskbar to make your plan more readable.

To modify the timescale, select the View tab, click the drop-down arrow next to Timescale in the Zoom group, and choose the time increments you want visible on the chart. If you select Timescale in the drop-down list, you can modify the information on any of the three tiers. Here's how:

1. **Click the View tab.**

2. **Click the Timescale format at the bottom of the Timescale drop-down menu.**

   The Timescale dialog box opens (refer to Figure 6-10).

3. **Click a tier tab and select a style for Units, Label, and Align.**

4. **Set the count.**

   For example, if your Units choice is weeks and you change the Count option to 2, the timescale appears in two-week increments.

5. To prevent the display of a certain tier, select One Tier or Two Tiers from the Show drop-down list in the Timescale Options section.

6. If you want Project to use fiscal-year notation in the timescale, select the Use Fiscal Year check box.

   For example, if your 2016 fiscal year begins July 1, 2016, 2017 applies to all months in the fiscal year. Set the fiscal year by choosing File ⇨ Options ⇨ Schedule.

7. To show marks at the beginning of each unit of time, select the Tick Lines check box.

8. Repeat Steps 2 through 6 for each tier that you want to modify.

9. Click the Non-Working Time tab.

10. In the Formatting options, select the one you prefer.

    Your choices are to have the shaded area for nonworking time appear behind taskbars or in front of taskbars or to simply not appear.

11. In the Color or Pattern list, select different options for the shading format.

12. Click the Calendar setting and select a different calendar on which to base the timescale.

    You can find out more about calendar choices in Chapter 8.

13. Click the OK button to save your new settings, which apply only to the timescale for the currently displayed view.

Use the Size setting on the three tier tabs to shrink the display proportionately and to squeeze more information on your screen or the printed page.

Zooming in and out

One way to modify the display of any Project view is to use the Zoom menu on the View tab of the Ribbon. This feature shows you a longer or shorter period in your project without your having to change the timescale settings manually. When you need to see several years at a time in your project, for example, click Zoom and then Zoom Out several times until as many months or years as you like can fit into the view.

You can also choose Zoom Entire Project in the Zoom group to show the entire project on the screen. Another nifty technique is to click the Zoom Selected Tasks button. The chart moves so that the bar representing the task is shown on the chart screen. Another quick (but less precise) way to zoom is to use the Zoom slider in the lower-right corner of the Project window. Drag it left to zoom out and drag right to zoom in.

Use these keystroke combinations to navigate the timescale:

✔ **Alt+Home:** Move to the beginning of the project.

✔ **Alt+End:** Move to the end of the project.

✔ **Alt+right arrow:** Scroll the timescale to the right.

✔ **Alt+left arrow:** Scroll the timescale to the left.

✔ **Alt+Page Down:** Move the timescale one page to the right.

✔ **Alt+Page Up:** Move the timescale one page to the left.

Displaying different columns

Each spreadsheet view has certain default columns of data that are stored in tables. Gantt Chart view with the Tracking table displayed, for example, has data related to the progress of tasks. The Resource sheet contains many columns of data about resources that can be useful for entering new resource information. In addition to choosing to display predefined tables of columns, you can modify any spreadsheet table to display any columns you like.

To insert a column, go to the Format tab. In the Columns group, click Insert Column. Another option is to follow this procedure to show selected columns of data:

1. **Scroll the table to the right, and click the Add New Column heading.**

   A list of available columns appears. The available columns are shown in alphabetical order — I'm only showing you 34 here and I'm not even through the Bs! So yes, as you can see in Figure 6-11 there are quite a few options to choose from!

2. **In the list, select the field that contains the information you want to include.**

   Typing the first letter of the field name scrolls the list more quickly.

3. **If you want to enter a different label for the field heading, right-click the field heading and choose Field Settings; type the name in the Title box and click the OK button.**

   The title in the current view appears in the column heading for this field.

4. **Move the mouse pointer over the column heading, drag the column to the left or right, and reposition the column where you want it relocated within the table.**

To hide a column, right-click its heading in the sheet pane and then choose Hide Column. Or, to insert a column at a particular location, right-click the column heading at that location and choose Insert Column. It's then inserted directly to the left of the selected column.

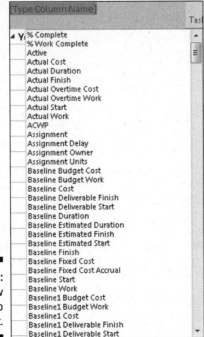

Figure 6-11:
New
columns to
insert.

You can display preset tables of sheet data, such as Tracking for recording progress on tasks or Entry for entering new task information: Simply choose View⇨Tables (in the Data group) and then click the name of the table you want to display.

Modifying Network Diagram view

Network Diagram view is useful for understanding the flow of tasks throughout your project, and it can help you understand which series of tasks determines the overall project duration. Known as the *critical path,* it's the longest chain of tasks (in duration, not in number of tasks) in your project. The tasks on the critical path are *critical* tasks; tasks that aren't on the critical path are *noncritical* tasks.

When you first display Network Diagram view, you see boxes of various types — one for each task in your project. You can modify the information contained in those boxes and modify the field formatting.

By default, a typical task contains the task name, task ID, start date, finish date, duration, and resource name. A milestone displays only the milestone date, milestone name, and task ID number.

Different categories of tasks (such as *critical* or *noncritical*) can contain different information, and you can modify the field information contained in any individual box or category of boxes.

See Chapter 4 for more on adding information about tasks and milestones.

Changing what's in the box

Sometimes, you want to see information about task timing, and at other times, you focus on other issues, such as resources. To accommodate these various information needs, Network Diagram view allows you to use various templates for the information contained in the diagram boxes.

To modify the information included in these boxes, follow these steps:

1. **Right-click anywhere in Network Diagram view outside any box and choose Box Styles in the right-click menu.**

   The Box Styles dialog box appears, as shown in Figure 6-12.

Figure 6-12:
You can use templates of data for task boxes in Network Diagram view.

2. **In the Style Settings For list, select a task category.**

3. **To modify the data included in the task boxes, select a different template from the Data Template list.**

   You can choose additional templates (and edit any template to include whatever data you like) by clicking the More Templates button.

   A preview of the data included in the template appears in the Preview area.

4. **Click the OK button to save the new template.**

You can also apply different templates to each box separately by right-clicking a box (rather than clicking outside it), choosing Format Box, selecting a different template from the Data Template drop-down list, and then clicking the OK button.

Beautifying diagram boxes

Are you the creative type? Do you dislike the shape or color of the boxes in Network Diagram view? Do you want to add shading to the box backgrounds? Project lets you do all this and more.

Follow these steps to modify the format of Network Diagram boxes:

1. **Right-click anywhere in Network Diagram view outside any box and choose Box Styles in the right-click menu.**

   The Box Styles dialog box appears, as shown in Figure 6-13.

Figure 6-13: The Box Styles dialog box in Network Diagram view.

2. **Click the Shape drop-down list and select a different shape from the list that appears.**

3. **Click the Color drop-down list in the Border section and select a different color from the list of colors.**

   Note: This choice specifies the color of the line that forms the box, not a background color. For that topic, see Step 5 in this list.

4. **Click the Width drop-down list and select a line width from the ones that are displayed.**

5. **Click the Color drop-down list in the Background section and select a color for the background that fills the inside of each box.**

6. **Click the Pattern drop-down list and select a pattern of lines to fill the interior of each box.**

7. **Click the OK button to save the new settings.**

Combinations of certain patterns and colors in backgrounds can make the text in the box difficult to read, so look at the preview in the Box Styles dialog box to ensure that your combination works.

You can also format *individual* boxes by right-clicking a box, choosing Format Box, and formatting the border, and background as described in the information on Box Styles earlier.

Modifying the Network Diagram layout

You can modify the layout of Network Diagram view by right-clicking outside a box and selecting Layout. As shown in Figure 6-14, you can either allow Project to position the boxes or position them manually. You can also define how to lay out the boxes and whether to show summary tasks.

Figure 6-14: Modifying the Network Diagram layout.

Cosmetic options include defining the link style and whether to show link labels or connector arrows. You can set the critical path to show in a specific color (red is the default) and change the background color.

A neat trick in Network Diagram view is to edit the layout to show link labels. (Right-click outside any task nodes, choose Layout, and then select the Show Link Labels check box.) A code, such as FS (for finish-to-start), is displayed to explain the type of dependency that each dependency line represents. You can also collapse the boxes so that only the task number appears. Simply right-click outside a box and select Collapse Boxes. You might also want to zoom the Network Diagram view to show as much information as you need. Figure 6-15 shows collapsed diagram boxes and the link labels on the dependency lines.

Figure 6-15:
The
modified
Network
Diagram
view.

Resetting the view

Most changes you make in a view apply as long as you have saved them. But if you've made so many changes that the view is now messy, you can reset it at any time: Click the Task tab on the Ribbon, click the bottom of the Gantt Chart button, and click Reset to Default. Once you click Yes, the view reverts to the default view.

Part II
Managing Resources

In this part . . .

✔ Identify all the resources you need to complete the project.

✔ Create and share resources.

✔ Assign resources to get the work done.

✔ Determine project costs.

Chapter 7

Creating Resources

· ·

In This Chapter

▶ Understanding work and material resources

▶ Creating resources to complete your project

▶ Setting resource availability

▶ Benefitting from resource groups and shared resources

· ·

*P*rojects utilize people, equipment, and materials, and these people, equipment, and materials are called project *resources.*

Using resources wisely is the delicate art of combining the right resources with the right skills and assigning those resources to invest the right amount of time (or units) for tasks. And you have to do this without overbooking anyone or anything at any point in the schedule.

A resource, because it affects timing and costs, is a big deal in Project. For this reason, many tools are available to help you create resources, specify how and when they'll work, assign them to tasks, manage their costs, and manipulate their workload. The first step in working with resources is to create them and enter certain information about them. That's what this chapter is all about.

Resources: People, Places, and Things

Many people hear the word *resources* and think that it means *people.* Well, people are indeed frequently used as project resources, but they're only part of the story. Resources can also consist of equipment you rent or buy or materials such as wood or iron. You can even create resources that represent facilities you have to rent by the hour, such as laboratories or meeting spaces.

Here are some typical project resources (and one not-so-typical resource):

- ✔ Engineer
- ✔ Office supplies
- ✔ Hotel ballroom
- ✔ Administrative assistants
- ✔ Furniture
- ✔ Computer software
- ✔ Graphical designer
- ✔ Rocket fuel

You get the picture. Resources can be practically anything or anyone that you use to complete your project.

You can also create a resource as a cost placeholder if you're tracking costs using Project. For example, you might assign a resource named Plant Visit a cost of $750 to cover airfare, hotel, and rental car charges for the visit.

Becoming Resource-Full

After you create and organize the tasks in your project, the next step, typically, is to create its resources. Before you create resources in Project 2016 willy-nilly, though, you must understand how they affect your project.

Understanding resources

First and foremost, a *resource* is an asset that helps accomplish a project, whether the asset is a person, a piece of equipment, a material, or a supply. One aspect of working with resources effectively is to manage the workflow of any resource that has limited time availability for your project. When you create resources, you indicate their availability by hours in the day or days of the week. For example, one person may be available 50 percent of the time, or 20 hours in the standard 40-hour workweek, whereas another may be available full time (40 hours). When you assign these kinds of resources to your project, you can use various views, reports, and tools to see whether any resource is overbooked at any point during the project. You can also see when people are sitting around, twiddling their thumbs, or when they may be available to help on another task. You can even account for resources that work on multiple projects across your organization and ensure that they're being used efficiently.

Another aspect of working with resources effectively is understanding how the number of resources you assign to work on a task affects the duration of that task. In other words, if you have a certain amount of work to perform but few people to do that work, a typical task takes longer to finish than if scads of folks are available.

The task type determines whether a task's duration changes based on the number of resources assigned to it. (Chapter 5 describes task types.)

Finally, resources add costs to a project. To account for costs in your project — such as a person working many hours on a task, computers that you have to buy, or services that require fees — you must create resources and assign them to one or more tasks. I discuss project costs in Chapter 9.

Resource types: Work, material, and cost

For the purposes of resource planning, Project recognizes only these three types of resources:

- **Work:** This person, such as a programmer or plumber, can be reassigned but not depleted. Work resources are assigned to tasks to accomplish work.

- **Material:** Material has a unit cost and doesn't consume working hours, but it can be depleted. Examples of material costs are steel, wood, and books.

- **Cost:** Using a cost resource gives you the flexibility to specify the applicable cost, such as travel or shipping, every time you use the resource.

Deciding which resource type to use when adding an external vendor or equipment resource to the project can be tricky. If you want to avoid adding hours of work to the project when that resource is being used, don't set up the resource as a work resource. Use a cost resource or fixed-cost approach instead.

How resources affect task timing

Under Project 2016's default settings, effort-driven scheduling is turned off for both manually and automatically scheduled tasks. So no matter how many work resources you assign, the task duration stays the same and Project piles on more hours of work for the task, to reflect more effort.

However, in some cases of a fixed-unit or fixed-work task type, the addition or removal of resources assigned to the task should have an impact on the time it takes to complete the task. In essence, the old maxim "Two heads are better than one" may be modified to "Two heads are faster than one."

Suppose that one person is assigned to the Dig Ditch task, which requires four hours of effort. Two people assigned to the Dig Ditch task will finish the job in two hours because two hours are being worked by each resource simultaneously, which achieves four hours of effort in half the time. To make scheduling a task work this way, you first have to change the task to an auto-scheduled task by using the Auto Schedule button in the Tasks group on the Task tab. Then you have to turn on effort-driven scheduling by double-clicking the task, clicking the Advance tab in the Task Information dialog box, selecting the Effort Driven check box, as shown in Figure 7-1, and then clicking the OK button. (I discuss effort-driven tasks in Chapter 5.)

Figure 7-1:
The Effort Driven check box.

Assigning additional people to tasks doesn't always shorten work time proportionately, even though that's how Project calculates it. When you have more people, you also have more meetings, memos, duplicated effort, and conflicts, for example. If you add more resources to a task, consider also increasing the amount of effort required to complete that task to account for inevitable workgroup inefficiencies.

Estimating resource requirements

You usually know how many material resources it takes to complete a task: In most cases, you can use a standard formula to calculate the number of pounds, tons, yards, or another quantity. But how do you know how much effort your work resources must invest to complete the tasks in the project?

Include a certain amount of extra material resources if you think you will need it for rework or scrap.

As with many aspects of information you put into a Project schedule, determining the level of effort rests to a great degree on your own experience with similar tasks and resources. Still, remember these caveats:

- ✓ **Skill counts.** A less skilled or less experienced resource is likely to take more time to finish a task. Experiment — increase the duration by 20 percent for a less skilled resource, for example, or reduce it by 20 percent for a more skilled resource.

- ✓ **History repeats itself.** Look at previously completed projects and tasks. If you've tracked people's time, you can likely see how much effort was required in order to complete various types of tasks on other projects and draw parallels to your project. This technique for estimating effort duration is similar to analogous estimating, covered in Chapter 5.

- ✓ **Ask and you shall receive.** Ask the resources themselves to estimate how long they think a task will take. After all, the people doing the work should know best how long it takes.

Allow for reserve time in a project to account for unforeseen circumstances, such as resources being less skilled than you had planned. To ensure that milestone dates are met, many people add a task called Contingency Reserve or Buffer to their schedules immediately before a milestone delivery or the end of a phase.

The Birth of a Resource

Just as someone fills out the birth certificate whenever a baby is born, a form is filled out whenever a resource in Project is born (that is, *created*). On the Resource Information form, you enter information such as the resource name, the availability, and the rate per hour or cost per use. You can also enter optional information, such as the group (company workgroup) to which the resource belongs or the resource's email address.

You can create a resource as a single person or entity, a generic resource (such as a skill set with no person assigned, such as Assistant or Engineer), or even a group of several resources that work together. Many times in the early stages of project planning, you know only the resource skill you need, to be replaced later by a named individual who has both the time and the qualifications to complete the task.

Creating one resource at a time

On the simplest level, a resource (a person, a piece of equipment, or a material) is created as a single entity — a particular person or a meeting room or a piece of equipment. You create the resource by entering information in the Resource Information dialog box.

When you create a resource, you must type, at minimum, the resource name, though you can also add as much information as you want. Some people prefer to create all the resources first and add contact and cost information later. In Chapter 9, I describe in detail how to add the cost information for resources.

To create a resource using the Resource Information dialog box, follow these steps:

1. **Click the bottom of the Gantt Chart button on the Task tab in the View group of the Ribbon, and click Resource Sheet.**

2. **Double-click a blank cell in the Resource Name column.**

   You can also click the Information button in the Properties group on the Resource tab.

   The Resource Information dialog box appears, as shown in Figure 7-2.

Figure 7-2: These four tabs can hold a wealth of information about any resource.

3. **Type a name in the Resource Name text box.**

4. **Click the down arrow in the Type box (on the right) to choose Work, Material, or Cost.**

The settings that are available to you differ slightly, depending on which option you choose. For example, a material resource has neither the Email nor Logon Account option, and a work resource or cost resource has no Material Label option.

5. **For a material resource, enter a description of the units in the Material Label field.**

   For example, you might enter pounds for a Flour resource or tons for a Steel resource.

6. **In the Initials field, type an abbreviation or initials for the resource.**

   If you don't enter anything, the first letter of the resource name is inserted when you save the resource.

7. **Continue to enter any information you want to include about the resource.**

   This information may include an email address, the group type (a department, division, or workgroup, for example), booking type (proposed or committed), or code (such as a cost-center code).

   If you enter information in the Group field, you can then use the Filter, Sort, and Group By features to look at sets of resources. (See Chapter 11 for more about filtering and working with groups.)

8. **Click the OK button to save the new resource.**

To enter information about several resources at a time, display Resource Sheet view and enter information in the columns. You can even paste resources copied from another source (such as an Excel spreadsheet) into this view.

Identifying resources before you know their names

In the planning stages of a project, you often find that not all resources are assembled. Even well into the project, sometimes you don't know what resource you'll be using; you know only that you need a resource with a certain skill set to complete upcoming tasks. In this case, consider creating certain resources as generic resources.

To create a generic resource, give it a name that describes its skill, such as Engineer, Designer, or even Meeting Space (rather than a specific resource named Conference Room B). Then, in the Resource Information dialog box, be sure to select the Generic check box.

You can then display a Yes/No column titled *Generic* to identify these resources, and you can create a resource filter to filter for a Yes or No entry in the Generic column to filter resources by this characteristic.

No formula exists for using the Generic setting to recalculate your schedule based on resource availability. However, many people find this setting useful when they use rolling wave planning or when they aren't responsible for specific resource assignments (for example, assigning a temporary worker to a task when a temporary-hiring agency will choose the specific worker). For a refresher on rolling wave planning, see Chapter 3.

You can replace a generic resource name with the name of the resource that's added to your project. For example, if you enter **Engineer 1** as a resource, you can replace it with **Jim Taylor**, the name of the engineer who will do the work. To make the switch, go to Resource Sheet view and, in the Resource Name column, click the cell for the resource, type the new name, and press Enter. Don't worry if you've already assigned the generic resource to tasks in the project. Project updates all assignments with the new name.

Many hands make light work

Rather than assign people individually to a task, you can assign a group of people who typically work together. Being able to make a single assignment of a *consolidated resource* rather than several separate resources and assignments can be a time-saver in larger projects.

Suppose that you need eight security personnel for the Youth Center event, and you create a Security Personnel resource. You will have eight resources, so in the Resource Information dialog box you enter **800%** in the Units column in the Resource Availability box to indicate eight full-time resources.

No special setting is used to designate a multiple resource. However, you may want to indicate the number of resources by adding it to the resource name. For example, name your security personnel resource Eight Security Personnel. The defining factor in this type of resource is the maximum number of assignment units: 800% signifies eight resources in the group. Figure 7-3 shows Security Personnel with the Generic check box selected and the units at 800%.

Assigning a resource at less than 100 percent units creates a part-time assignment. Of course, another option is to keep the resource in the pool at 100 percent and assign them only part time to a task. It's your choice.

Figure 7-3:
Consolidated
resource.

Managing Resource Availability

Lots of Project 2016 features handle resources — in particular by helping you spot resource overallocation. *Overallocation* is a calculation, based on the resource's calendar and availability, indicating that too much work has been assigned based on this availability.

Consider Monica Mendez, an engineer who works a standard eight-hour day based on her calendar. Monica is assigned to the Write Final Report task at 50 percent of her availability and to the Create Design Specs task — which occurs at the same time as the report task — at 100 percent of her availability. Monica is now working at 150 percent of her availability, or 12 hours per day. Poor Monica is overbooked. Be careful — she might even quit the project.

A resource is assigned to a task at 100 percent availability (or units) by default, but you can modify that setting if you know that a resource will be assigned to several tasks and can only spend a limited amount of time working each one.

Estimating and setting availability

Availability is easier to estimate for some resources than for others. A manager is unlikely to devote an entire day to any single task, because he has to deal with all the employees who report to him and also sign authorizations, attend meetings concerning various projects, and develop budgets, for example. A production worker's availability may be simpler to pin down to a single task: If one manufacturing job spends three days on the line and one person is working on the line the entire time, it's more accurate to say that she is working on that task full time.

One mistake made by Project beginners is to overthink availability. Of course, no one spends eight hours every day on a single task in a project. Employees spend part of their workdays reading email, chatting with coworkers, and answering phone calls about issues unrelated to their projects. A resource may spend seven hours on a task one day and only three hours the next. Don't get hung up on a day-by-day resource schedule when estimating availability. If, over the life of a task, the employee focuses on it, 100 percent availability is an appropriate setting. If that person works only five days on a ten-day task, however, that's 50 percent availability, whether she works four hours per day for ten days or five full days at any point.

The Units (availability) setting helps you spot the overbooking of a resource who may work on multiple tasks at the same time in a project schedule.

To set default resource units to specify availability, follow these steps:

1. **Display the Resource Sheet view.**

2. **Click the Max column for the resource.**

3. **Type a number representing the percentage of time that the resource is available to work on the project.**

   For example, type **33** for a resource who's available one-third of the time or **400** for a resource who can provide four full-time workers. (Entries greater than 100 percent represent resources that provide a group or team to handle assignments.) The most common entry (the default) is 100 for a single resource working full time on assignments in the project.

4. **Press Enter or Tab.**

   The entry is completed.

Note that this only works for resources whose type is set to Work.

When a resource comes and goes

In addition to being available to a project only a certain percentage of the time (say, 50 percent of the project's entire duration), a resource may be available for only a certain period of time (perhaps April–June) during the life of the project — commonly, when you use a resource borrowed from another department or when you're working with a freelancer who's squeezing in your project with others. Another possible resource is one who's available half time for the first few days of the project and then full time for the remainder. In this case, you enter a date range in the Available From and Available To columns of the Resource Availability area in the Resource Information dialog box, as shown in Figure 7-4, to specify varying availability.

Figure 7-4:
Time periods and units of availability.

To specify a limited period during which a resource is available to work on your project, follow these steps:

1. **Display the Resource Sheet view.**

2. **Double-click a resource.**

   The General tab of the Resource Information dialog box appears (refer to Figure 7-4).

3. **Use the Available From and Available To columns (in the Resource Availability area) to specify the period of availability.**

4. **In the Units column in the same row, either click the arrows to raise or lower the availability in 50 percent increments, or type a number.**

   Press Enter to finish the entry.

5. **Repeat Steps 3 and 4 to specify additional periods of availability on subsequent rows in the Resource Availability area.**

6. **Click the OK button to save the setting.**

Sharing Resources

Many organizations manage lots of projects at the same time. Sometimes, a project is the only project of its type in a company, such as organizing an office move. Others, such as a building design project in an architectural firm, happen simultaneously with several other, similar projects and draw on many of the same resources, such as architects and draftspeople.

When an organization engages in projects of a similar nature at the same time, drawing from a centralized resource pool can save it time because it doesn't have to create resources that already exist. Tracking resources across projects can also be helpful.

You can use another time-saving Project feature to pull existing resources from a company address book or from your own Address Book in Outlook.

Skimming from resource pools

If you use Project throughout your company, you may have a *resource pool,* a centralized repository of common resources that allows project managers to assign those resources to their various projects. By using a resource pool, you can form a more realistic idea of how busy resources are across all projects at any time.

Creating sharer files

Both individual resources and generic resources can be created in a blank project as a resource pool and saved to an accessible location on your company network. Then any project manager can assign those resources to her own projects. These projects are then referred to as *sharer files* because they share resources from the resource pool. For example, if you have a pool of maintenance people whom everyone in your manufacturing company assigns to projects, create a Project file named `Resource Pools` and enter all the resources to share in Resource Sheet view. Or create the resource pool file named `CEO` and let everyone who is managing projects that require the CEO's involvement and assign him from that central location. Then use the resource-sharing tools in Project to assign these resources to tasks within your plan.

When anyone uses resource assignments from a sharer file, that information is also saved in the resource pool file. Then anyone can use that file to look at resource allocations across all projects in the organization.

TIP

Don't confuse resource pools with *enterprise resources,* which require that you set up Project Professional, Project Server, and Microsoft Office Project Web App. A resource pool is simply a Project file that contains only a list of resources in Resource Sheet view and is saved on a shared network drive for your workgroup or on your company server. Anyone with access to the resource pool file can assign the resources it contains to projects. A resource pool saves everybody the trouble of having to repeatedly create these resources in his or her individual projects.

To access a resource that's available to your entire organization, follow this procedure:

1. **Open the resource pool file and then open the file that will be the sharer file.**

   See the earlier sidebar "Creating sharer files" for information about the resource pool and sharer file.

2. **Working in the sharer file, choose Resource ⇨ Resource Pool ⇨ Share Resources.**

   The Share Resources dialog box appears.

3. **Specify the resources for the project.**

   If you want to specify that a project will use only its own resources (the default setting), select the Use Own Resources option. If you want to share resources, select the Use Resources option and then choose a project from the From list.

4. **Specify what Project should do when a conflicting resource setting, such as the resource base calendar, exists.**

   If your project's setting will take precedence, select the Sharer Takes Precedence option. If you want the pool setting to rule, select Pool Takes Precedence.

5. **Click the OK button to complete the process.**

   All resources in the specified resource pool are added to your own project's resource list, ready to be assigned to tasks.

After you add a shared resource to your project, you can update shared resource information, in case the person who maintains those shared resources has made a change, such as increasing the resource's rate per hour. To do this, choose Resource ⇨ Resource Sharing ⇨ Refresh Resource Pool.

Drowning in the resource pool

Drawing resources from resource pools saves you time because you don't have to repeatedly re-create those resources. However, you may wonder whether you should track your resource's time in the resource pool file to see whether the resource is overbooked. Most projects in the real world use resources that aren't solely dedicated to a single project. New users of Project are often confused because almost every person working on their projects spends time on other work, from general communication with coworkers and clients to efforts invested in other projects. Should these beginners build resource pools to account for time shared among several projects at one time?

Generally speaking, trying to track every minute of every resource's day to see whether resources are working 100 percent or 50 percent on your tasks or are being shared among multiple projects amounts to chaos. Ask yourself this question: When this resource works on a task in your project, will he put his entire focus on that task at that time? If so, you may not need to fool around with tracking shared resources across many projects. Especially on shorter tasks, resisting the urge to micromanage the efforts of your resources outside your own project usually works well. If, on the other hand, you have resources working only half the time or splitting time between two projects routinely, consider using shared resource tools to keep track of those resources across projects.

If you combine separate projects into one master project at any point, Project allows you to have duplicated resources. If you link the combined projects and then delete a duplicate resource in the master project, it's deleted in the subproject as well. A better practice is to have all the separate projects share resources from a resource pool so that no duplicate resources exist when you create the master project file.

Importing resources from Outlook

Project allows you to save yourself the time spent entering resource information by allowing you to pull resources from Outlook.

To pull resources from Outlook, you must have it specified as your default email program: Open Outlook, and when you're asked whether you want it to be your default program, say yes.

When you insert one or more Outlook resources into your project, they're added to your project list, using the resource name and email address as they exist in the Outlook Address Book. The default first-letter initial and

work type are also preassigned. You can then add to the resource any
details you like.

To insert resources from your Outlook Address Book, display Resource Sheet
view and follow these steps:

1. **Go to the Resource Tab on the Ribbon. In the Insert group, click Add
   Resources, and then click Address Book.**

   The Select Resources dialog box appears.

2. **Click the name of a resource in the Name list.**

3. **Click Add to place the selected name in the Resources list.**

4. **Repeat Steps 2 and 3 to add to your project all the resource names you
   want to import.**

5. **When you're finished, click the OK button.**

The names now appear in the project resource list, ready for you to assign
them to tasks.

Chapter 8

Working with Calendars

In This Chapter

▶ Exploring the base, project, resource, and task calendars

▶ Understanding how calendars work together

▶ Setting calendar options and working times

▶ Choosing the project calendar

▶ Working with task calendars

▶ Using resource calendars

▶ Creating your own calendar templates

▶ Copying calendars to another project

Most people live their lives based on responding to their clocks and calendars. Think about it: You wake up, and your first thoughts are about what day it is, what time it is, and whether it's a workday.

You have a typical workday, whether you're a 9-to-5 person or your particular job calls for you to work from midnight to 8 a.m. You probably also vary from that routine now and then, when you complete a 12-hour marathon session in a crunch or slip away after half a day to go fishing on a nice summer day.

In a way, Project 2016 calendars resemble your work life: They set standards for a typical working time and then allow for variation. Unlike you, however, Project 2016 has several types of calendars to account for.

Mastering Base, Project, Resource, and Task Calendars

One piece of information to consider when assigning resources is *when* people can work. You adjust resource working time in calendars. As I describe in Chapter 2, when you first open a new project, you enter information about the project either in the Project Information dialog box or in the File Tab in the Project Information section. One option under project information is the Project Calendar.

You have three calendar options:

✔ The **Standard** (default) calendar shows a typical 9-to-5 workday and a 5-day workweek, with no exceptions such as holidays. You can think of it as the company calendar, which reflects its operating hours (when the "doors are open").

✔ **Night Shift** shows an 8-hour workday, scheduled between 11 p.m. and 8 a.m., with an hour off for a meal, from Monday through Friday — no exceptions. You can select this calendar for resources who work the same company days but different hours.

✔ The **24 Hours** base calendar shows continuous time, 24 hours per day and 7 days per week.

Project 2016 has four calendar types: base, project, resource, and task. Mastering the calendar types can be tricky, but understanding how calendars work is essential to mastering the software. Tasks are scheduled and resources are assigned based on the calendar settings you make.

You can manage calendars in a project in one of three ways: Use a project calendar that sets the working dates and times for all resources and tasks, modify calendars for specific resources, or assign and modify calendars for specific tasks.

Don't become confused by my use of the term *project* as it refers to the software, the project calendar type, and your project. I use *Project 2016* to indicate the software itself, *project calendar* to specify the calendar type, and plain *project* to refer to your project.

How calendars work

Not everyone in a company works the same schedule, and not every task can be performed in the same eight-hour workday. To deal with the variations in schedules that occur in most workplaces, Project 2016 offers various calendar settings. Here's the lowdown on the role of each of the four calendar types in Project 2016 (the next section details how they interact):

✔ **Base:** The template on which all other calendars are built. Three base calendars are available: Standard, Night Shift, and 24 Hours. (You can read more about them later in this chapter, in the section "Working with Task Calendars and Resource Calendars.")

- **Project:** The default calendar for scheduling. You choose which base calendar template your particular project should use.

- **Resource:** Combines the base calendar settings with any exceptions (nonworking times, such as vacation time) that you set for a particular resource.

- **Task:** Provides a spot where you can set exceptions for a particular task.

When you create tasks and assign resources to work on them, Project 2016 has to base that work on a timing standard. For example, if you say that a task should be completed in one workday, Project 2016 knows that a *workday* means 8 hours (or 12 hours or whatever) because that's how you set up a standard workday in the project calendar. Likewise, suppose that you assign a resource to work two weeks on a task in a company that uses a standard five-day workweek. If that resource's own calendar is set for a standard four-day workweek, the two weeks of work by that resource defer to the timing of the resource calendar for a total of only eight workdays.

The nature of a task can affect resource time. A two-week, effort-driven task isn't complete until its resources have invested two weeks (according to the project calendar or task calendar) of effort. You can find out more about effort-driven tasks in Chapter 5.

How one calendar relates to another

All calendars in a project are controlled, by default, by the project calendar setting. Here's the tricky part, though: When you change a task calendar or resource calendar (known as an *exception*), you have to understand which setting takes precedence.

Here's how the precedence concept works:

- With no other settings made, the base calendar template you select for the project calendar when you first create the project controls the working times and days of all tasks and resources.

- If you make changes in the working hours for a resource, those settings take precedence over the project calendar for that resource when you assign it to a task. Likewise, if you assign a different base calendar for a task, that calendar takes precedence over the project calendar for that task.

- If you apply one calendar to a resource and a different calendar to a task that the resource is assigned to, Project 2016 uses only common hours to schedule the resource. For example, if the task calendar allows work from 8 a.m. to 5 p.m. and the resource calendar allows work from 6 a.m. to 2 p.m., the resource works from 8 a.m. to 2 p.m., which is the only period the calendars have in common.

✔ You can set a task to ignore resource calendar settings by opening the Task Information dialog box (double-click the task name in Gantt Chart view) and selecting the Scheduling Ignores Resource Calendars check box on the Advanced tab. (This setting isn't available if the task calendar is set to None.) You might make this setting if you know that all resources are required to be involved in a task (such as a quarterly company meeting), regardless of their usual work hours.

Scheduling with Calendar Options and Working Times

In this section, I throw two more timing elements at you: calendar options and working times.

Calendar options are used to change the standard settings for a working day, week, and year. You can set a project calendar to Standard, for example. By default, that's 8 a.m. to 5 p.m., five days a week.

Working time is used to adjust the time available for work on a particular date or days. Suppose that you make a change to the calendar options so that you have 8-hour days and 32-hour workweeks. Also check your working time to ensure that you specify 3 nonworking days of the 7-day week, to jibe with the 32-hour week. If you want to set a certain date as *nonworking* for your project, such as the company offsite meeting day, you can do that using the working-time settings.

To ensure that the project is scheduled accurately from the get-go, make all changes to calendar options and working times *before* you add tasks to the project.

You have to change the calendar options and calendar settings for *every* new project file you create. However, you can set up a calendar that can be used for all your projects and shared in a single global location, as explained later in this chapter, in the section "Sharing Copies of Calendars."

Setting calendar options

When you make changes to a resource calendar or task calendar, you simply adjust the times that a resource is available to work or the time during which a task occurs; you don't change the length of a typical workday for the project. A day is still 8 hours long if that's the project calendar setting, even if you say that a task that takes place on that day uses the 24-hour base calendar template.

To change the length of a typical workday to ten hours rather than eight, for example, you must do so on the Calendar tab of the Options dialog box.

Follow these steps to modify the calendar options:

1. **Select the File tab on the Ribbon and click the Options button.**

   The Project Options dialog box appears.

2. **Click the Schedule category on the left side of the Project Options dialog box, as shown in Figure 8-1.**

Figure 8-1:
Define the typical working day, week, month, and year.

3. **From the Week Starts On drop-down list, choose a day.**

4. **To modify the start of the fiscal year, select a month from the Fiscal Year Starts In drop-down list.**

5. **To change the working hours in a typical day, type new times in the Default Start Time and Default End Time fields.**

   If you change the default start or end time setting, change the corresponding working time also, as described in the following section.

6. **Modify the Hours Per Day, Hours Per Week, and Days Per Month fields as needed.**

7. **Click the OK button to save these settings.**

Worrying about every calculated hour can be tedious. Most professional schedulers avoid changing the default calendar settings. Unless you truly want to track the scheduling of tasks to the hour, simply manage tasks to the day or week and keep track of scheduled deliverables in this manner.

Setting exceptions to working times

To change the available working hours for a particular day (such as December 24), you use the working-time settings. For example, if the day before Thanksgiving is half a workday, you can modify the working-time settings for that day; then any resources assigned to a task on this date spend only half a day working. You also use these settings to specify global working and nonworking days to match the calendar options settings.

Here's how to change working times:

1. **On the Project tab, go to the Properties group and click the Change Working Time button.**

   The Change Working Time dialog box opens, as shown in Figure 8-2.

Figure 8-2:
The standard calendar shows the default working times.

2. **On the calendar, click the day you want to change.**

3. **Click the Exceptions tab to display it; then click the Name cell in a blank row, type a name for the exception, and press Enter.**

4. **Click the exception name you entered in Step 3 and then click the Details button.**

   The Details dialog box for this exception opens, as shown in Figure 8-3. This example shows Thanksgiving Eve with the workday ending at 2 p.m.

Figure 8-3:
Modifying
the default
calendar.

5. **Select either the Nonworking or Working Times radio button.**

6. **Enter a time range in the From and To fields.**

   To set nonconsecutive hours (for example, to build in a lunch break), you have to insert two or more sets of numbers (such as 8 to 12 and 1 to 5) in the From and To fields.

7. **Select a recurrence pattern and then set an interval in the Recur Every *x Time Period* field.**

   For example, if you select Weekly and click the arrows to set the interval field to 3, this pattern recurs every three weeks.

8. **Set the range of recurrence.**

   Either enter Start and End By dates or select the End After radio button and set the number of occurrences there. This example ends after one occurrence.

9. **Click the OK button to close the Details dialog box and click OK again to close the Change Working Time dialog box. Save your changes.**

Working with Task Calendars and Resource Calendars

You can set a task calendar to use a different base calendar template from the one you selected for the project calendar. Doing so takes precedence over the project calendar for that task. Suppose that you select the Standard calendar template for a project and a 24 Hours task calendar template. If you then specify that the task has a duration of one day, it's one 24-hour day (assuming that the assigned resources also use a calendar allowing for a 24-hour schedule, such as machinery).

To modify the settings for a task calendar, follow these steps:

1. **In the Gantt Chart view, double-click the task name.**

   The Task Information dialog box appears.

2. **Click the Advanced tab.**

3. **From the Calendar drop-down list, choose a different base calendar.**

4. **Click the OK button to save the new calendar setting.**

If a resource assigned to a task has a modified calendar, the resource works only during the specific hours that the task calendar and resource calendar have in common.

Setting resource calendars

Only work resources have their own calendars. That's because material resources are charged not by time worked but by units used, and a cost resource is assigned a set cost that doesn't relate to any time worked on a task.

Even the most resourceful resources have only so many hours in a day to work. When you have to deal with variations in resource schedules, consider modifying the resource calendars.

You can change the base calendar template for each work resource and set specific dates as working or nonworking. These exceptions take precedence over the project and task calendars, and control when a specific resource can work.

Unless a resource has a truly unique working schedule, don't change its base calendar template. For example, if a resource usually works a day shift but works a night shift for only a few days during the life of the project, don't change that resource's base calendar template to Night Shift. If one person works from 10 a.m. to 7 p.m. because the company allows him to, you probably don't have to vary his schedule from the typical 8-to-5 work schedule that's set in the project calendar, because he works eight hours a day, like everyone else does. Unless your project deals with the most detailed level of time, where hours and not days are the typical units of measure for tasks, making these types of changes is more work than it's worth.

Making the change to a resource's calendar

To modify a resource's calendar settings, follow these steps:

1. **Display a view that includes a resource column, such as the Resource Sheet view.**

   Simply select the view from the drop-down list that appears when you click the bottom of the Gantt Chart button on the Task tab of the Ribbon. Chapter 6 covers how to display different views.

2. **Double-click a resource name.**

   The Resource Information dialog box appears.

3. **Click the Change Working Time button on the General tab to display the Change Working Time dialog box.**

   The Exceptions and Work Weeks tabs have settings that are identical to the ones in the Change Working Time dialog box for tasks, but changes made here affect this resource rather than the task.

4. **In the Click on a Day to See Its Working Times calendar section, click the day that you want to change.**

5. **Click the Work Weeks tab to display it; then click a blank row, enter a name for the exception, and press Enter.**

   The Start and Finish dates populate with the date you chose. If you want to edit the default workweek for all weeks of the year, leave [Default] selected instead. If you want to mark a single holiday, use the Exceptions tab instead.

6. **Click the exception you just created, and click the Details button.**

   The Details dialog box for this exception appears.

7. **Select the day or days to modify in the Select Day(s) list on the left side.**

   You can click the first day and then Shift+click to select a range of adjacent days, or Ctrl+click to select nonadjacent days.

8. **To set working times for these exceptions, select either the Nonworking or Working radio button. If you chose nonworking time, click OK.**

9. **If you chose to set specific working times in Step 8, enter a time range in the From and To fields. Click OK.**

   To delete a row in the From and To area, click the row number and press Delete.

   To set nonconsecutive hours (for example, to build in a lunch break), put two or more sets of numbers (such as 8 to 12 and 1 to 5) in the start and finish columns.

10. **Set the range of recurrence.**

    Change the Finish date to meet your needs.

    Figure 8-4 shows how a resource's vacation is shown in the Change Working Time dialog box.

Figure 8-4:
Changing
working
time on a
resource
calendar.

11. **Click the OK button to close the Change Working Time dialog box and save these changes.**

Micromanaging nonworking time for your resources can leave you no time to do anything else, so avoid this urge. For example, if someone takes off half a day for a doctor's appointment, don't block off a day. However, if a resource takes a two-week vacation or a three-month sabbatical, you should probably modify that resource's calendar.

Resources can work overtime even if their calendars say that they're 9-to-5ers, though you have to tell Project 2016 to schedule overtime work. You can also set a different rate to be charged for overtime work for that resource. To find out more about overtime, see Chapter 10.

Creating a Custom Calendar Template

Although the three Project 2016 base calendar templates cover most working situations, you might want to create your own calendar template. For example, if the project involves a telemarketing initiative and most project resources work six hours, from 4 p.m. to 10 p.m. (that's when they all call me anyway!), consider creating a new calendar template named Telemarketing. Another reason to create a custom template is that the three Project 2016 calendars have no holidays specified. You may need to ensure, at minimum, that company holidays are indicated in the calendar you use to ensure that Project 2016 accurately schedules around those dates.

If you want to save some time when creating a template, start with an existing base calendar template that most closely fits your needs. Then modify it as you like by making changes to the working times and calendar options (see the section "Scheduling with Calendar Options and Working Times," earlier in this chapter) to ensure that they're in agreement. After you create a new calendar template, it's available for you to apply in all three calendar types: project, task, and resource.

Because the project calendar is the basis of the entire project, it should represent the most common working schedule in the project. If only certain resources in the project work odd hours, change the resource calendars and not the project calendar.

Follow these steps to create a new calendar template:

1. **Click the Project tab, go to the Properties group, then click Change Working Time.**

   The Change Working Time dialog box appears.

2. **Click the Create New Calendar button.**

   The Create New Base Calendar dialog box appears.

3. **In the Name box, type a unique name for the new calendar.**

4. **Select either the Create New Base Calendar or the Make a Copy of *x* Calendar radio button; then select an existing base calendar from the list on which to base the calendar template.**

If you choose Create New Base Calendar, Project 2016 creates a copy of the Standard calendar with a new name. If you choose Make a Copy Of and select 24 Hours or Night Shift, the new calendar is based on that choice. Whichever you choose, it's your starting point, and you can make changes to make the calendar unique after making this choice.

5. **Click the OK button to return to the Change Working Time dialog box.**

Now make changes to the working time for the new calendar template.

6. **Click the OK button to save the new calendar settings.**

If you haven't already done so, change the calendar options to match the working times of the custom calendar you created. You can do this from the Change Working Time dialog box, using its Options button.

Sharing Copies of Calendars

You can make a calendar available for multiple projects by using the *Organizer;* it serves as the control center for custom items such as calendars you create in your project files. Using the Organizer, you can copy a custom calendar from one project file into another. Or you can copy a custom calendar into a template that provides default settings to every new, blank project file you create.

To copy a calendar from one project to another, follow this procedure:

1. **Open the project to which you want to copy a calendar and the project file that holds the custom calendar to copy.**

2. **Choose File ➪ Info.**

Backstage view opens.

3. **Click the Organizer button.**

The Organizer dialog box appears.

4. **Click the Calendars tab.**

5. **From the Calendars Available In drop-down list (in the lower-left corner), select the Project 2016 file that contains the calendar you want to copy.**

6. **In the Calendars Available In drop-down list (in the lower-right corner), choose whether you want to make the calendar available in another open project (by selecting that project) or the Global template (by selecting** `Global.MPT`**).**

7. **In the list on the left, click the calendar you want to copy and then click the Copy button, as shown in Figure 8-5.**

    The calendar is copied to the current project.

Figure 8-5:
Copying a
calendar to
other
projects.

8. **If you want to give the calendar a different name, make sure that it's selected in the list, click the Rename button, type a new name in the Rename dialog box that appears, and then click the OK button.**

9. **Close the Organizer by clicking the X (Close) button in the upper-right corner.**

Follow these pointers to copy calendars from project to project:

✔ **Give the calendar a descriptive name.** Providing an appropriate name helps you remember the calendar's general parameters.

✔ **If your company has standard calendars, have a single resource create and disseminate them.** If ten versions of a management calendar float around and you grab the wrong one, it can cause problems.

✔ **Add the project manager's initials to every calendar template name you create.** That way, you know which ones you created.

Chapter 9

Assigning Resources

. . . .

In This Chapter

▶ Identifying the right resource

▶ Making resource assignments

▶ Checking resource availability

▶ Using Team Planner view

. . . .

After you enter tasks and resources, you start assigning tasks to resources. That is when the fun begins! The duration of some tasks may change, and you may start to see evidence of people who are overbooked on several tasks that happen around the same time. Understanding how these results occur is the key to making intelligent assignments and balancing the project scope with your milestone obligations and resource availability.

In fact, assigning resources, balancing scope, schedule and cost, and replanning is an ongoing process throughout a project. As usual, Project provides the tools to help you manage the resource assignment process so you can arrive at an optimal solution.

Finding the Right Resource

Sometimes, no one in the world can perform a certain task like Albert does, and you'll persuade Albert to do that job if it kills you. At other times, almost anyone can handle the work.

If any Tom, Dick, or Mary with a certain skill level (or a certain rate per hour) can do the job, you can use Project 2016 features to find the right resource and ensure that she has enough time to take on "just one more" task.

Needed: One good resource willing to work

You've probably used the Find feature in other software to find a word or phrase or number. That's child's play compared with Project's Find feature, which can find you a backhoe, a corporate jet, or even a person! You can use Project's Find feature to look for resources with certain rates or in a certain workgroup. You can search for resources by their initials, their maximum assignment units, or their standard or overtime rate, for example.

Suppose that you need to find a resource whose standard rate is less than $50 per hour. Or you want to find someone who can spend extra time working on a task, so you search for any resource whose maximum units are greater than 100 percent. (In other words, the resource can work a longer-than-usual day before she is considered *overallocated.*) Perhaps you need to find a material resource that is a chemical measured in gallons, but you can't remember its exact name. In this case, you can search for resources whose material label includes the word *gallons.*

To find resource information, you must be working in a resource-oriented view. To find task information, you must be working in the task-oriented view.

First, display any resource view and then follow these steps to find resources in Project:

1. **On the Task tab, click Find in the Editing group.**

   The Find dialog box appears, as shown in Figure 9-1.

2. **In the Find What box, type the text you want to find.**

   For example, type **75** if you want to search for a resource with a standard rate of $75 per hour or less, or type **water** if you want to find a resource whose material label contains that word.

Figure 9-1:
Using the
Find feature.

Find		
Fi_n_d what:	75	
_L_ook in field:	◉ Selected	Standard Rate ▾
	◯ All Visible	
_T_est:	is less than ▾	
_S_earch:	Down ▾	☐ Match _c_ase
	_R_eplace...	_F_ind Next	Close

3. **From the Look in Field list, choose the name of the field in which you want to search.**

   The default field is Name. When you click the drop-down arrow, you see all kinds of different fields you can search. For example, to search for resources that have a maximum unit-assignment percentage of more than 100 percent, choose the Max Units field. Or choose Standard Rate to search based on the resource's hourly rate.

4. **In the Test box, select a criterion.**

   The default value is contains, but when you click the drop-down arrow, you see lots of options. For example, if you're looking for maximum units of more than 100 percent, Is Greater Than is the best choice. For a rate less than $75 per hour, try Is Less Than.

5. **If you prefer to search backward from the current location (that is, the selected cell in the task list) instead of forward, choose Up from the Search box.**

6. **If you want to match the case of the text, select the Match Case check box.**

7. **To begin the search, click the Find Next button.**

8. **Continue to click Find Next until you find the instance you're looking for.**

Custom fields: It's a skill

When assigning resources, you often need to consider a person's skills. If a person with less skill or experience could work on a particular task (and save you money because she charges a lower rate per hour), wouldn't it be nice to be able to find these resources easily?

Well, Project doesn't include a Skill field, but it does allow you to add fields of your own. You can use these fields for anything, but one useful way is to code resources by skill level. You can use a rating system such as A, B, and C or use terms such as *Exp* for an experienced worker and *Beg* for a beginning-level worker.

Here's how to add a custom field:

1. **Display the Resource Sheet (or whatever sheet in which you want to view the custom field).**

2. **Scroll to the right on the sheet until you get to the end of the columns and click the Add New Column column heading.**

3. **Type a name for the field and press Enter.**

You can enter whatever you like in this column for each resource in the project. Then you can search for specific entries in that field using the Find feature or turn on a filter to display only resources with a certain skill level in that field. (Read more about filters in Chapter 11.)

The custom field that's created using this method uses one of the placeholder fields Text 1 through Text 30 that's available for you to customize. You can customize other types of placeholder fields, such as cost fields or flag fields. To access more custom fields, right-click a field column heading and click Custom Fields.

Some organizations designate custom fields for certain company information, such as an accounting code or a vendor rating. If a Project administrator is in charge of these enterprise-wide standards, check with her before you choose a custom field to designate skill level.

Making a Useful Assignation

In a project where entering tasks isn't complex, defining the relationship, assigning a resource, and entering the duration is sufficient for developing a working schedule. But when you work in an organization that has many projects competing for limited resources and those projects are complex in nature, you're better served using software to help you manage its complexities.

Alas, the more complex the environment, the more variables that affect the schedule. For example, you can't simply enter a series of tasks; you need to determine the type of task (such as fixed units, fixed work, or fixed duration) and determine whether the task is effort driven. The task type affects the duration of the task after you assign resources. I describe task types in Chapter 5.

When you assign resources, pay attention to the resource type (work, material, or cost) and the resource availability. In addition, consider whether the project calendar, task calendar, and resource calendars affect the tasks assigned to resources. You can use a couple of methods to assign resources to tasks and also specify the resource assignment units. These assignment units differ slightly between work resources and material and cost resources, as explained in the next several sections.

Determining material and cost-resource units

Work resources, which are typically people, are assigned to a task using a percentage: for example, 50 percent or 100 percent. When you assign a resource at a percentage, the assignment is based on the resource calendar. A resource with a Standard calendar spends eight hours a day working if you assign it at 100 percent assignment units.

A *material resource* is assigned in units, such as gallons, consulting sessions, yards, or tons. When you assign a material resource to a task, you designate how many units of that resource are devoted to that task. Project doesn't act like job-costing software, deleting units from an inventory; it isn't affected by how many units are used against the total available. (You can't use it in this manner.)

A *cost resource* is one that incurs a variable cost every time you assign it. For example, if you create the Permit Fee cost resource, every time you assign a permit fee to a task, you can designate the actual cost for that assignment, whether it's $25 or $125.

Making assignments

You have three main ways to assign resources in Project (although you can use other methods while working in various views):

- ✔ Select resources from the Resources tab of the Task Information dialog box.
- ✔ Enter resource information in the Resource column in the Entry table (displayed in Gantt Chart view).
- ✔ Use the Assign Resources dialog box.

Regardless of which method you use, you work in a task-based view, such as Gantt Chart view, to make the assignments.

Which method you use depends to some extent on your own preferences. Follow these guidelines:

- ✔ **Resource column:** By default, you assign resources at 100 percent availability. If you want to assign a different percentage, don't use this method; it's more difficult if you need to assign multiple resources.

✔ **Assign Resources dialog box:** Replace one resource with another (using the handy Replace feature) or filter the list of available resources by a criterion (for example, resources with a cost of less than a specified amount). This method is useful for assigning multiple resources.

✔ **Task Information dialog box:** Having the task details handy (such as task type or the constraints contained on other tabs of this dialog box) is helpful when you make the assignment.

Selecting resources from the Resource column

You can add resources from the Resource column, whether it's from Gantt Chart view or Tracking Gantt view.

Even though Task Usage view lists tasks in its sheet pane and can even display a Resource column, this view can't be used to add resource assignments.

Follow these steps to assign resources at a default percentage:

1. **Display Gantt Chart view by clicking the Gantt Chart button on the Task tab or View tab of the Ribbon.**

2. **Click the View tab. In the Data group click Tables. From the drop-down menu click Entry.**

3. **Click in the Resource Names column for the task on which you want to make a resource assignment.**

   An arrow appears at the end of the cell.

4. **Click the arrow to display a list of resources.**

5. **Click the resource you want to assign.**

   The resource name appears in the Resource column, assigned at 100 percent.

You can always change the assignment units later by opening the Task Information dialog box and changing the assignment units on the Resources tab.

Using the Assign Resources dialog box

To assign a work resource or material resource to a task, you can select a task and then use the Assign Resources dialog box to make assignments. This unique dialog box is the only one you can leave open and continue to scroll within the project, making it easy to switch between selecting a task and making an assignment. This method is easy to use for assigning material and cost resources. To use the Assign Resources dialog box, follow these steps:

1. **Click the Assign Resources button in the Assignments group of the Resource tab on the Ribbon.**

   The Assign Resources dialog box appears, as shown in Figure 9-2.

2. **Click a task to select it.**

   The Assign Resources dialog box can remain open while you select tasks in the task list. Then you can make assignments to a variety of tasks without the need to close and reopen the dialog box repeatedly.

3. **Click the Units column for the work or material resource you want to assign or the Cost column for the cost resource you want to assign, and then specify the assignment units or cost for the resource.**

   Click the spinner arrows in the box to increase or decrease the setting. If you don't select units for a work resource, Project assumes that you're assigning 100 percent of the resource. The spinner arrows show 50 percent or 100 percent, or you can simply type a percentage. For a material resource, use the spinner arrows in the Units column to increase or decrease the unit assignment, or type a number of units. For a cost resource, type the expected cost for that particular assignment.

4. **Click the Assign button.**

5. **Repeat Steps 2 through 4 to add all resources.**

6. **If you want to replace one resource with another, click an assigned resource (indicated with a check mark), click the Replace button, select another name on the list, set its units, and click OK.**

7. **Click the Close button to save all the assignments.**

Adding assignments in the Task Information dialog box

You can assign resources on the Resources tab of any Task Information dialog box by following these steps:

1. **Double-click a task name in Gantt Chart view.**

   The Task Information dialog box appears.

2. **Click the Resources tab to display it.**

3. **Click in a blank Resource Name box and then click the arrow that appears on the right side of the box.**

   A drop-down list of resources appears.

4. **Click the resource you want to assign.**

5. **For a work or material resource, click the Units column and use the spinner arrows to set an assignment percentage; for a cost resource, click the Cost column and enter the cost.**

   If you're assigning a material resource, the Units default setting is a single unit. (If your units are pounds, the default assignment is 1 lb.) Use the spinner arrows in the Unit field or type a value there to assign additional material units.

6. **Repeat Steps 3 through 5 to assign additional resources.**

7. **Click the OK button.**

Shaping the contour that's right for you

When you make a work resource assignment, Project spreads out the work evenly over the life of the task. However, you can modify the level of work that takes place during the life of an autoscheduled task — its *work contour* — so that more work takes place near the beginning, middle, or end of the task.

For example, if you know that the employees on a task to install a new computer network will have to spend some time up front studying the manuals and reviewing the schematics for the wiring before they can begin to make measurable progress on the installation, you may use a late-peaking contour. Or if you know that employees are likely to put in a lot of work up front on a survey — and then sit back and wait for the results to come in — you may choose an early-peaking contour.

Using a different contour on a particular resource's task assignment can free that resource to work on a second task that occurs during the life of the first task. This strategy can help you resolve a resource conflict.

The contour you select will have slightly different effects, depending on the task type. Trust me: Most project managers don't even want to try to understand this complex equation. Simply try a different contour to see whether it solves your problem and doesn't make too dramatic a change to the task duration or another resource assignment. Realize that most all the applied work contours result in a greater task duration.

To set a task's contour, follow these steps:

1. **Display Task Usage view.**

   This view shows resource assignments by task.

2. **Double-click a resource assignment.**

   The Assignment Information dialog box appears.

3. **On the General tab, from the Work Contour drop-down menu, choose a preset pattern.**

   The Work Contour options are shown in Figure 9-3.

4. **Click the OK button to save the setting.**

Figure 9-3: Work Contour options.

If none of these patterns fits your situation, you can manually modify a resource's work by changing the number of hours the resource puts in day by day on a task in Task Usage view.

Before you save, ensure that your modifications equal the number of hours you want, or else you can inadvertently change the resource's assignment.

TIP

Resource Usage view is useful for reviewing resource hours across a timeline at this stage of planning. This view gives a side-by-side comparison between a single resource's workload and all the tasks taking place during a particular period in the project.

Benefitting from a Helpful Planner

One thing you may notice after making resource assignments is that a little Person icon appears as an indicator beside certain tasks in Gantt Chart view. If you switch to a resource-oriented view, you may see that certain resource names now display in red. These changes are Project's way of indicating resources in danger of being overbooked in the plan.

Team Planner view you can help ensure that you've distributed work among resources in a manageable way. To change to Team Planner view, click the Resource tab and click the Team Planner button on the far left side. This view enables you to move assignments among resources, assign tasks that haven't been assigned, and even schedule tasks that haven't been scheduled. Figure 9-4 shows Team Planner view.

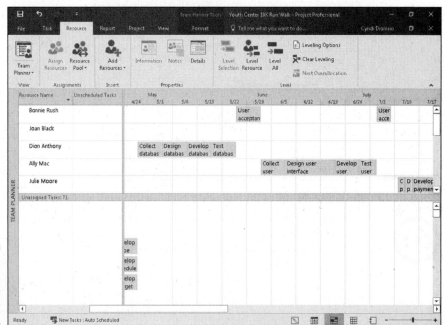

Figure 9-4:
Team
Planner
view.

When two or more tasks assigned to a resource overlap and cause the resource to be overbooked (or *overallocated*), thin red bars appear above and below the overbooked period. Team Planner view also shows you any tasks that are unassigned or lack enough schedule information to be scheduled.

To view unassigned tasks, drag the bar at the bottom that shows the number of unassigned tasks up, dropping it to split the view the way you want.

From there, you can drag and drop to correct a number of schedule issues, and you can use the following techniques in any combination:

✔ **To fix a resource overallocation:** Drag an overlapping task to the left or right to change its schedule. If you want to reassign the task to another resource, drag the task up or down to that resource.

✔ **To assign an unassigned task:** Drag the task up to the row for the resource to which you want to assign the task.

✔ **To schedule an unscheduled task:** Drag the task to the right, to the timescale portion of the view, and then drop the task into a schedule position.

Team Planner view is only one tool you can use to handle overbooked resources. Chapter 12 presents even more methods for fixing workload issues.

Dragging horizontally in Team Planner view changes the task schedule, whereas dragging vertically from one resource to another changes the task assignment.

After you have a workable version of the project schedule, ensure that your resources agree to their assignments. You can send the entire project plan to resources as an email attachment or sync it with SharePoint.

Chapter 10

Determining a Project's Cost

In This Chapter

▶ Understanding how costs accrue

▶ Establishing work resource rates

▶ Specifying unit costs

▶ Adding fixed costs

▶ Allowing for overtime

▶ Adding up all the costs

*T*here's no such thing as a free lunch — and if you use Project to track costs, there's no such thing as a free resource, because Project uses resources working on tasks as a way of calculating most of the costs of the project.

When you set up a resource, you specify a work resource rate (by default, this rate is calculated by hour) or a material resource per use cost. You can also create *cost resources* — a variable cost that isn't calculated using a per-use or hourly rate but that may be used several times in a project, such as travel expenses. For example, if you assign a resource to work ten hours on a task, give that resource an hourly rate of $20, and you've added a $200 cost to the project. Create a resource named *cement,* give it a unit cost of $200, and assign ten units (for example, ten tons of cement), and you've added a whopping $2,000 to the bottom line.

Some other factors come into play as well, such as how many hours a day a resource is available to work and any overtime rates. At the end of the day, all these settings come together to comprise the project cost.

This chapter helps you explore the relationship between resources and costs, and shows you how to set resource standard and overtime rates and create fixed costs.

How Do Costs Accrue?

Project helps to account for costs on various tasks with a combination of costs per hour, costs per use, costs per unit, fixed costs, and costs for specific assignments of cost resources. Before you begin to flesh out cost information about resources, you have to understand how these calculations work.

Project provides two main pictures of the budget in a project: one at the moment you freeze the original plan (a *baseline plan*) and the ongoing picture of actual costs that comes from the activity and material usage you record as the project moves along. You record a certain amount of work effort on tasks, and tasks with costs assigned to them then add up costs based on the effort expended or units of materials used.

Adding up the costs

The best way to understand how costs add up in the project is to look at an example. John Smith (not his real name) is managing a project that involves the building of a new gourmet ice-cream packaging plant. Here are the costs that John anticipates for the task he has created, Install Ice-Cream Mixers:

- ✔ About ten person-hours of effort to complete the installation
- ✔ A cost per use of $500 paid to the mixer manufacturer to oversee the installation and to train workers to use the machine
- ✔ Twenty pounds of ice-cream ingredients to test the mixers
- ✔ Shipping expenses of $150 for the mixers and supplies
- ✔ A fixed cost of $2,500 for the mixers themselves

The ten hours of effort will be expended by work resources. The total cost for the ten hours is a calculation: 10 × the resource rate. If the resource rate is $20, this cost totals $200. If two resources work on the task, one at a rate of $20 and one at a rate of $30, then (with effort-driven scheduling turned off by default) Project adds 20 hours of effort between them, and the resulting cost is $500.

The cost per use of $500 is a fee to the manufacturer, which is also created as a work resource. This cost doesn't change based on the number of resources or the time involved.

The cost of 20 pounds of ice cream (any flavor you like) is calculated as 20 × the unit cost of the ice-cream ingredients. If the unit cost is $2, this cost is $40.

Shipping the new equipment and ice-cream supplies to you results in a charge of $150. Shipping was created as a cost resource because it has no associated work, and different shipping costs may apply to other tasks in the project.

Finally, the $2,500 cost for the mixers themselves was entered separately, as a fixed cost in the Cost table of Gantt Chart view.

And that's how costs are assigned and how they add up on projects. When working in Project, you soon discover that although it has quite capable costing features, they're probably some of the most underutilized.

You can create and assign resources that have no associated costs. For example, if you want your boss to be available to review status reports but your company doesn't require that your boss's time be charged to the project, you can simply use those resource assignments to remind you about the need for your boss's availability on that day or at that time.

When will this hit the bottom line?

In business, you rarely get to choose when you pay your own bills. In Project, however, you can choose when your costs affect your budget.

Resources can be set to accrue at the start or end of the task that they're associated with or to be prorated throughout the life of the task. If a task of three months begins April 1, a $90 cost resource can be added to the actual costs to-date on Day 1, on Day 90, or at a dollar per day until the end of the task. Use the Accrue At field in Resource Sheet view or on the Costs tab of the Resource Information dialog box to set the accrual method.

This scenario isn't exactly a purely realistic reflection of how you have to pay for costs because, let's face it: Most bills come due 30 days after they hit your desk. It's more a factor of when you want that cost to show up for the purposes of tracking costs and reporting expenses against the project. My preference is to accrue cost at the same rate at which work is performed. This keeps costs and work aligned.

Specifying Cost Information in the Project

Most projects involve a combination of cost types: work, material, and cost (that is, fixed cost). Before you can enter the information at the task or resource level, you have to do your homework to find out the fixed costs as well as the hourly or unit rates for all your resources.

During the planning stages, you may not be able to anticipate exactly what a particular cost will be or know every resource's rates. In this instance, you may need to develop an estimate and progressively elaborate the estimate as you know more. For example, if you know that you have a project to upgrade the lighting, painting, and landscaping for the community in a property own-er's association, you might start with a high-level estimate for the landscap-ing. As you find out more about the type of trees, shrubs, flowers, and labor you need, you can define costs at a more detailed and more accurate level. By starting with an estimate, at least some cost will be reflected in the plan, and you can enter more accurate information later, as soon as you know it.

Use a field in the Resource Sheet, such as Code, to designate resources as having estimated rates or costs so that you can easily go back to those tasks and update the estimates as the plan progresses.

You can't avoid fixed costs

Maybe it's that huge fee for the consulting company your boss insisted you use, even though you knew that the report wouldn't tell you a thing you didn't already know. Or perhaps it's the $2,000 for a laptop computer you talked your boss into buying so that you could manage the project when you're on the road. Whatever it is, it's a cost that doesn't change, no matter how many hours the task continues or how many people work on the task. It has no unit cost or rate per hour, and no actual hours of work are tracked. It's a *fixed cost.*

You can specify this type of cost by entering **Cost** in the Type field in the Resource Sheet. Every time you assign the resource to a task, you specify the actual cost associated with it.

You can also simply enter a fixed cost associated with a task without having to create and assign a cost resource to it. To do so, you can use the Cost table in the sheet in Gantt Chart view.

A *table* is a preset column combination that simplifies entering certain information in a sheet pane.

Follow these steps to enter a fixed cost for a task:

1. **Display the project in Gantt Chart view.**

2. **Click the View tab, and in the Data group, choose Tables ⇨ Cost.**

   The table of columns appears, as shown in Figure 10-1. You can insert the Fixed Cost column into any sheet, but the Cost table is ready for you to use.

3. **Click the Fixed Cost column for the task to which you want to assign the cost and then enter the amount.**

Figure 10-1:
The Cost table.

	Task Name	Fixed Cost	Fixed Cost Accrual	Total Cost	Baseline	Variance	Actual	Remaini
99	⊿ Safety	$0.00	Prorated	$3,800.00	$0.00	$3,800.00	$0.00	$3,800.00
100	⊿ Medical	$0.00	Prorated	$3,800.00	$0.00	$3,800.00	$0.00	$3,800.00
101	Set medical procedures	$0.00	Prorated	$1,800.00	$0.00	$1,800.00	$0.00	$1,800.00
102	Medical training event	$0.00	Prorated	$1,200.00	$0.00	$1,200.00	$0.00	$1,200.00
103	Purchase medical supplies	$500.00	Start	$500.00	$0.00	$500.00	$0.00	$500.00
104	Set up medical location	$0.00	Prorated	$150.00	$0.00	$150.00	$0.00	$150.00
105	Tear down medical location	$0.00	Prorated	$150.00	$0.00	$150.00	$0.00	$150.00

That's all there is to it, but because you can enter only one fixed-cost amount for a task, you should also enter a task note where you can itemize fixed costs if you have more than one. Note also that the default fixed-cost accrual method is prorated: If you prefer to have fixed costs hit the budget at the start or end of a task, use the Fixed Cost Accrual column in this table to select another option. Figure 10-1 shows the task to purchase supplies as having costs accrue at the start of the task.

Entering hourly, overtime, and cost-per-use rates

Whether it's minimum wage or the astronomical fees your lawyer charges you every time you sneeze, most people are paid a certain amount per hour. To represent most people involved in the project, you create work resources and charge them to the project at an hourly rate. Some resources also charge an additional flat fee for each use. For example, a plumber may charge a trip charge or "show up" fee of $75 and then add the cost per hour. This flat fee is a cost per use, added every time you assign the resource to a task, no matter how many hours are involved in completing the task.

The first cost you enter is a resource's hourly rate and an overtime rate (if the resource has one). After a resource has an hourly rate, you can enter the estimate of how many hours that person will work on each task he's assigned to, and Project totals his estimated costs in your plan and adds any cost per use. When you track actual effort expended on tasks, a calculation of actual effort multiplied by the hourly rate plus any cost-per-use returns actual costs.

By comparing estimated costs and actual costs, you form an ongoing picture of whether the project is within budget.

To set resource rates per hour and cost per use for a work resource, follow these steps:

1. **Display Resource Sheet view.**

2. **Click the Std Rate column for the resource to which you want to assign a cost.**

3. **Enter a dollar amount.**

   If you're entering a rate for a unit other than hours, type a slash (/) and then the unit (for example, **year** or **month**).

4. **Press Tab to go to the Ovt column.**

5. **Enter a dollar amount.**

6. **Press tab to move to the Cost/Use column.**

7. **Type a dollar amount.**

   This amount is the flat-fee amount that will be added every time you assign the resource to a task.

8. **Press Tab.**

   The entry is completed.

Figure 10-2 shows the work resources with their standard hourly rates.

In many projects, you don't track the cost per resource for internal resources because people's salaried rates are generally considered confidential. Sometimes, a standard midrange or loaded-resource rate is used to track employee rates by job grade.

Figure 10-2:
Entering
resource
costs.

	ⓘ	Resource Name	Type	Material	Initials	Group	Max.	Std.	Ovt.	Cost/Use	Accrue	Base
1		Bonnie Rush	Work		BR		100%	$100.00/hr	$0.00/hr	$0.00	Prorated	Standard
2		Joan Black	Work		JB		100%	$75.00/hr	$0.00/hr	$0.00	Prorated	Standard
3		Dion Anthony	Work		DA		100%	$65.00/hr	$0.00/hr	$0.00	Prorated	Standard
4		Ally Mac	Work		AM		100%	$50.00/hr	$0.00/hr	$0.00	Prorated	Standard
5		Julie Moore	Work		JM		100%	$50.00/hr	$0.00/hr	$0.00	Prorated	Standard
6		David Smith	Work		DS		100%	$65.00/hr	$0.00/hr	$0.00	Prorated	Standard
7		Calvin Daley	Work		CD		100%	$40.00/hr	$0.00/hr	$0.00	Prorated	Standard
8		Jack Beck	Work		JB		100%	$40.00/hr	$0.00/hr	$0.00	Prorated	Standard
9		Chip Lee	Work		CL		100%	$40.00/hr	$0.00/hr	$0.00	Prorated	Standard
10		Darren Scott	Work		DS		100%	$40.00/hr	$0.00/hr	$0.00	Prorated	Standard
11		Erica Mendoza	Work		EM		100%	$30.00/hr	$0.00/hr	$0.00	Prorated	Standard
12		Dr. Golden	Work		DG		100%	$150.00/hr	$0.00/hr	$0.00	Prorated	Standard
13		Dan Johnson	Work		DJ		100%	$70.00/hr	$0.00/hr	$0.00	Prorated	Standard
14		Jamie Wong	Work		JW		100%	$50.00/hr	$0.00/hr	$0.00	Prorated	Standard
15		Cliff Reardon	Work		CR		100%	$40.00/hr	$0.00/hr	$0.00	Prorated	Standard
16		Water	Material	gallons	W			$1.00		$125.00	Start	
17		Food	Cost		FD						Start	
18		Beverages	Material	gallons	BV			$2.00		$85.00	Start	

Assigning material resources

Calculating the cost of a material resource might take you back to solving
problems in your old high school algebra class. Fortunately, if you aren't an
algebra whiz, Project makes a straightforward calculation to arrive at the
cost of using a material resource.

When you assign a work resource to a task, Project multiplies its standard
hourly rate by the hours of work for the assignment. But material resources
don't have hours of work: You pay for them by the unit quantity, not by the
hour. So when you set up a material resource, you specify a standard rate
for a single unit (per yard, or ton, or gallon, for example) and assign a certain
number of units to each task. The cost is the number of units multiplied by
the cost per use.

To assign a standard unit rate for a material resource, follow these steps:

1. **Display Resource Sheet view.**

2. **If you haven't already done so, click the Material Label column for
   that resource and then type a unit name (such as** gallon**).**

3. **Click the Std Rate column for the resource you want to set and then
   type a dollar amount (such as the cost per gallon).**

4. **Press Enter or Tab to finish the entry.**

Figure 10-2 shows that the water and beverages are set up at a cost per gallon, with a setup fee for the company to deliver and set up the water and beverage stations.

You can also make cost-rate entries in the Resource Information dialog box. The Costs tab of this dialog box, shown in Figure 10-3, offers columns labeled Standard Rate, Overtime Rate, and Per Use Cost.

Figure 10-3: Setting rates in the Resource Information dialog box.

Note that you can also use the Resource Information dialog box to enter as many as five standard unit rates with effective dates to account for fluctuations in unit cost over the life of the project.

How Your Settings Affect Your Costs

In Chapter 9, I describe how to assign resources to tasks and how to assign those resources in certain units (percentages for work resources and quantity consumed for material resources). All these factors work together in calculating the cost of the resource when assigned to tasks.

Suppose that you want to assign a mechanic to a task with the following parameters:

Base calendar: Night Shift (eight hours, six days per week, between 11 p.m. and 8 a.m.)

Cost per hour: $20

Overtime cost: $30

Availability: 100 percent

Assigned to a two-day task: 50 percent

Here's how to calculate the cost of this resource: Two days at half-time availability based on an eight-hour calendar is a total of eight hours (four hours per day). The resource incurs no overtime, so the cost is $8 \times \$20 = \$160$.

Change two settings for the same resource to see what happens:

Assigned to a two-day task: 150 percent

Amount of overtime authorized: 8 hours

Now the resource is working 12 hours per day (150 percent of 8 hours) over two days. With 16 total hours at the standard rate ($20) and 8 hours of overtime ($30), this person will cost $(16 \times \$20) + (8 \times \$30) = \$560$.

The great thing about Project is you don't have to worry about completing the calculations; Project does them for you. After you specify settings for your resources, Project does the work of tallying and showing total costs to you.

Part III
Before You Baseline

Visit www.dummies.com/extras/project2016 to read about working with risk.

In this part . . .

✔ Work with filters, groups, and the Task Inspector.

✔ Manage the project constraints.

✔ Format the Project schedule to add pizzazz to the project.

✔ Set an interim plan and a baseline.

Chapter 11

Fine-Tuning Your Plan

● ●

In This Chapter

▶ Viewing timing and resource issues with filters

▶ Grouping information

▶ Using the Task Inspector pane to determine task drivers

▶ Issuing warnings and suggestions to fix task schedules

● ●

A s they say, the best-laid schemes of mice and project managers go oft awry, and the schedule is no different. After you take your best shot at laying out the project schedule, creating every task, and assigning every resource — and you think you're ready to start your project — think again.

A close look at almost any schedule reveals issues that you should resolve before you baseline. These issues may include a schedule that ends a month after the projected finish date, human resources who are assigned to work 36-hour days, or a budget that exceeds the national debt. (Details, details. . . .)

Even if you see no glaring problems related to time, workload, or cost, you should ensure that the project schedule is as realistic as possible before you commit to it. Take a moment to give the project the once-over by using filters to focus your attention on potential problem areas. You can also use the Task Inspector to pinpoint issues with the schedule or resources. If these options aren't enough, Project identifies problem areas and suggests solutions.

Everything Filters to the Bottom Line

The first step in solidifying the project schedule is simply to look at it from a few different perspectives — similar to circling a car to inspect all its features before you fork over the down payment. Filters help you gain that kind of perspective.

At this stage, you can use filters to examine two major problem areas:

- **Overallocated resources:** Those resources working more than the number of hours you specified.

- **Tasks on a critical path:** The *critical path* consists of the series of tasks in the project that must be completed on time for the project to meet its final finish date.

One way to look at the critical path is that it's the one with the least amount of slack (or *float*). Any task that has *slack* — that is, any length of time that the task could be delayed without affecting a milestone or the project end date — is not on the critical path. If the project has multiple critical paths, or near-critical paths, delays on those paths are likely to cause a problem as well. You can say that for every day the critical path slips, the project delivery date slips a day. Therefore, you can see the necessity of not only knowing the project's critical (and near-critical) paths, but also being able to easily check their status.

Setting predesigned filters

Filters work similarly to the Zoom feature in a word processor: They give you a close-up look at various aspects of your plan and help you spot clues about problems, such as overallocated resources. You can set a filter to highlight tasks or resources that meet certain criteria or to remove from view any tasks or resources that don't meet the criteria.

Project provides predesigned filters that you can simply turn on for tasks or resources, using criteria such as

- Tasks with a cost more than a specified amount

- Tasks on the critical path

- Tasks that occur within a certain date range

- Milestone tasks

- Tasks that use resources in a resource group

- Tasks with overallocated resources

Several filters, such as Slipping Tasks and Over-Budget Work, help you spot problems after you've finalized the schedule and are tracking progress. (See Chapter 15 for more about tracking.)

You can access filters in a couple of ways. When you use the Filter drop-down list, you choose built-in filters from a list. The filters act to remove from view any tasks that don't meet specified criteria and display the ones that do.

To turn on these filters from the View tab of the Ribbon, follow these steps:

1. **Display a resource view (such as Resource Sheet view) to filter for resources or a task view (such as Gantt Chart view) to filter for tasks.**

2. **In the Data group on the View tab, click the Filter drop-down list and choose a criterion.**

   The Filter list is a drop-down list; when no filter is applied, the list displays All Tasks or All Resources. If you choose a filter that requires input, you see a dialog box, such as the Resource Range one shown in Figure 11-1. The dialog box will be different depending on which filter you choose. Otherwise, the filter is applied immediately, and it removes from view any resources or tasks that don't match your criteria.

Figure 11-1:
Entering
filter
parameters.

3. **If a dialog box is displayed, fill in the required information and click the OK button.**

   The filter is applied.

To redisplay all tasks or resources, click the Filter drop-down list on the View tab and then select the No Filter option.

Putting AutoFilter to work

The Project 2016 AutoFilter feature is turned on by default for all new schedule files. Arrows appear in the column headings in the displayed sheet. When you click the arrow in the Resource Names column, for example, the name of every resource assigned to tasks in the project is listed in alphabetical order, along with other filtering and sorting choices. See Figure 11-2 for an example. In the AutoFilter list for a column, select check boxes to control which items appear onscreen. Selected items appear, and deselected items are hidden by the filter. If you want to display only a few items, clear the Select All check box first to deselect all items and then select the check boxes next to individual items to reselect them. Then click OK and your filter is applied.

Figure 11-2:
Deselect the
check box
beside
any item to
hide it.

You can also choose the Filters option from an AutoFilter menu to access predefined filters. For example, Figure 11-3 shows the predefined Is Greater Than filter that's available to the cost-related fields in the Cost table. In this case, the filter shows any task with a cost (total cost) between $2,000 and $4,000.

Figure 11-3:
AutoFilter
choices are
specific to
each field.

Follow these steps to use AutoFilter:

1. **Display the view and table that contain the fields (columns) you want to filter.**

   Arrows appear at the top of every column.

2. **Click the arrow on the column you want to filter.**

3. **Use the Filters submenu to select a filter.**

   Select a predefined filter. For example, if you're filtering for task cost, you can choose filters in the Total Cost column that look for costs greater than, equal to, or less than specified amounts. You can also set up another filter that looks for costs between two specified amounts. The Clear Filter from *Field Name* choice removes a previously applied filter.

4. Click the OK button.

Any task that doesn't meet your criteria temporarily disappears from the view.

To apply highlighting to items that meet your filter criteria rather than remove nonmatching items from view, use the Highlight list in the Data group on the View tab. This list works like the filter does except that it highlights the applicable tasks.

Creating do-it-yourself filters

You don't have to use predesigned filters: You can get creative and design your own filters. To define a new filter, you specify a field name, a test, and a value.

For example, the following line filters for any task on the critical path:

Critical (field name) **Equals** (test) **Yes** (value)

You can also include additional qualifiers to the filter. The following example filters for tasks that are on the critical path *and* have a baseline cost of more than $5,000:

Critical (field name) **Equals** (test) **Yes** (value)

and

Baseline Cost (field name) **Is Greater Than** (test) **5000** (value)

Here's how to build your own filter definition:

1. Choose View ➪ Filter ➪ More Filters.

The More Filters dialog box appears, as shown in Figure 11-4. It lists all available filters — built-in and custom.

Figure 11-4: The More Filters dialog box lists all available filters.

2. **Select either the Task or Resource radio button to specify in which list of filters you want the new filter to be included.**

3. **Click the New button.**

   The Filter Definition dialog box appears.

4. **In the Name field, type a name for the filter.**

   If you want the filter to be easily accessed in the drop-down lists, select the Show in Menu check box.

5. **Click the first line of the Field Name column and then click the down arrow that appears to display the list of choices, as shown in Figure 11-5.**

Figure 11-5: Give the new filter a name that describes what it does.

6. **Click a field name to select it.**

7. **Repeat Steps 5 and 6 for the Test and Value(s) columns.**

   - *Test* is a condition that must be met, such as Does Not Equal or Is Greater Than.

   - *Value(s)* is either a value you enter, such as a specific date or cost, or a predetermined value, such as baseline cost.

8. **If you want to add another condition, choose And or Or from the And/Or column and then make choices for the next set of Field Name, Test, and Value(s) boxes.**

   Note that you can cut and paste rows of settings you've made to rearrange them in the list, or use either the Copy Row or Delete Row button to perform those actions for filters with several lines of criteria.

9. **Click the Save button to save the new filter and then click Apply to apply the filter to your plan.**

Click the Organizer button in the More Filters dialog box to copy filters you've created from one Project file to another file or to make them available in all your files by copying the new filter into the Global.mpt.

Gathering Information in Groups

Project 2016 uses the Group feature to chunk information into logical groupings based on predefined criteria. (You may recall working with the work breakdown structure, or WBS, in Chapter 2, where I show you how to decompose the project into logical chunks of work.) For example, you can use the Group feature if you want to see resources organized by work group, or you may organize tasks by their duration, from shortest to longest.

Organizing tasks or resources in this way may help you spot a potential problem in the project — for example, if you find that the majority of resources at the project startup are unskilled or that most of the tasks at the end of the project are on the critical path. Like filters, groups come predefined, or you can create custom groups. Groups also have a function similar to outlining, in which you can collapse and expand groups to better zero in on the tasks or resources that you want to examine more closely.

Applying predefined groups

Predefined groups, which are quick and easy to apply, cover a host of common requirements in projects. Follow these steps to apply a predefined group structure to the project:

1. **Display either a resource view (such as Resource Sheet view) to group resources or a task view (such as Gantt Chart view) to group tasks.**

2. **On the View tab, click the Group By list in the Data group and then choose a criterion.**

   The information is organized according to your selection. Figure 11-6 shows Gantt Chart view grouped by milestone. Tasks that aren't milestones are collapsed.

Figure 11-6:
Tasks grouped as milestones.

❶	Task Name	Predecesso	Duration
	◢ **Milestone: Yes**		**149 days**
	Charter signed		0 days
	Planning complete	6,7,8,9,10,11	0 days
	Registration Available	48,42	0 days
	Start ad campaign	55,73SS,61,6	0 days
	Race		0 days
	▷ **Milestone: No**		**160 days**

To redisplay all tasks or resources in their original order, click the arrow in the Group list on the View tab to display the list. Then select the No Group option. (When no group is applied, the Group box displays `[No Group]`.)

Devising your own groups

Custom groups include three elements: a field name, a field type, and an order. For example, you may create a group that shows the field name (such as Baseline Work) and the field type (such as Task, Resource, or Assignment) in a certain order (descending or ascending). A group that shows Baseline Work for tasks in descending order, for example, would list tasks in order from the greatest number of work hours required to the least number required. Other settings you can specify for groups control the format of the group's appearance, such as its font and font color.

Follow these steps to create a custom group:

1. Choose View ➪ Group ➪ More Groups.

The More Groups dialog box appears, as shown in Figure 11-7.

2. Select either Task or Resource to specify in which list of groups you want to place the new group.

3. Click the New button.

The Group Definition dialog box appears, as shown in Figure 11-8.

Figure 11-8:
The % Work
Complete
group.

4. **In the Name field, type a name for the group.**

5. **Click the first line of the Field Name column, click the down arrow that appears to display the list of choices, and then click a field name to choose it.**

6. **Repeat Step 5 for the Field Type and Order columns.**

    Note that if you want the Field Type option of grouping by assignment rather than by resource or task, you must first select the Group Assignments, Not Tasks check box to make that field available to you. Otherwise, the field type of Task or Resource appears by default.

7. **If you want to add another sorting criteria, click a Then By row and make choices for the Field Name, Field Type, and Order columns.**

8. **If you want the new group to be shown in the list when you click the Group box on the Formatting toolbar, select the Show in Menu check box.**

9. **Depending on the field name you've chosen, you can make settings for the font, cell background, and pattern to format the group.**

    I tell you more about formatting the project schedule in Chapter 13.

10. **If you want to define intervals in which to organize the groups, click the Define Group Intervals button.**

    This step displays the Define Group Interval dialog box, as shown in Figure 11-9. Use these settings to specify a starting time and an interval. For example, if the Group By criterion is % Work Complete, and you select Interval as the Group On setting and then enter a group interval of 10.00, groupings are in 10 percent intervals (those between 0 and 10 percent in one grouping and those between 11 to 20 percent in another, and so on).

Figure 11-9:
Group
interval
options.

> **11.** Click the Save button to save the new group and then click Apply in the More Groups dialog box to apply the group to your plan.

If you want to make changes to an existing predefined group, choose View➪Group By➪More Groups. In the More Groups dialog box, make sure that the group is selected and then click the Edit button. The Group Definition dialog box then appears so that you can edit all those settings for an existing group.

Figuring Out What's Driving the Project

With all the activity taking place in a project — perhaps hundreds of tasks, thousands of dependencies, and calendars, for example — identifying the factors driving a project can be difficult. Three features in Project 2016 can help you see what's driving the project and make those all-important tweaks before finalizing the project plan:

- ✔ **Task Inspector pane:** Identifies the factors driving the timing of tasks in the project, pinpoints problems, and suggests solutions

- ✔ **Task warnings and suggestions:** Help you identify possible schedule issues in manually scheduled tasks

- ✔ **Multiple Undo:** Lets you try different approaches and then undo several changes in a row

Inspecting tasks

When you play a round of golf, several factors can affect your game: an oncoming cold, bad weather, or a defective club. (These are the reasons I give myself, anyway.) Likewise, the timing of every task in a project is affected by certain conditions, known as *task drivers.* The Task Inspector pane can help you recognize these conditions, which can include

✓ **Manual start dates or assignments:** You have manually entered a start date, or you have assigned a resource to a task and the resource isn't available.

✓ **Calendars:** You have assigned a different calendar to the task or resource, or both, and the calendar differences are causing a scheduling conflict.

✓ **Leveling delay:** If you've turned on leveling to handle resource overallocation, the leveling may have caused a task to be delayed. (I discuss leveling in Chapter 12.)

✓ **Constraints:** You apply a constraint to a task, such as forcing it to finish on a certain date.

✓ **Summary tasks:** Their timing is driven by the timing of their child tasks or subtasks.

✓ **Dependency relationships:** A predecessor task can cause changes in a task's timing.

Even though you specify start and finish dates for manually scheduled tasks, you can use the Task Inspector to ensure that the task schedule you've established works in conjunction with other tasks. Project performs behind-the-scenes calculations to determine when each manually scheduled task is likely to occur based on predecessors and its duration. If Project detects that the task is likely to get off track, it warns you about the potential problem and suggests a solution.

To display the Task Inspector pane, change to a task-oriented view such as Gantt Chart view and simply click the Inspect button in the Task group on the Task tab. The Task Inspector pane appears. Click the task that you want to inspect, and the pane explains the various conditions driving the timing of the selected task, as shown in Figure 11-10. If the Task Inspector pane includes schedule change options such as the two shown in the figure, you can click the button for a solution to apply it to the task. Click the Close button in the Task Inspector pane when you're done.

Handling task warnings and suggestions

When you work with auto-scheduled tasks, Project can reschedule them for you when you establish task dependencies. Because the start and finish dates of manually scheduled tasks are hard-wired (fixed), Project loses the useful ability to move them around when predecessor task schedules change. Even though Project can't automatically move manually scheduled tasks, it performs forecasted calculations for completing each manually scheduled task based on the task's links and other drivers. If Project finds that a potential scheduling problem may occur with a manually scheduled task, it alerts you — even when the Task Inspector pane isn't open.

Figure 11-10:
The Task
Inspector
pane shows
you the
influences
on the
timing of
a task.

These alerts appear in the form of warnings (a red diamond with an exclamation point inside) and suggestions. Warnings represent problems that are likely to cause the project to finish off schedule, suggestions give you ideas for optimizing the schedule, perhaps improving on the projected finish date.

Figure 11-11 shows a warning that the task will go past its deadline. You can see that there is also an overallocation icon that indicates that the task has overallocated resources.

Figure 11-11:
A task with
a warning
icon.

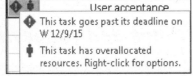

Right-click the task with the warning to display a shortcut menu with options for addressing the potential schedule problem at the top, as shown in Figure 11-12. If you want to apply a schedule change option, click it on the shortcut menu.

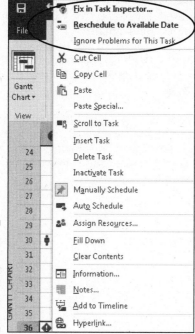

Figure 11-12:
Right-click a
cell that
shows a
warning
icon.

Here's a rundown of the choices you may see:

- ✔ **Reschedule to Available Date:** If an overallocated resource is assigned to the task, this choice reschedules all or part of the task to a time frame when the resource is available to handle the work.

- ✔ **Respect Links:** This warning solution moves the task based on the timing of its predecessor task. In most cases, this solution moves the task later based on the predecessor task's schedule.

- ✔ **Switch to Auto Schedule:** This warning solution typically appears for manually scheduled summary tasks. It also appears as a suggestion solution for subtasks. Choosing this schedule change causes the summary task to recalculate based on the roll-up values of its subtasks. For subtasks, the switch typically means that the task can move to an earlier spot in the schedule, potentially improving the schedule for any successor tasks, too.

- ✔ **Fix in Task Inspector:** Clicking this choice opens the Task Inspector pane so that you can review the drivers and other scheduling factors for the task before choosing a schedule change.

✔ **Ignore Problems for This Task:** This option allows the overallocated resources to remain overallocated. It will keep the warning indicator if the task is still expected to go past its deadline.

Schedule warnings appear by default. To view suggestions, select the Task tab and click the drop-down arrow on the Inspect Task button in the Task group. Then choose Show Suggestions.

Task scheduling warnings and suggestions typically don't appear unless you've outlined the task list, creating summary tasks. Because some of the warning and scheduling calculations are based on summary task information, you should follow the good practice of organizing the schedule using the work breakdown structure (described in Chapter 2).

Chapter 12

Negotiating Project Constraints

• •

In This Chapter

▶ Adding contingency reserve to tasks

▶ Making adjustments to shorten the schedule

▶ Managing costs

▶ Resolving resource conflicts

▶ Moving a project to a better time

• •

*A*fter you know which issues are affecting the project schedule, you can start to develop ways to address them. Sometimes, you simply have to recognize that events (especially on projects) don't always play out as planned. A sprinkling of contingency reserve may resolve the issue.

After you work out the initial version of the schedule, budget, and resource assignments, you meet with stakeholders to negotiate changes based on their priorities. For example, you might ask these questions:

✔ Can the schedule be altered to contain costs?

✔ Can in-house resources be added to expedite the work?

✔ Can less-expensive resources be hired to save money?

In this chapter, I describe multiple options for negotiating the various constraints of time, resources, scope, and costs that affect the project.

It's about Time

Suppose that the boss asks you to commit to completing a project by a certain date. Your palms get sweaty and the pit of your stomach feels queasy, but then, for cover, you tack on a week to the targeted finish date and promise to deliver the impossible.

You hope that you can do it. You want to do it. But *can* you do it?

Project helps you feel confident about committing to a time frame, because you can see how long every task takes to complete. Before you make promises to the boss, you had better know the total length of time to complete the project and its *critical path* — the longest series of tasks that must be completed on time in order to meet the overall project finish date.

The timing data for the project summary task tells you how long the entire project will take to complete. Simply display Gantt Chart view and look at the Duration, Start, and Finish columns. If the finish date isn't feasible, you have to modify tasks or resources or negotiate a different date.

Before you commit to an unreasonable date, remember Murphy's Law: Anything that can go wrong will go wrong. And it *thrives* on projects. To lessen Murphy's influence, you allocate contingency reserve, as described in the next section "Applying contingency reserve."

Applying contingency reserve

Contingency reserve is either time or money that is factored into the schedule or the budget to mitigate identified risks. A *risk* is an uncertain event or condition that, if it occurs, affects the schedule (or another project objective, such as cost, resources, or performance). The proper way to deal with uncertainty on a project is to conduct a thorough risk analysis, as described in the later sidebar "Working with risk."

For those risks you accept, because you either choose not to develop a response or can't further mitigate their probability or impact, you can set aside contingency reserve to address the event when and if it occurs. No prescribed equation can determine the appropriate amount of reserve to set aside; every project is different. Here's a list of factors that generally indicate you should set aside more reserve:

✔ New or unproven technology

✔ Complex projects with numerous interfaces

✔ Projects that are unfamiliar to your organization

✔ Resources unfamiliar with the type of work to be done

✔ A constrained budget

✔ Business-critical or high-profile project

To provide contingency reserve in the schedule, an unresourced task is commonly added at the end of every project phase or before a major deliverable is due. This strategy increases the likelihood that you'll meet the due date of a milestone or phase. Figure 12-1 shows how a task called Registration Contingency was added to reduce the probability that a slip on any task in the Registration work packages would delay the Registration Available milestone. If everything goes as planned, then the contingency won't be used. However, if there are tasks that need to be reworked, or if there are problems with a resource, or if a stakeholder isn't available for feedback, there is some reserve built in.

Set aside contingency reserve for both the schedule and the budget.

Figure 12-1:
Adding contingency in the schedule.

⊿ Registration		67 days	T 4/28/16	F 7/29/16
▷ Database		25 days	T 4/28/16	W 6/1/16
▷ User Interface		27 days	T 6/2/16	F 7/8/16
▷ Payment		12 days	M 7/11/16	T 7/26/16
▷ Confirmation		10 days	M 7/11/16	F 7/22/16
Registration Contingency	48	1 wk	M 7/25/16	F 7/29/16
Registration Available	48,42,49	0 days	F 7/29/16	F 7/29/16

Working with risk

All projects have risk. There are too many unknown factors for you to be able to expect your project to go exactly as planned. To account for these unknown elements, take the time to follow these steps:

1. **Work with your team to create a list of all possible risks.**

   Analyze the WBS, schedule, budget, technical documentation, and any other documentation you can get your hands on.

2. **Calculate the probability that the risks you've identified will occur, and determine their impact.**

   For example, risks may affect the schedule, budget, scope, quality, stakeholder satisfaction, or another objective.

3. **Prioritize the risks by those that have the greatest impact and probability.**

4. **Develop a response plan for risks that are likely to have a significant impact if they occur.**

   Responses may include these strategies: Avoid the risk altogether, find a different way to perform a task, eliminate the risky part of the project, reduce the probability or impact of the event (or both), transfer the risk to someone else (such as a vendor) to handle, or accept the risk.

5. **Update the project schedule.**

   Include the work, resources, time, and funding that are necessary to implement the risk responses as appropriate.

Completing a task in less time

If you do your homework and add contingency reserve to the project (refer to the preceding section), you're making the plan realistic but also adding time to the project. When the project finish date just won't work for the powers that be, you have to try a few tactics to chop the timing down to size.

Checking dependencies

The timing of the plan is determined by the duration of each task and by its *dependencies* — the relationships you build between tasks. Ask yourself whether you've built all dependencies in the best way possible. Perhaps one task didn't start until another was finished but the second task could have started two days before the end of its predecessor. Building in this type of overlap (known as *fast tracking*) can save you time.

Use the Task Inspector pane, covered in Chapter 11, to scope out dependencies.

Here's an example: You created a finish-to-start relationship for the Do Research and Write Speech tasks, such that you couldn't start writing the speech until your research was finished. But is that true? Couldn't you do a first draft of the speech starting three-fourths of the way through the research? Especially when you have two different resources working on those tasks, initiating the second task before the first is complete can save you time.

Over the life of a project with hundreds of tasks, adding that kind of overlap to even a few dozen tasks can save you a month of time or more.

You can take a refresher course in creating and changing dependencies in Chapter 4.

Managing the availability of resources

Another factor that drives timing is the availability of resources. Sometimes in a dependency relationship, one task can't start before another ends, simply because the resources aren't available until the predecessor task is over. Look for these potential problems with resource-dependent timing:

- ✔ You delayed the start of a task because a resource wasn't available. But perhaps another resource can do the work. If so, switch resources and let the task start sooner.

- ✔ Project calculates the duration of auto-scheduled tasks (Fixed Work and Fixed Units with effort-driven scheduling) according to the number of resources available to do the work. If you add resources to these tasks, Project shortens their duration.

✔ If you assign a more highly skilled resource to certain tasks, you may be able to reduce the hours of work required to complete the task, because the skilled person can finish the work more quickly.

✔ Assigning more resources to tasks on the critical path can shorten those effort-driven tasks.

✔ You have money but no time or resources. Consider hiring an outside vendor to handle the work.

Chapter 9 covers the mechanics of making and changing resource assignments.

Cutting to the chase: Deleting tasks

When all else fails and you've reduced as much time as possible using the methods described in the preceding sections, it's time to cut some specific corners. First, consider skipping nonvital tasks. Then ask whether you can revisit the goals of the project with stakeholders and perhaps reduce its scope so that you can jettison tasks from the schedule. You can even negotiate for less-stringent quality or performance levels.

Never eliminate all slack in the schedule. Slack is your friend; it provides scheduling flexibility around resources.

Trading time for cost

Sometimes, the most critical objective in a project is the schedule. If that's the case on your project, you may be able to negotiate for a larger budget to reduce the overall duration. You then use the extra funds to pay for overtime, add resources, expedite shipping, or increase the hourly commitment of existing resources. Reducing the schedule by throwing money (in the form of resources) at the problem is called *crashing*. However, not all tasks can be crashed. Tasks that have truly fixed durations take as long as they take, regardless of the number of resources you throw at them.

To crash the schedule, start by analyzing tasks to see where you can deduct the most time from the schedule for the least cost. After you exploit this task, move to the next least-expensive task, and so on.

Focus only on the tasks that are on the critical path. Reducing the duration of tasks that aren't on it does no good if you're trying to reduce the overall length of the project.

At some point, you'll reduce the duration of the critical path to the extent that you have a different critical path. Then you can go to work on the new critical path.

The more you fast-track, crash, and de-scope the project, the more likely it is to be late. That's right: At some point, you'll have compressed as much time as possible from the schedule and it will have multiple critical paths and near-critical paths. If any task on any of those paths slips, the project will need to use some contingency reserve. And if you aren't careful, you'll use it all up and make the project late.

Getting What You Want for Less

After you assign all resources to tasks and set all fixed costs, sticker shock may set in. Project tallies all those costs and shows you the project's budget. If those numbers simply won't work, follow these tips for trimming the bottom line:

- **Use less-expensive resources.** A high-priced engineer may be assigned to a task that can be performed by a junior engineer, for example. Or you may have assigned a high-priced manager to supervise a task that can be handled by a lower-salaried line supervisor.

- **Lower fixed costs.** If the budget allows for the travel costs associated with four plant visits, calculate whether you can manage with only three, and try to book flights ahead of time to get cheaper airfares. Look for a vendor who can sell you that piece of equipment for less than the $4,000 you allocated — or make the old equipment last for one more project.

- **Reduce overtime.** If resources who earn overtime are overallocated, reduce their hours or use resources who are on straight salary for those 14-hour days.

- **Complete the task in less time.** The resource cost is a factor of task duration, hourly wage, or number of units. If you change tasks so that fewer work hours are needed in order to complete them, tasks cost less. However, don't be unrealistic about the time it *truly* takes to complete the work.

The Resource Recourse

Before you finalize the plan, consider resource workload. As you delved into assigning resources to tasks in the project, you probably created situations where resources must work around the clock for days on end. The first step in finalizing your resources is to spot those overallocations — then you have to help those poor folks out!

Checking resource availability

To resolve problems with resource assignments, you have to first figure out where the problems lie by taking a look at a few views that focus on resource assignment.

Resource Usage view, shown in Figure 12-2, and Resource Graph view, shown in Figure 12-3, are useful in helping you spot overbooked resources. In Resource Usage view, the overbooked resource is shown in red, and the overallocation icon (a little red person in the Indicator column) appears. In Resource Graph view, the graph bars are shown in red for any allocation over the units allowed for the resource. In this case, Bonnie is overallocated for five days.

Figure 12-2:
Resource Usage view spells out the workload day by day.

ⓘ	Resource Name	Work	Details	T	F	S	May 29, '16 S	M	T	W	T
⚑	⊿ **Bonnie Rush**	**1,280 hrs**	Work	16h	16h			16h	16h	16h	8h
	Team management	280 hrs	Work	2h	2h			2h	2h	2h	2h
	Risk management	280 hrs	Work	2h	2h			2h	2h	2h	2h
	Change management	280 hrs	Work	2h	2h			2h	2h	2h	2h
	Stakeholder management	280 hrs	Work	2h	2h			2h	2h	2h	2h

Figure 12-3:
Resource Graph view gives you a visual clue to overworked resources.

Keep in mind that resources are flagged as overallocated in these Resource views based on their assignment percentages and calendars. A resource based on a standard calendar showing 8-hour days, assigned at 100 percent to a task, will work 8 hours a day on it. If you assign the same resource at 50 percent to another task that happens at the same time, the resource will put in 12-hour days (8 plus 4) and be marked as overallocated.

In Resource Usage view, any overallocated resource has the exclamation point in the Indicator column. The total hours that the resource is working each day on his combined tasks are summarized on the line that lists the resource's name. In Resource Graph view, work is summarized in the Peak Units row at the bottom, and all work that exceeds the maximum allowable amount is highlighted in the bar graphic.

Deleting or modifying a resource assignment

Suppose that you discover that a resource (I'll call her Janet) is working 16 hours on Tuesday and 14 hours on Friday. You have several options to rectify the workload:

✔ **Remove Janet from a few tasks to free up some time.** This option is good if she's working on noncritical tasks, especially if other resources are working on those same tasks.

✔ **Change Janet's Resource calendar to allow for a longer workday — for example, 12 hours.** A 100 percent assignment will therefore have Janet working 12 hours on any single task in a day. If you stretch a resource's workday, reduce the resource's assignments also. For example, if someone frequently spends 16 hours on two tasks in one day (based on an 8-hour calendar) and two 100 percent assignments, change to a 12-hour calendar and 50 percent assignments (6 hours on each of the two tasks, totaling 12 hours a day). However, if the resource typically works an 8-hour day and 12- or 16-hour days *are the exception,* don't change the resource's base calendar; it will affect *all* assignments for that resource. And if an overtime pay rate applies, remember to authorize (add) it.

The first two options in this list may lengthen the tasks that the resource is assigned to, regardless of whether you remove the resource or reduce the resource's assignment.

✔ **Change Janet's availability by increasing her assignment units to more than 100% in the Resource Information dialog box.** For example, if you enter **150%** as her available units, you're authorizing her to work 12 hours a day, and Project then doesn't consider her overallocated until her working time exceeds 12 hours.

✔ **Use Team Planner view to shuffle some of Janet's tasks to other resources.** When you're making the switch, Team Planner view provides the best visibility into how changes affect various resources.

✔ **Ignore the problem.** I don't mean this statement facetiously; sometimes, a resource can reasonably work 14 hours *for a day or two* during the life of a project, and you don't need to change the resource's usual working allocation to eliminate the exclamation point in the indicator column. (However, let Janet order pizza on the company's tab on those long workdays — and don't let them become the norm.) A resource who is scheduled for even a few minutes more than the calendar allows is flagged as overallocated. As the project manager, it isn't worth the effort for you to attempt to resolve tiny overallocations that don't affect the project schedule.

Beating overallocations with quick-and-dirty rescheduling

Gantt Chart view also clues you in to overbooked resources. When a task has an overallocated resource assigned, the Overallocation icon appears in the Indicator column. To fix the overallocation, you can right-click the icon and choose Reschedule to Available Date (refer to Figure 11-12 in the preceding chapter). This method reschedules all or part of the task to a period when the resource is available to fix the overallocation, if possible. You can always undo the change if you disagree with its impact on the overall project schedule. This method can't fix all overallocations, so if the icon remains after you choose Reschedule to Available Date, look at other methods to resolve the problem. Right-clicking the icon again and choosing Fix in Task Inspector from the menu enables the Task Inspector to give you ideas for fixing the overallocation.

Finding help

When one person is overworked, you have to look for help. You can free resources in several ways.

For starters, you can assign someone to help on a task and thus reduce the overbooked resource's workload. Reduce the resource's work assignment on one or more tasks, perhaps by reducing 100 percent assignments to 50 percent. You do this in the Task Information dialog box on the Resources tab or by selecting the task and clicking the Assign Resources tool to open the Assign Resources dialog box.

Quickly check a work graph for any resource by clicking the Graphs button in the Assign Resources dialog box.

You'll also find that by adding resources to certain tasks, you shorten the task duration. You may, therefore, free the resource in time to eliminate a conflict with a later task in the project.

Experiment with changing the work contour of the resource. By default, Project has a resource work on a task at the same level, or *flat-loaded,* for the life of the task. You can modify the work contour, for example, so that a resource invests the highest level of effort at the start of a task, which frees the resource's workload later when a conflict with another assignment might occur. See Chapter 9 for information about how to apply a work contour to a resource assignment.

Leveling resources

Project calculates *resource leveling* to try to resolve resource overallocations in the project. The feature works in two ways: by delaying a task until the overbooked resource is freed up or by splitting tasks. Splitting a task involves (essentially) stopping it at some point, thereby freeing the resource, and then resuming it later, when the resource is available.

You can make these types of changes yourself or let Project make the calculation. Project first delays tasks that involve overallocated resources to use up any available slack. When no more slack is available on these tasks, Project makes changes based on any priorities you've entered for tasks, dependency relationships that are affected, and task constraints (such as a Finish No Later Than constraint).

Don't worry: You can turn on leveling to see which changes Project would make and then clear the leveling to reverse those actions if you don't like the results.

To level the resources in the project, follow these steps:

1. **From the Resource tab, go to the Level group and select Leveling Options.**

   The Resource Leveling dialog box appears, as shown in Figure 12-4.

2. **Choose whether to allow Project to level automatically or manually:**

   - *Automatic* tells Project to level every time you change the plan.

   - *Manual* requires you to click the Level All button in the Resource Leveling dialog box or use the Level All button on the Resource tab.

Figure 12-4:
The
Resource
Leveling
dialog box.

3. **If you choose to level automatically, select the Clear Leveling Values before Leveling check box if you want previous leveling actions to be reversed before you level the next time.**

4. **Set the leveling range to one of these options:**

   - *Level Entire Project*
   - *Level <a date range>*

   If you choose the latter option, fill in a date range by making choices in the From and To boxes.

5. **From the Leveling Order drop-down list, click the down arrow and make a choice:**

   - *Standard* considers slack, dependencies, priorities, and constraints.
   - *ID Only* delays or splits the task with the highest ID number — in other words, the last task in the project.
   - *Priority, Standard* uses task priority as the first criterion in making choices to delay or split tasks (rather than using up slack).

6. **Select any of the five check boxes at the bottom to control how Project levels:**

   - *Level Only within Available Slack:* No critical tasks are delayed, and the current finish date for the project is retained.

- *Leveling Can Adjust Individual Assignments on a Task:* Project removes or changes assignments.

- *Leveling Can Create Splits in the Remaining Work:* Certain tasks are placed on hold until resources are freed up for work.

- *Level Resources with the Proposed Booking Type:* Booking type (proposed or committed) relates to the firmness of your commitment to using that particular resource. *Allowing resource leveling to consider a resource's booking type* means that committed resource assignments are considered more sacred than proposed assignments when Project makes changes.

- *Level Manually Scheduled Tasks:* Project moves the task even if you've scheduled it manually.

7. **Click the Level All button to have Project perform the leveling operation.**

To reverse leveling, choose Resource Tab⇨Clear Leveling.

When you have only a few instances of overallocated resources, go to the Resource tab and choose Level Group⇨Level Resource. Select the resource from the Level Resources dialog box (shown in Figure 12-5) and then click Level Now.

Figure 12-5: The Level Resources dialog box.

To level or not to level?

As both a process and a program feature, resource leveling has pros and cons. It can make changes that you may not want it to make — for example, removing a resource from a task where you absolutely need that person's unique skills. Leveling frequently delays the project's finish date, which may not be acceptable to you (or your boss).

The safest setting for resource leveling (the one that makes the least drastic changes to the

timing) is to level only within slack. This setting may delay certain tasks, but it doesn't delay the project completion date.

If you can't live with the changes resulting from resource leveling, the capability to turn it on and off is vital. After you turn on this feature, look at its changes to resolve resource problems, and then turn it off and manually institute the portions of the solution that work for you.

To be successful, take the time to find the best combination of all these methods. Solving problems is often a trial-and-error process. Although you may initially look for a single quick fix, the best solution usually results from making lots of small changes.

Rescheduling the Project

From time to time, you have to hit the brakes on a project. For example, you may set up an entire project schedule, and just as you're ready to start rolling, the project is put on hold, caused by a budget shortfall, priorities that have changed, resources being pulled to another project, or cold feet on the part of stakeholders. It happens, but it also happens that projects have a way of coming back to life. The good news for you is that if the essential facts of the project (such as its scope and the resources you've planned to use) haven't changed, you can simply reschedule the entire project to start from a later date rather than rebuild the plan from scratch. This process reschedules both auto-scheduled and manually scheduled tasks so that you don't even have to use your thinking cap.

To reschedule the project, follow these steps:

1. **Choose Project, Go to the Schedule Group, then click Move Project.**

    The Move Project dialog box appears, as shown in Figure 12-6. You can use it to reschedule an entire project that was put on hold.

Figure 12-6:
The Move
Project
dialog box.

2. **Enter the new project start date in the New Project Start Date field, or choose a date from the drop-down calendar.**

3. **Select the Move Deadlines check box if you want Project to move any deadlines that are assigned to tasks.**

4. **Click the OK button.**

Chapter 13

Making the Project Look Good

In This Chapter

▶ Formatting the Gantt chart

▶ Formatting Network Diagram task boxes

▶ Dressing up task boxes

▶ Modifying the layout of a view

▶ Changing the gridlines in a view

▶ Adding graphics to the project

▶ Creating a custom field

*Y*ou may know the saying "Clothes make the man." Well, in the same spirit, sometimes the look of the schedule makes the project. Having a project that looks good serves two purposes: It impresses people with your professionalism and people can look at the project on the screen and on hard copy to easily discern the different boxes, bars, and lines.

Project uses default formatting that's helpful in most cases. However, if you have certain company standards for reporting — say, representing baseline data in yellow and actual data in blue, or more frequent gridlines to help the nearsighted CEO read Project reports more easily — Project has you covered.

Whatever you need, Project provides tremendous flexibility in formatting various elements in the plan.

Looking Good!

Microsoft has decided to capitulate to the artist in all of us by allowing users to modify shapes, colors, patterns, and other graphical elements in the Project schedule. You gain great flexibility in determining how the schedule looks.

When you print a Project view (as covered in Chapter 18), you can print a legend on every page. The legend helps readers comprehend the meaning of the various colors in the plan (or the shading, if it's printed in black and white) along with shapes that you set for elements.

All the views and formatting choices that Project offers you aren't confined to the screen; you can print the schedule or reports. Whatever information is displayed onscreen when you print a view is also printed. So knowing how to make all kinds of changes onscreen allows you to present information to team members, managers, vendors, and clients on hard copy too.

By using all the improved methods of collaborating on projects, such as sharing documents via Project Web App, you can make a visually appealing schedule available to even more people across the web.

Printing in color is useful because you can provide the full visual impact and nuance of the various colors used for graphical elements, such as taskbars and indicators. If you print in black and white, you may find that certain colors that look good onscreen aren't distinct when you print them. When you modify the formatting, the project can look good in color *and* in black and white, and onscreen and in print.

Formatting the Gantt Chart

Project 2016 allows you to customize the Gantt chart in several ways. You can choose different taskbars, add text inside taskbars, and supply different ends. You can highlight the critical path so that it stands out, and you can change the font styles in the sheet section of the schedule.

Formatting taskbars

Taskbars are the horizontal boxes that represent the timing of tasks in the Chart pane of Gantt Chart view. You can format a bar individually, change the formatting settings on different types of taskbars, or apply a new style that controls bar formatting on the entire chart.

You can change several characteristics about taskbars:

✔ **The shape that appears at the start and end of the bar:** The ends can be formatted with different shapes, such as arrows and triangles.

✔ **The shape, pattern, and color of the middle of the bar:** You can change the shape's type and color.

> ✔ **The text that you can set to appear in five locations around the bar (to the left or right of the bar or above, below, or inside it):** You can include text in any or all of these locations; just don't add so many text items that they become impossible to read. As a rule, use only enough text to help readers of the plan identify information, especially on printouts of large schedules where a task may appear far to the right of the Task Name column that identifies it by name in the sheet area.

When you track progress on a task, a progress bar is superimposed on the taskbar. You can format the shape, pattern, and color of the progress bar. The goal is to contrast the progress bar with the baseline taskbar so that you can see both clearly.

By formatting taskbars, you can help readers of the plan identify various elements, such as progress or milestones. If you make changes to individual taskbars, people who are accustomed to the standard formatting in Project may have trouble reading the plan. In other words, don't get carried away.

To create formatting settings for various types of taskbars, follow these steps:

1. **From the Format tab, select Format in the Bar Styles group and then choose Bar Styles.**

   The Bar Styles dialog box appears, as shown in Figure 13-1.

Figure 13-1: The Bar Styles dialog box.

2. **On the spreadsheet, along the top in the Name column, select the type of task that you want to modify (Split, Progress, or Milestone, for example).**

   To modify the styles used for all summary tasks, for example, select Summary. The choices on the Bars tab in the bottom half of the dialog box change based on the selected task type.

3. **Click in the Show For Tasks column for the task type you want to modify and then select criteria for the task, such as Critical or Finished, from the drop-down list that appears.**

4. **Click the Bars tab at the bottom of the dialog box to display your options, and then click the down arrows next to the following options:**

   • *Shape:* Modify the shape of either end or the middle of the taskbar.

     Shapes on either end may be any one of 24 shapes (as shown in Figure 13-2), though you may commonly see an arrow, a diamond, or a circle. The shape in the middle consists of a bar of a certain width.

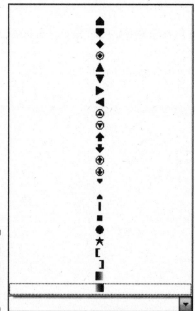

Figure 13-2: Various bar-style end shapes.

   • *Color:* Modify the color used on either end or in the middle of the taskbar.

     Project now enables you to choose among various theme colors (as in the other Office applications).

- *Type:* Modify the type of formatting for the shape on either end of the taskbar.

    This setting controls how the shape is outlined: framed with a solid line, surrounded by a dashed line, or filled in with a solid color.

- *Pattern:* Select another pattern for the middle of the bar.

5. Click the Text tab and then

> *a. Click any text location.*
>
> An arrow appears at the end of that line.
>
> *b. Click the down arrow to display an alphabetical list of possible data fields to include and then click a field name to select it.*
>
> *c. Repeat Steps 5a and 5b to choose additional text locations.*
>
> Figure 13-3 shows how resource names are selected for the right side of the bar and how the WBS is selected inside the bar.

6. Click the OK button to accept all new taskbar settings.

Figure 13-3:
Add text to
as many as
five loca-
tions in and
around
taskbars.

Text	Bars	
	Left	
	Right	Resource Names
	Top	
	Bottom	
	Inside	WBS

If you want to make the same types of changes to an individual taskbar rather than to all taskbars of a certain type, right-click the taskbar and choose the Format Bar option. The Format Bar dialog box appears, offering the same Text and Bars tabs found in the Bar Styles dialog box, without the options at the top to select the type of item to format.

Zeroing in on critical issues

The Gantt chart doesn't show the critical path by default. All subtask taskbars appear in blue, no matter the specifics surrounding the task. To give the critical path visibility, you can make the bars for critical paths appear in a color that stands out, such as dark red.

Displaying the critical path is a snap: Simply click the Gantt Chart Tools Format contextual tab on the Ribbon and then select the Critical Tasks check box in the Bar Styles group. Whenever Critical Tasks is selected, Project applies the special color to the critical taskbars.

Restyling the Gantt chart

If those boring red and blue Gantt bars are cramping your style, not to worry: You can try a new look, including a different color scheme, by applying a new Gantt Chart style. Working in Gantt Chart view, click the Gantt Chart Tools Format contextual tab. Then click the More drop-down button in the Gantt Chart Style group to display the available styles, as shown in Figure 13-4. Select the style you want, and Project reformats the whole project. It doesn't get much simpler!

Figure 13-4: Project 2016 offers over-all Gantt chart styles.

If you want to format the sheet portion of Gantt Chart view, too, start by clicking the Gantt Chart Tools Format contextual tab. Click the Text Styles button in the Format group to open a dialog box for changing the text font, size, and other options. Figure 13-5 shows a customization of critical tasks to have a bold Calibri 12-point font with a purple color. You can choose any font, style, size, color, pattern, or background for the font style. You aren't limited to changing only critical tasks; you have 18 other types of tasks you can change, including milestones, summary tasks, and bar styles. You can also use the Wrap Text button in the Columns group to control whether text automatically wraps in a particular cell or column.

Formatting Task Boxes

Network Diagram task boxes use different shapes to help you spot different types of tasks:

- ✔ **Summary tasks** use a slightly slanted box shape and include a plus sign (+) or minus symbol (–), depending on whether the summary task's subtasks are hidden or displayed. Click the symbol to hide or display subtasks.

- ✔ **Subtasks** show up in simple rectangular boxes.

- ✔ **Milestones** are shown in boxes with points on both ends.

You can change the formatting of each task box individually or by type. To change the formatting of task boxes displayed in Network Diagram view, follow these steps:

1. **Display Network Diagram view.**

2. **Right-click the task box that you want to change and then choose Format Box.**

   Alternatively, right-click anywhere outside the task boxes and then choose Box Styles to change the formatting of all boxes of a certain style.

The Format Box dialog box (or the Box Styles dialog box) appears, as shown in Figure 13-6.

Figure 13-6:
Changing
styles for a
single box in
the Format
Box dialog
box.

3. **To modify the border style, make selections in the Shape, Color, and Width lists.**

4. **To modify the background area inside the box, make a selection in the Color list or Pattern list, or both (at the bottom of the dialog box).**

5. **Click the OK button to save these new settings.**

When you modify the formatting of individual boxes in Network Diagram view, the standard settings of slanted summary tasks no longer serve as visual guides to *all* tasks. If you make changes and decide to restore a task box to its default setting, click the Reset button in the Format Box dialog box.

Adjusting the Layout

In addition to displaying particular columns and formatting taskbars, you can make certain changes to the layout of the view. These options vary a great deal, depending on the view. The layout of Calendar view and Network Diagram view is quite different from the layout choices offered in Gantt Chart view, for example.

To display the Layout dialog box for a view, right-click the area (for example, the chart area in Gantt Chart view) or anywhere in Calendar view or Network Diagram view and then choose Layout from the menu that appears. Alternatively, regardless of the view, you can select the Layout option from the Format Group on the Format tab. The appropriate dialog box appears. Figures 13-7, 13-8, and 13-9 show the various layout choices available in different views.

Figure 13-7:
The Layout dialog box in Gantt Chart view.

Figure 13-8:
The Layout dialog box in Network Diagram view.

Figure 13-9:
The Layout
dialog box in
Calendar
view.

The settings in these Layout dialog boxes generally reflect how the elements on the page are arranged and how dependency link lines are displayed.

Table 13-1 describes the layout settings. You could likely spend a week or so experimenting with all these settings to see what they look like, and I could spend a few days writing about the various options. The tools that Project offers to modify the formatting of elements such as taskbars and task boxes provide helpful flexibility.

Table 13-1		Layout Options
Layout View	*Option*	*How It's Used*
Calendar	Use Current Sort Order	Project uses the latest sort order you've applied to tasks.
	Attempt to Fit as Many Tasks as Possible	The sort order is ignored, and as many tasks as possible are fitted into a date box.
	Show Bar Splits	When a task includes a period of inactivity, the task can be shown as being split into different parts over time.
	Automatic Layout	Project modifies the layout in response to the insertion of additional tasks.
Network Diagram	Layout Mode area	Automatic or manual positioning is allowed.
	Box Layout area	These settings arrange and align boxes; adjust alignment, spacing, and height; and modify the display of summary tasks.
	Link Style area	The style for dependency link lines and labels is modified.
	Link Color area	The color for links is set both on and off the critical path.
	Diagram Options area	The background color and pattern of boxes as well as page breaks and task progress are controlled.

Layout View	Option	How It's Used
Gantt Chart	Links	The style of lines indicating dependency links are set.
	Date Format	The format of the date used to label taskbars is modified.
	Bar Height	The height of taskbars is set in points.
	Always Roll Up Gantt Bars	When this option is selected, taskbar details roll up to the highest-level summary task.
	Round Bars to Whole Days	When you use portions of days, bars are allowed to represent the nearest whole-day increment.
	Show Bar Splits	A task that includes a period of inactivity can be shown as split into different segments over time.
	Show Drawings	Drawings are displayed onscreen and on the printout.

Now that you know the options available for modifying view layouts, I have some advice: Stick with the default settings unless you have a specific reason to make a change (such as when you want to highlight certain types of information for a project presentation). When you no longer need a layout change, return to the default settings. Or if you want to make changes, make them globally across the organization and stick to them. Then someone reading the project plan can more easily interpret the different kinds of information presented in views. Generally speaking, if you tinker too often with the way Project displays information, it only makes your own learning curve steeper — and confuses those who know the default settings in Project.

Modifying Gridlines

Just as phone numbers are divided into several shorter sets of numbers to help you remember them, visual elements are often broken up graphically to help you understand information in chunks. Tables use lines, calendars use boxes, football fields use yard lines, and so on.

Several views in Project include gridlines to indicate certain elements, such as a break between weeks or the status date (that is, the date to which progress has been tracked on a project). These lines help someone reading the plan to discern intervals of time or breaks in information; for example, gridlines can be used to indicate major and minor column breaks. You can modify these gridlines in several ways, including changing the color and style of the lines and the interval at which they appear.

To modify gridlines, use the Gridlines dialog box and follow these steps:

1. **Right-click any area of a view that contains a grid (for example, the chart area of Gantt Chart view or Calendar view) and then choose Gridlines.**

   The Gridlines dialog box appears, as shown in Figure 13-10. You can also display the Gantt Chart Tools Format contextual tab, select Gridlines in the Format group, and then click Gridlines to open the dialog box.

Figure 13-10: The Gridlines dialog box.

Gridlines
Line to change:
Gantt Rows
Bar Rows
Middle Tier Column
Bottom Tier Column
Current Date
Sheet Rows
Sheet Columns
Title Vertical
Title Horizontal
Page Breaks
Project Start

Normal — Type: — Color: Automatic
At interval — ● None ○ 2 ○ 3 ○ 4 ○ Other: 0
Type: — Color: Automatic
Help — OK — Cancel

2. **In the Line to Change list, select the gridline you want to modify.**

3. **Use the Normal Type and Color lists to select a line style and color.**

4. **If you want to use a contrasting color at various intervals in the grid to make it easier to read, follow these steps:**

   a. *Select an interval at which to include a contrasting line.*

      This setting is typically used with a different style or color from the Normal line setting to mark minor intervals for a grid. Note that not every type of gridline can use contrasting intervals.

   b. *Choose the type and color of that line from the lists.*

5. **Click the OK button to save these settings.**

You make choices for modifying gridlines one by one, and you have no Reset button to revert to the original settings. Gridlines modified in one view don't affect gridlines in any other view.

Recognizing When a Picture Can Say It All

Words, numbers, taskbars, and task boxes work well in the plan, but you may want to add elements of your own, such as drawing a circle around a task to draw attention to it or adding a simple drawing to show a process or working relationship.

You can use a drawing tool on the Gantt Chart Tools Format contextual tab of the Ribbon to draw images in the chart area of Gantt Chart view. Follow these steps to add a drawing:

1. **Display Gantt Chart view.**

2. **Click the Gantt Chart Tools Format tab and then, in the Drawings group, click Drawing.**

   The menu of available shapes and commands appears, as shown in Figure 13-11.

Figure 13-11: Using drawing tools to add basic shapes.

3. **Click the drawing tool that represents the type of object you want to draw, such as an oval or a rectangle.**

4. **At the location on the chart where you want to draw the object, drag the mouse until the item is drawn approximately to the scale you want.**

5. **Release the mouse button.**

When you draw an object over an element such as a taskbar, the drawn object is solid white and covers up whatever is beneath it. You have a couple of choices if you want the item underneath to show through:

- Right-click the object, choose Properties, and click None in the Fill section of the Format Drawing dialog box to remove the fill.

- Right-click the object, choose Arrange, and choose Send to Back to place the object behind the chart elements.

At this point, you have these options:

- **Add text:** If you drew a text box, you can click in it and then type whatever text you want.

- **Resize objects:** Resize any object you've drawn by selecting it and then dragging any of the resize handles (the little black boxes) around its edges outward to enlarge it or inward to shrink it.

- **Move objects:** Move the mouse over the object until the mouse pointer becomes a four-way arrow. Then drag the object elsewhere on the chart.

Creating a Custom Text Field

The tables that Project offers for sheet views often restrict you to particular types of entries. For example, you have to enter a numerical value in any cost-related field. Project offers a number of placeholder fields that you can customize for your own purposes and add to any task or resource table. You can customize the text, cost, number, flag, and other types of fields. A neat shortcut is to create a custom field with a lookup table.

You can use a *lookup table* to create a drop-down list of values to select to create a custom field. That is, when you click a cell in the field, you can then click the drop-down list arrow that appears and select predefined entries. Suppose that you want to add a field that indicates whether an invoice has been submitted, paid, or posted. Creating a custom field with the lookup table offering the possible states of payment can make data entry faster and also help prevent data-entry mistakes that can occur if the field has no restrictions. By default, only the entries in the lookup table may be entered for the field.

To create and use a custom text field with a lookup table, follow these steps:

1. **Display the task- or resource-oriented view and then display the table that you want to customize.**

   You display tables by choosing Tables from the View tab and selecting a table from the list that appears.

2. **Right-click any field column heading and choose Custom Fields from the menu that appears.**

   The Custom Fields dialog box appears.

3. **Select the type of field you want from the list of options, as shown in Figure 13-12.**

Figure 13-12:
Custom field
types.

4. **Click Rename, type a name for the field in the Rename Field dialog box, and click the OK button.**

5. **Back in the Custom Fields dialog box, click the Lookup button.**

   The Edit Lookup Table dialog box appears, as shown in Figure 13-13.

6. **Enter a possible value (such as a date for a date field or a dollar amount for a cost field) in the Value column.**

   You can enter a description for each value in the Description column if necessary.

Figure 13-13:
Setting
values for
the field.

7. **Repeat Step 6 to enter additional values for this field.**

8. **To set an entry as the default setting for the field, select the check box labeled Use a Value from the Table As the Default Entry for the Field, click a value in the list, and click the Set Default button.**

9. **Click the Close button; then click OK to save the list and close all dialog boxes.**

10. **Add the field to the location you want in the table.**

   Click the column to the right of where you want to insert the new column. Choose Format ⇨ Insert Column and then select the column from the drop-down menu that appears.

   Figure 13-14 shows a custom text field with a lookup table added to Resource Sheet view in a project.

Figure 13-14:
The Value
list from the
Training
field.

Task Name	Remaini ▾	Actual Cost ▾	Invoice Status	Add New Column ▾
◢ **Registration**	$32,000.00	$0.00		
◢ **Database**	$14,400.00	$0.00		
Collect database requirements	$2,600.00	$0.00	▾	
Design database	$2,600.00	$0.00	Not invoiced Work is done, but not invoiced	
Develop database	$2,600.00	$0.00	Invoiced Invoice has been submitted, but not paid	
Test database	$2,600.00	$0.00	Paid Invoice has been paid, but no posted	
User acceptance	$4,000.00	$0.00	Posted Amount paid has been posted	

Chapter 14

It All Begins with a Baseline

In This Chapter

▶ Saving plan information with a baseline

▶ Making use of multiple baselines

▶ Setting and resetting baselines

▶ Saving interim plans

*W*hen you go on a diet (hasn't everyone?), you step on the scale the first day to record your starting weight. Then, as the diet progresses, you have a benchmark against which you can compare your dieting ups and downs.

Project lets you benchmark project data so that you can compare the actual activity that takes place on tasks against the original plan. This saved version of the plan data, or *baseline,* includes all information in the project, such as task timing, resource assignments, and costs.

The *interim plan* in Project is essentially a timing checklist. It includes the start and finish dates of tasks, and the estimated start and finish dates for tasks not yet started.

This chapter shows you when, why, and how to save a baseline and an interim plan for the project.

All about Baselines

After you complete all the planning necessary to develop a robust schedule (and other documents) for a project, and after you've made the schedule presentable, it's time to baseline it. The *baseline* represents the project at the moment you consider the plan final and you're ready to commit to it before you begin any activity. The baseline, which is saved in the original Project file, exists alongside the progress you record on tasks in the project.

Key data that a baseline captures includes the baseline start, finish, duration, work, and cost information for each task. After you save a baseline and track activity against it, you can get baseline data and actual data, as well as visual indications of your progress.

You can use a baseline to debrief yourself or the team at any point in a project. The baseline is especially useful at the end of a phase, when you can compare actual progress against estimates from many weeks or months ago. You can then improve your planning skills and learn to make more accurate estimates up front. You can also use a baseline and the actual activity that you track against it to explain delays or cost overruns and to illustrate the impact of significant scope changes to employers or clients by using a wide variety of reports and printed views.

It's a good practice to revisit the baseline and estimates at the end of each phase of the project. If the project lasts longer than six months, however, you're missing out on an opportunity to learn as you go. Plus, you'll likely forget what you were thinking when you produced the original estimates.

Finally, you can also save and clear baselines for only selected tasks. If one task is thrown off track by a major change, for example, you can modify its estimates and leave the rest of the baseline alone.

Saving a baseline

You can save a baseline at any time by opening the Set Baseline dialog box. After you save a baseline the first time, the baseline data of a summary task is updated if you make changes to a subtask below it, such as changing the start date for a task or deleting a task. However, when you're saving the baseline for only a selection of tasks, you can change that functionality by making a choice about how the baseline *rolls up,* or summarizes, data. You can choose to have modifications rolled up to all summary tasks or only from subtasks for any summary tasks you select. This second option works only if you've selected summary tasks and haven't selected their subtasks.

To use rolling wave planning, save a baseline for only selected tasks. In other words, perhaps you've sufficiently detailed the early tasks in the first phase or first month or two of a large project, and you're ready to commit to that part of the plan, but the latter detail still remains to be hammered out. Saving a baseline for earlier tasks allows you and the team to get working on those tasks while allowing for the progressive detailing of later tasks down the line.

To save a baseline, follow these steps:

1. **To save a baseline for only certain tasks, select them by dragging over their task ID (row) numbers.**

2. **Click the Project tab, and in the Schedule group, click the Set Baseline drop-down arrow, and choose Set Baseline.**

   The Set Baseline dialog box appears, with the Set Baseline option selected, as shown in Figure 14-1.

Figure 14-1: Setting baselines and interim plans.

3. **Select either the Entire Project or the Selected Tasks radio button.**

4. **If you chose Selected Tasks in Step 3, make selections for how the baseline rolls up changes to task data.**

   You can summarize changed data in all summary tasks or for only selected summary tasks.

5. **Click the OK button to set the baseline.**

Saving more than one baseline

The concept of multiple baselines seems almost contrary to the definition of a baseline. After all, the purpose of a baseline is to set the proverbial stake in the sand and measure progress against it. You might keep multiple baselines for several purposes. Consider these reasons:

- ✓ **You have a baseline plan for a customer and another one for the internal team.** In other words, you might want to steer the team to a tighter deadline than the promised delivery date.

- ✓ **You have multiple scenarios for the project.** Maybe you're unsure whether you'll need an extra widget for the gadget you're building. You can set one baseline that assumes the extra widget is unnecessary and set another baseline that assumes it's vital.

- ✓ **You're anticipating a risk event taking place.** You want to develop a recovery plan or response plan in one baseline version of the plan.

- ✓ **You're analyzing the effect of a change to the project schedule (or another element of the project plan) that affects the project or product scope.** You can set a different baseline to see the before-and-after effect of the change, though in this case you may prefer to reset the baseline. I discuss resetting the baseline in the later section "Clearing and resetting a baseline."

The Set Baseline dialog box includes a list of these baselines, with a date stamp of the last date each was saved, as shown in Figure 14-2. When you save a baseline, you can save without overwriting an existing baseline by simply selecting another one of the baselines in this list before saving.

Figure 14-2:
Multiple
baseline
options.

If you save multiple baselines or interim plans, you can view them by displaying columns in any sheet view for those plans. For example, if you want to display information for a baseline you saved with the name Baseline 7, you would insert the column named Baseline 7 into the Gantt Chart view sheet.

You can view multiple baselines at one time by going to View in the Task Ribbon, clicking to show the drop-down menu, selecting More Views, and then selecting Multiple Baselines Gantt. Then click Apply.

When calculating variances (whether the schedule is early or late or costs are over or under budget), Project uses only the first baseline that's saved (the one named Baseline, not Baseline1). If the project schedule and other parameters change dramatically, such as when a project is delayed and later revived, you produce more valid variance data by clearing and resetting the baseline, as described in the next section.

The more baselines you save, the larger the Project file becomes and the more it can slow performance.

Clearing and resetting a baseline

A baseline is intended to be a frozen picture of the project plan that remains sacrosanct and never changes. Well, that's the theory. In practice, events can make an original baseline less than useful — and even obsolete.

For example, if a project that spans four years from beginning to end, you may want to save a new baseline every year because costs increase or resources change. Then you can see incremental versions of the estimates that reflect the changes you made based on changes in the real world.

In contrast, a project that starts with a well-thought-out baseline plan can change a week later when the entire industry shuts down from a massive strike that lasts for three months. All original timing estimates then become bogus, so you would adjust the plan, save a new baseline, and move ahead after the strike is resolved.

To clear an existing baseline, follow these steps:

1. **To clear the baseline for only certain tasks, select them.**

2. **Click the Project tab and, in the Schedule group, click the Set Baseline drop-down and choose Clear Baseline.**

   The Clear Baseline dialog box appears, with the Clear Baseline Plan option selected by default.

3. **From the Clear Baseline Plan drop-down list, choose a baseline to clear, as shown in Figure 14-3.**

Figure 14-3:
Clearing the
baseline or
the interim
plan.

4. **Select either the Entire Project radio button to clear the baseline for the entire project or the Selected Tasks radio button to clear selected tasks.**

5. **Click the OK button.**

The project baseline is cleared or selected tasks are cleared.

In the Interim

An interim plan is sort of a "baseline light," in which you save only the actual start and finish dates of tasks that have had activity tracked on them, as well as the baseline start and finish dates for all tasks that haven't started.

An interim plan saves only timing information. If that's all you need, all the data about resource assignments and costs, for example, aren't saved. (When you save a large number of baselines, the Project file is *huge*. Saving an interim schedule makes the schedule less bulky.)

Because a baseline holds a great deal of data, the baseline can eventually become obsolete. An interim plan can be saved to record date changes but not overwrite the original baseline cost data.

Finally, you're allowed to save as many as 11 baseline plans (the original baseline plus baselines 1–10). If you need more than 11, consider using interim and some baseline data to expand the number of sets of data you can save.

Don't go crazy for baselines and interim plans. Even in a long-term project, saving too many sets of plans can become confusing. To keep track of a plan when you save it, print a copy for your records, and note when and why the plan was saved.

Saving an interim plan

Interim plans and baselines are saved using the same dialog box. The difference is that you have to specify where the data in an interim plan originates. For example, if you want to save the start and finish dates from the Baseline2 plan to the third interim plan, you copy from Baseline2 to Start/Finish3. If you want the current scheduled start and finish dates for all tasks, choose to copy from Start/Finish.

If you want to change currently scheduled start and finish dates in a baseline, but you don't want to change all the other data that's typically saved in a baseline, you can copy from Start/Finish to the baseline plan that you want to change.

Follow these steps to save an interim plan:

1. **To save an interim plan for only certain tasks, select them.**

2. **Click the Project tab and, in the Schedule group, click the Set Baseline drop-down arrow, and choose Set Baseline.**

   The Set Baseline dialog box appears.

3. **Select the Set Interim Plan radio button.**

4. **From the Copy drop-down list box, select the set of data that you want to copy to the interim plan.**

5. **From the Into drop-down list box, select the fields in which you want to store the interim plan data, as shown in Figure 14-4.**

6. **Select the appropriate radio buttons to save the plan for the entire project or selected tasks.**

7. **If you choose to save the plan for selected tasks, use the check boxes to indicate how roll-up baseline options should work.**

8. **Click the OK button to save the plan.**

By using the Copy and Into fields in the Set Baseline dialog box, you can save as many as ten interim plans based on either baseline or actual data.

Figure 14-4:
Copy
settings
from any
saved
baseline to
an interim
plan.

Clearing and resetting an interim plan

Ten interim plans may seem like a lot when you're starting out in Project, but in the thick of a busy and ever-changing project, ten may fall short of the number you need. You may eventually need to clear one and resave it.

Project piggybacks baseline and interim plan settings, so you choose the Clear Baseline menu command to clear an interim plan.

To clear an interim plan, follow these steps:

1. **To clear only certain tasks in an interim plan, select them.**

2. **Click the Project tab and, in the Schedule group, click the Set Baseline drop-down arrow, and choose Clear Baseline.**

   The Clear Baseline dialog box appears, as shown in Figure 14-5. You can use it to clear and reset interim plans as often as you like.

Figure 14-5:
The Clear
Baseline
dialog box.

Clear Baseline	⊗
○ Clear baseline plan	Baseline ▼
● Clear interim plan	Start1/Finish1 ▼
For ○ Entire project ● Selected tasks	
	OK Cancel

3. Select the Clear Interim Plan option, and then, from the accompanying list, choose the plan that you want to clear.

4. Click to clear the specified interim plan for the entire project or for any tasks you've selected.

5. Click the OK button to clear the plan.

You can now save a new set of information to that interim plan, if you like.

You may want to save a backup copy of various versions of the file with interim and baseline data. If you clear a baseline or an interim plan, its data disappears forever.

Part IV
Staying on Track

In this part . . .

- ✔ Collect data to determine the project's status.
- ✔ Track resource usage to ensure delivery that's on time and on budget.
- ✔ Compare planned accomplishments to actual accomplishments.
- ✔ Find out about basic earned-value concepts.
- ✔ Figure out how to recover when a project doesn't proceed as planned.
- ✔ Create reports to communicate project status.

Chapter 15

On the Right Track

● ●

In This Chapter

▶ Planning communications

▶ Using tracking tools

▶ Recording actual activity on tasks

▶ Specifying the amount of work complete

▶ Updating fixed costs

▶ Moving a task

▶ Using Update Project to make changes to the big picture

▶ Consolidating multiple projects

● ●

After a project moves from the planning stage into action, it's a continually changing game that features rules, goals, a general time frame — and chaos.

Whether a task happens as planned or wanders off in an unexpected direction, your job after the planning stage is to record what is happening. In other words, you're *tracking* the progress. Tracking starts when team members report their progress on the project. Then you (or someone else assigned to tracking) record the progress of every task in Project.

When you track activity, you'll be amazed at the data Project returns to you. Some of it's good news, and some of it's bad, but all of it's useful in managing the project.

Developing a Communications Management Plan

When you're planning a project, consider what information you (or any other stakeholder) need to track, who has the information, how it will be delivered, and how often it needs to be updated. Frequently, this information is stored in a separate document known as the *communications management plan*. Table 15-1 shows a simple example.

Table 15-1	Communications Management Plan		
Stakeholder	*Information*	*Method*	*Frequency*
Project manager	Status report	Email	Weekly
Team members	Project status	Meeting	Biweekly
Sponsor	Progress report	PowerPoint	Monthly

The communications management plan can be complex — or as simple as a Word table or an Excel spreadsheet. You enter the name or position of each stakeholder in the leftmost column, and then, across the top, enter the information that's needed, its method, and frequency of delivery.

It isn't rocket science, but you still have to determine up front which information you might want to track, when you might want it, and in which form.

Gathering data

The first step in tracking progress on a project is to gather information about what's been going on. The simpler it is to report progress on a project, the better, because people will *do* it. The more routine you can make the reporting — such as every Friday, on a specific form turned into the same person — the easier it is to gather data.

You can then input that information into Project in several ways: Use various views and tables to enter information in sheets of data, enter information in the Task Information dialog box, or use the tracking tools in the Schedule group of the Task tab on the Ribbon.

The amount of data you collect is determined by the information you need to track and the level of detail. For example, some people use Project only to create a timeline for their activities. Others use resources and track their total work on tasks, just not to the level of detail that scrutinizes hourly work performed. For some people, simply marking one task 50% complete and another 100% complete — and letting Project assume that all resources completed their estimated amounts of work — is fine.

Applying a tracking method

You have to identify the best tracking method for you, which is determined by the amount and type of information you need to monitor. Microsoft provides four tracking methods in Project 2016:

- ✔ Task – total
- ✔ Task – time phased
- ✔ Assignment – total
- ✔ Assignment – time phased

I guide you throughout the rest of this chapter, but you can begin to understand these methods by comparing task tracking and assignment tracking. You can track information by *task,* indicating to the present time (or a status date you select) the total work completed or costs for the task. Or you can track information by *assignment,* which is a more detailed tracking that shows you the total work completed or costs by each resource.

Suppose that the Test Electrical Components task is estimated to take 12 hours of work, according to the project baseline. An Engineer, Electrician, and Assistant — three human resources — are assigned at 100% of their time. Tracking by *task – total,* you can simply note that the task is 75% complete, which translates into nine hours of work finished.

Project assumes that the three resources split the work equally — three hours for each resource. In reality, however, the Engineer spent one hour, the Electrician spent six, and the Assistant spent two. Therefore, the *time phased* variable enters the picture. Time-phased tracking uses specific time increments, whether you choose to track work by task or work completed by individual resources on the task.

So in the Test Electrical Components task, you can use the *task – time phased* approach to track the nine hours on a daily basis. Or you can use the *assignment – time phased* approach to track each resource's work, hourly or daily.

If the project or organization doesn't require detailed assignment or time-phased tracking, you're better off using the *task – total* method. Then you can spend less time entering information into Project and more time managing the team and the stakeholders.

Using the tracking tools

Sometimes, it seems that Project provides a handy button for everything you need to do on a project, so why should tracking be any different? The tracking tools at the top of the Schedule group on the Task tab perform updates on selected tasks in any sheet view. Figure 15-1 shows the tracking tools. The five on the left are the percent complete buttons, and the button on the right allows you to mark on track or update tasks.

Figure 15-1:
The tracking
buttons.

These tools make specific updates to selected tasks:

✔ **Percent Complete:** Click this tool to quickly mark a task's progress using a calculation of the percentage (from 0% to 100%) of hours of work completed.

✔ **Mark on Track:** Selecting a task and clicking this tool records activity automatically to the status date as you scheduled it in the baseline. (See the later section "Specifying the status date" to set a status date.)

✔ **Update Tasks:** To display a dialog box that contains tracking information about the progress, duration, start, and finish dates, find this tool on the menu that opens when you click the down arrow on the Mark on Track button. For example, you can indicate whether a task's actual start date varied from its current start date. Figure 15-2 shows the Update Tasks dialog box.

Figure 15-2:
The Update
Tasks dialog
box.

Update Tasks	
Name: Design database	Duration: 1w
% Complete: 0%	Actual dur: 0w	Remaining dur: 1w

Actual		Current	
Start: NA		Start: T 5/5/16
Finish: NA		Finish: W 5/11/16

| Help | Notes... | OK | Cancel |

You can use a few more tools, found elsewhere in Project, to track and illustrate progress:

- ✔ **Update Project:** Mark all tasks in a project as complete to a specific status date. You can also use this tool to reschedule uncompleted work. The section "Update Project: Sweeping Changes," later in this chapter, explains how to perform overall updates.

- ✔ **Move Task:** Reschedule all or part of a selected task. You can use this tool, found in the Tasks group on the Task tab on the Ribbon, to move a task forward or backward or to reschedule parts of it by the status date. The "Moving a Task" section, later in this chapter, explains how to use this tool.

- ✔ **Add Progress Line:** Turn on a type of drawing tool. On the Format tab, in the Format group, choose Gridlines. Click the down arrow and select Progress Lines. A dialog box appears so that you can, at particular dates, set up *progress lines:* They indicate which tasks are ahead of or behind schedule by way of a vertical line that connects in-progress tasks.

For everything, there's a view

You may already know that Project has a view for everything you want to do. For example, you can use Task Sheet view and Task Usage view (as shown in Figures 15-3 and 15-4, respectively) to easily update either task or resource information. So many variations are available that you may believe Microsoft charges by the view.

Figure 15-3:
Task Sheet
view.

		Task Mode	Task Name	Work	Duration	Start	Finish	Add New Column
24			◢ **Registration**	512 hrs	64 days	T 4/28/16	T 7/26/16	
25			◢ **Database**	200 hrs	25 days	T 4/28/16	W 6/1/16	
26			◢ Collect database requirements	40 hrs	1 wk	T 4/28/16	W 5/4/16	
			Dion Anthony	40 hrs		T 4/28/16	W 5/4/16	
27			◢ Design database	40 hrs	1 wk	T 5/5/16	W 5/11/16	
			Dion Anthony	40 hrs		T 5/5/16	W 5/11/16	
28			◢ Develop database	40 hrs	1 wk	T 5/12/16	W 5/18/16	
			Dion Anthony	40 hrs		T 5/12/16	W 5/18/16	
29			◢ Test database	40 hrs	1 wk	T 5/19/16	W 5/25/16	
			Dion Anthony	40 hrs		T 5/19/16	W 5/25/16	
30			◢ User acceptance	40 hrs	1 wk	T 5/26/16	W 6/1/16	
			Bonnie Rush	40 hrs		T 5/26/16	W 6/1/16	

Figure 15-4:
Task Usage
view.

When tracking using the Task Sheet view, I insert a column that shows %
complete. To insert the column, simply right-click a column head and choose
Insert Column⇨Select % Complete.

Depending on the tracking method you need (see the section "Applying a
tracking method," earlier in this chapter), different views serve different purposes. Table 15-2 specifies the best view to use for each tracking method.

Table 15-2	Tracking Views	
Tracking Method	*Best View*	*Table or Column That's Displayed*
Task	Task Sheet	Tracking table
Task – time phased	Task Usage	Actual Work row
Assignment	Task Usage	Tracking table
Assignment – time phased	Task Usage	Actual Work row

When you find the appropriate view with the correct columns displayed,
entering tracking information is as simple as typing a number of hours, a
dollar amount for fixed costs, or a start or finish date in the appropriate
column for the task you're updating.

Tracking Work for the Record

To track progress on a project, you enter several types of information. First,
you tell Project as of when you want to track progress: By default, it records
information as of the current date based on your computer's date-and-time

settings. However, if you want to record progress as of, say, the end of the company's quarter, you can do that, too.

You can record the actual start and finish dates of a task, the percent complete (for example, 75% complete), and the actual work performed (the number of hours that resources spent on each task). If you believe that the task will take less or more time than you anticipated, based on progress to date, you can modify the remaining duration of the task. You can also enter units of materials used and fixed-cost information for expenditures incurred, such as equipment rental or consulting fees.

Specifying the status date

If you don't know the day of the week, you can't very well gauge whether you're making headway on the week's work. Tracking is like that: First, establish the *status date,* or the date as of which you're tracking progress.

By default, Project uses the date-and-time setting on your computer as the date for entering actual activity information. However, sometimes you want to time-travel. Suppose that the boss asks for a report showing the status of the project as of the last day of the quarter, December 31. You've gathered time sheets from all resources through that date, but you didn't enter those updates into Project until three days after the quarter ended. You can set the status date in Project to December 31 and then enter the tracking data. Even better, certain automated tracking tools work along with the status date. For example, if you know that all tasks in the project were on schedule as of the status date, use the Update Project tool to mark all scheduled work as complete up to that date.

After you set the status date and enter information, Project uses that date to calculate *earned value,* which is the value of work completed to date. Also, any task-complete or percent-complete information records as of that date and progress lines in the chart area reflect that timing. Any reports or printouts of views that you generate paint a picture of the status of the project as of that date.

Here's how to set the status date:

1. **Select the Project tab and then click the calendar in the Status group of the tab.**

   A Status Date window will appear.

2. **Click the down arrow to display the calendar.**

3. **If you want to set the status date in another month, click the right or left arrow in the upper-right corner of the calendar to navigate to that month.**

4. **Click the date you want.**

5. **Click the OK button.**

Now you're ready to start entering tracking data.

Remaining on track

When you're determining the project status, and you find that a task was, or will be, on schedule as of the status date, you can use a tool to mark the task as partially complete through the status date. Project assumes an even distribution of work over time and calculates the percentage complete as of the status date. It then marks the percent complete accordingly. To use this tool, simply select tasks to update and click the Mark on Track button in the Schedule group on the Task tab.

Determining the percent complete

When I'm asked how to determine whether a task is 25%, 50%, or even 36.5% complete, I usually refer people to their own intuition. If the boss asks you how that report is coming along, you typically make a quick, internal calculation and supply a rough estimate. A rough estimate, based on your experience and the information your resources provide about their progress, is often good enough.

You can also calculate the percent complete in more precise ways. For example, if you estimate that a task should take ten hours of effort, and your resources report performing five hours of effort, you can say that the task is 50% complete. Be careful, though: Just because people have spent half the allocated time doesn't mean that they have accomplished half the work.

Cost is another way to estimate the percent complete: If you originally estimated that four resources assigned to a four-day task would tally $4,000 in costs, and the total time that the resources report spending on the task is $3,000, you can *guess* that the task is 75% finished. But again, just because you've spent three quarters of the money doesn't mean that you've accomplished three quarters of what you set out to do.

Determining the percentage of work that's done is easier when the deliverable is measurable. For example, if your task is to produce 100 cars on the assembly line in four days, and you've produced 25 cars, the task may be about 25% finished. Or if you were supposed to install software on ten computers in a computer lab, and the installation is complete on five of them, that's an easy 50% estimate.

But not every task can be calculated as neatly. If you know it'll be hard to gauge the percent complete when you're in the planning phase, collaborate with the team member on the interim measurements to allocate 25%, 50%, 75%, and 100% complete. For example, if you want to determine interim measurements for the three-week task Develop Medical Protocols, you might agree that when a complete list of protocols is needed and they've been assigned to development, the task is 25% complete. When 50% are drafted, the task is 50% complete. When the protocols are 100% drafted, the task is 75% complete. When the list has been edited and someone in charge has signed off on it and approved it, the task is 100% complete.

To avoid finding out (usually, at the last minute) that a team member's version of "almost complete" is significantly different from yours, agree up front that you'll sign off on 75% complete only after specific criteria are met.

Here's the simplest and quickest way to update the percent complete on a task: Click the task name to select it in any task-related view and then click the 0%, 25%, 50%, 75%, or 100% button on the Task tab. Alternatively, you can double-click any task to open the Task Information dialog box and then enter the Percent Complete value on the General tab there. You can also select a task, open the Mark on Track drop-down list, and click Update Tasks to open the Update Tasks dialog box and make the change there. If you want to enter a percentage in increments other than 25%, you'll have to enter it in the Task Information or Update Tasks dialog box or the % Complete column in any sheet view.

Don't let tracking become too detailed

Does it make sense to track 2.25% of progress every other day on a two-month task? Probably not. Except on the lengthiest tasks, entering a percent complete that's more specific than 25, 50, 75, or 100 probably isn't worth the trouble. That's partly because multiweek tasks can often be divided into subtasks for ease of tracking and partly because reporting is one purpose of tracking. If your boss or board of directors or client couldn't care less about reaching exactly 33.75% complete, you shouldn't care, either.

On the other hand, if the project must include (for a reason known only to you) a six-month task and you can't break it into subtasks, you may use percentages such as 10, 20, 30, 40, 50, and so on to prevent having to wait a month between updates with (apparently) no progress to show.

Recording start and finish information

If you note that a task is complete, and you don't enter the actual start date, Project (ever the optimist) assumes that you started on time. If you didn't start on time, and you want to reflect the actual timing, modify the actual start date; if you finished late, enter the actual finish date. However, if you don't modify the task duration, and you enter an earlier finish date, be aware that the start date is calculated to have occurred earlier.

You have two options to track this information:

> ✔ **Use the Update Tasks dialog box.** To open it (refer to Figure 15-2), click the Mark on Track button in the Schedule group on the Task tab.

> ✔ **Display a sheet view with Actual Start and Actual Finish columns (such as Tracking Gantt or Gantt Chart view) with the Tracking table displayed.** Then use the drop-down calendar in the Actual Start or Actual Finish column to specify a date. If you need to change the actual start date, you must mark the task as partially complete first. When you need to change both the Actual Start and Actual Finish dates, mark the task as 100% complete before specifying the dates.

A few conditions can cause a warning message to appear when you enter an actual start date or finish date — for example, when the actual start date precedes the start date of the project or when the actual start date causes a conflict with a dependent task. When this warning message appears, you have these options:

> ✔ Cancel the operation.

> ✔ Allow the conflict to exist (or the task to start) before the project starts.

To cancel the change, correct the problem (for example, by modifying the project start date), and then go back and enter the actual information. Or you can force the conflict and let it stand.

Knowing what to do when John works three hours and Mary works ten

To get to the blow-by-blow level of tracking, you record exactly how many hours each resource spends on tasks. This process can be about as much fun as typing all the names in the New York City phone book into a database, but it has certain benefits: After you track the number of actual hours, you can produce tallies of the total hours each resource invests in the project by day, week, or month. If you have to bill clients based on resource hours (for example, contract work by the hour), you have a clear record to refer to.

If you're tracking a budget in detail, multiplying resource hours by their individual rates provides an accurate accounting of costs as finely as computing them day by day.

If you don't enter specific hours, Project simply calculates the hours of work completed on the task as a percentage of the total hours assigned. It assumes that every person assigned to the task has completed the same percentage of work. For many people, this strategy works well; other people need more detail. If you're in the detail camp, specify actual resource hours as a total by task or day by day through the life of each task.

To enter resource hours, follow these steps:

1. **Display Task Usage view.**

2. **Scroll down to locate the task that you want to track and its resource assignments.**

   Each assigned resource is listed on a separate row underneath the task name.

3. **Enter the number of hours completed by the resource:**

   - *To enter only total hours:* Insert the Actual Work column into the sheet by right-clicking a column, choosing Insert Column, and selecting the Actual Work column. Enter total hours in the newly displayed column.

   - *To enter hours on the task day by day:* Right-click the chart pane and then choose Actual Work to display the row labeled Act. Work. Figure 15-5 shows this row in Task Usage view with actual values entered. Click the Act. Work cell on a day on which the resource worked, and enter a number. Repeat this step for every day that the resource worked on the task.

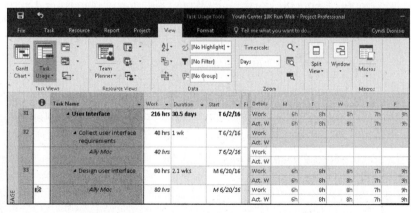

Figure 15-5:
Track resource activity day by day in this view.

If the hours you enter for a resource total more or less than the baseline estimate for that resource on that task, here's what happens:

- ✔ When you enter an amount in the Act. Work row and press Enter, the Actual Work column total recalculates to reflect the total number of hours worked on that task.

- ✔ A little pencil symbol appears in the ID column for that task, indicating that the assignment has been edited.

- ✔ A Person icon appears in the Indicators column to the left of the task name, indicating a resource overallocation.

You can change the entries in the Work column or the time-phased work row for a task or an assignment. If you do so, Project changes the task schedule accordingly. Then, if you mark actual work, it's tracked compared with the edited working hours.

To easily look up the total hours spent by each resource on the project, check the summary number of work hours listed next to the resource in the Resource Name column in Resource Usage view. This view is another handy way to track assignments.

Uh-oh — we're in overtime

When you enter 16 hours of work in a single day for a resource, even though the resource's availability is based on a calendar with an 8-hour day, Project doesn't recognize those hours as overtime. It's one instance of having to lead Project by the hand and tell it to specify overtime work.

When you enter hours in the Overtime Work field, Project interprets them as the number of total work hours that are overtime hours. So if you enter **16** hours of work on a task in the Work column and then enter **4** in the Overtime Work column, Project assumes 12 hours of work at the standard resource rate and 4 hours at the overtime rate.

To enter overtime hours, follow these steps:

1. **Display Resource Usage view.**

2. **Right-click a column heading and choose Insert Column.**

    The list of columns appears.

3. **Select Overtime Work in the list.**

4. Click in the Overtime Work column for a specific assignment for a resource and then click the spinner arrows to specify the overtime hours.

Figure 15-6 shows that you have allocated two hours of overtime for Dion Anthony.

If you specify overtime, Project assumes that effort-driven tasks have a shorter duration. After all, if the task were to take three 8-hour days (24 hours of work) to complete, and you recorded the resource working 12 hours for two days in a row, Project figures that all the effort was accomplished in less time. The duration of the task *shrinks*. If that's not what happened, you have to manually modify the task duration.

Specifying remaining durations for auto-scheduled tasks

Tracking information for auto-scheduled tasks has a weird and wonderful relationship in Project. For example, Project tries to help you by calculating the duration based on other entries you make, such as actual start dates and finish dates. In that particular case, Project calculates task duration according to those dates. (This process works in reverse, too: If you enter the task duration, Project recalculates the finish date to reflect it.)

You may instead want to enter the duration yourself. For example, if you have entered a start date and 20 hours of work on a task that has a baseline of 16 hours of work, Project can't comprehend that the scope of the task has changed, and that now the task is incomplete and requires another 20 hours of work. You have to tell Project about it.

To modify the duration of a task either in progress or completed, follow these steps:

1. **Display Gantt Chart view.**

2. **Click View, and in the Data group, click Tables and then click Tracking.**

   The Tracking table is displayed, as shown in Figure 15-7.

	Task Name	Act. Start	Act. Finish	% Comp.	Phys. % Comp.	Act. Dur.	Rem. Dur.	Act. Cost	Act. Work
24	⊿ **Registration**	T 4/28/16	NA	79%	0%	1.64 days	3.36 days	$29,400.00	468 hrs
25	⊿ **Database**	T 4/28/16	W 6/1/16	100%	0%	25 days	0 days	$14,400.00	200 hrs
26	Collect database requirements	T 4/28/16	W 5/4/16	100%	0%	1 wk	0 wks	$2,600.00	40 hrs
27	Design database	T 5/5/16	W 5/11/16	100%	0%	1 wk	0 wks	$2,600.00	40 hrs
28	Develop database	T 5/12/16	W 5/18/16	100%	0%	1 wk	0 wks	$2,600.00	40 hrs
29	Test database	T 5/19/16	W 5/25/16	100%	0%	1 wk	0 wks	$2,600.00	40 hrs
30	User acceptance	T 5/26/16	W 6/1/16	100%	0%	1 wk	0 wks	$4,000.00	40 hrs
31	⊿ **User Interface**	T 6/2/16	T 7/14/16	100%	0%	1.25 days	0 days	$12,400.00	216 hrs
32	Collect user interface requirements	T 6/2/16	W 6/8/16	100%	0%	1 wk	0 wks	$2,000.00	40 hrs
33	Design user interface	M 6/20/16	M 7/4/16	100%	0%	2.05 wks	0 wks	$4,000.00	80 hrs
34	Develop user interface	M 7/4/16	M 7/11/16	100%	0%	1 wk	0 wks	$2,000.00	40 hrs
35	Test user interface	M 7/11/16	T 7/14/16	100%	0%	3 days	0 days	$1,200.00	24 hrs
36	User acceptance	T 7/5/16	F 7/8/16	100%	0%	4 days	0 days	$3,200.00	32 hrs
37	⊿ **Payment**	M 7/11/16	NA	54%	0%	6.5 days	5.5 days	$2,600.00	52 hrs
38	Collect payment requirements	M 7/11/16	T 7/12/16	100%	0%	2 days	0 days	$800.00	16 hrs
39	Design payment function	W 7/13/16	T 7/14/16	100%	0%	2 days	0 days	$800.00	16 hrs
40	Develop payment function	F 7/15/16	NA	50%	0%	0.5 wks	0.5 wks	$1,000.00	20 hrs
41	Test payment function	NA	NA	0%	0%	0 days	2 days	$0.00	0 hrs
42	User acceptance	NA	NA	0%	0%	0 days	1 day	$0.00	0 hrs

3. **Click in the Actual Duration column of the task you want to modify and then use the arrows to adjust the actual duration up or down.**

4. **If you want to enter a remaining duration, click in the Rem. Dur. (Remaining Duration) column, and type a number and an increment symbol.**

   For example, you may type **25d** (where *d* is the increment symbol for days). If the remaining duration is greater than the original estimate and the task is on the critical path, Project warns you that the task is linked to a task constraint or linked to a task that can't move. You can either continue and allow the scheduling conflict or cancel and allow the scheduling conflict.

If you enter the percent complete for a task and then modify the duration to differ from the baseline, Project automatically recalculates the percent complete to reflect the new duration. For example, if you enter 50% complete on a 10-hour task and then modify the actual duration to 20 hours, Project considers those 5 hours (50% of 10 hours) being only 25% of the 20 hours.

Entering fixed-cost updates

Fixed costs are costs that aren't influenced by time, such as equipment purchases and consulting fees. Compared with the calculations and interactions of the percent completes and the start and finish dates for hourly resources, fixed-cost tracking will seem like simplicity itself!

Here's how to track fixed costs:

1. **Display Gantt Chart view.**

2. **Click View, and in the Data group, click Tables and click Cost.**

   The Cost table is displayed.

3. **Click in the Fixed Cost column for the task you want to update.**

4. **Type the fixed cost, or a total of several fixed costs, for the task.**

That's it! However, because Project lets you enter only one fixed-cost amount per task, consider adding a note to the task to itemize the costs you've included in the total.

The fixed cost assigned to the task is only the scheduled cost for the task. For this cost to become the planned cost, the task has to be baselined. Also, updates to the % Complete column update actual costs, depending on the accrual method that's selected for the task: Prorated is the default setting, but the start and finish dates of the task also influence the actual costs when the percent complete is applied.

Consider using some of the ten customizable Cost columns for itemized fixed-cost entry. Rename one Equipment Purchase, and another Facility Rental, for example, and then enter the costs in those columns. Of course, these columns of data may not perform calculations such as rolling up total costs to the summary tasks in the project, but they serve as reminders about itemized fixed costs.

In Project 2016, you can designate a resource type as a cost and assign a cost every time you assign the resource. The Cost column calculation of total cost includes the amount spent for cost resources on tasks. See Chapter 7 for more about resource types.

Moving a Task

If you've ever managed the subcontractors on any type of construction project, you've probably heard these dreaded words: "My current job is running long, so I'll get to your job in about a week." What you'd rather hear from a subcontractor (or any other type of resource) is this: "My schedule opened up, so I can start work on this assignment a week early." Project helps you easily reschedule an entire task or reschedule part of a task as of the status date.

Here's how to use the Move Task tool to move a task:

1. **Display Gantt Chart view.**

2. **If the task is partially complete and you want to move its uncompleted portion, select the Project tab. In the Status group, choose the Status Date drop-down and set a status date.**

3. **Select the task to move.**

4. **Click the Move button in the Tasks group on the Task tab.**

   The choices for rescheduling the task appear, as shown in Figure 15-8.

Figure 15-8:
Moving
a task.

5. Specify how to move the task:

- *To move the task forward or back by a default amount:* Click 1 Day, 1 Week, or 4 Weeks in either the Move Task Forward or Move Task Back section.

- *To move the task by a custom time frame:* Click the appropriate Custom option, specify the number of working days by which to move the task in the dialog box that appears, and click the OK button.

- *To reschedule part of the task according to the status date:* Choose the Incomplete Parts to Status Date option to split the task and move the uncompleted portion to resume later, starting on the status date. Choose the Completed Parts to Status Date option to split the task and move the completed portion earlier, before the status date.

- *To reschedule the task based on the availability of the assigned resources:* Choose the appropriate Custom option, specify the number of working days by which to move the task in the dialog box that appears, and click OK.

When you're moving a task that's auto-scheduled, a constraint is applied, to honor the newly scheduled task. Be aware that constraints apply restrictions to task scheduling and can make it challenging to manage the dates.

Update Project: Sweeping Changes

If it's been a while since you tracked activity, and you want to update the schedule, Update Project may be for you. This feature lets you track chunks of activity for specified periods. Update Project works best, however, if most tasks have been completed on schedule.

This type of tracking isn't finely tuned: It's similar to recording in your checkbook the balance that the bank sends in your mailed statement rather than accounting for your balance check by check. Doing so assumes that all your checks and deposits align with the bank's version as of that date; therefore, going forward, you're back on track.

Here are the settings options that Update Project offers you:

> ✔ **Update Work As Complete Through:** You can update the project in one of two ways through the status date you specify in this box. The Set 0% – 100% Complete setting lets Project calculate the percent complete

on every task that should have begun by that time. By choosing this option, you tell Project to assume that the tasks started and progressed exactly on time. The Set 0% or 100% Complete Only setting works a little differently: It tells Project to record 100% complete on tasks that the baseline indicated would be complete by now and to leave all other tasks at 0% complete.

✔ **Reschedule Uncompleted Work to Start After:** This setting reschedules the portions of tasks that aren't yet complete to start after the specified date.

To use Update Project, follow these steps:

1. **Display Gantt Chart view.**

2. **To update only certain tasks, select them.**

3. **In the Project tab, in the Status group, choose Update Project.**

   The Update Project dialog box appears, as shown in Figure 15-9.

Figure 15-9:
You can update only selected tasks or the entire project.

4. **Choose the update method you prefer: Set 0% – 100% Complete or Set 0% or 100% Complete Only.**

5. **If you want a status date other than the one shown or you didn't previously set one, set the date to use in the field in the upper-right corner.**

6. **If you want Project to reschedule any work rather than update work as complete, select the Reschedule Uncompleted Work to Start After option and then select a date from the list.**

7. **Choose whether you want these changes to apply to the entire project or to only selected tasks.**

8. **Click the OK button to save the settings and have Project make updates.**

If you want, you can use Update Project to make certain global changes, such as to mark as 100% complete all tasks that should be complete according to the baseline. Then you perform more detailed task-by-task tracking on individual tasks that are only partially complete.

Tracking Materials

Tracking the amount of materials used on tasks involves tracking actual units at the level of material resources. If you create a resource named Rubber and assign it to the Manufacture Tires task at 500 tons, for example, and then you use only 450 tons, you enter the actual units used.

This situation resembles the way you track work resource hours on tasks. To make it happen, simply follow these steps:

1. **Display Resource Usage view.**

2. **Locate the material resource in the list, and under the resource name, double-click the assignment for which you want to enter the actual units.**

   The Assignment Information dialog box appears (see Figure 15-10).

Figure 15-10: You can use the Assignment Information dialog box to enter actuals, too.

3. **Click the Tracking tab.**

4. **Enter the actual units used in the Actual Work field.**

5. **Click the OK button.**

If you need to enter actual units for multiple assignments, you can use the method I describe in the earlier section "Knowing what to do when John works three hours and Mary works ten." Right-click the right side of the view and choose Actual Work to display the row labeled Act. Work. You can then plug in the actual data. If you assign the material resource of 500 tons to a five-day task, for example, remember that Resource Usage view shows Project spreading out the usage — 100 tons for each of the five days of the task. If you don't care on which day the materials were used, you can simply increase or decrease one setting to make up for any difference in actual usage.

Tracking More Than One: Consolidated Projects

Often, projects are related in some fashion (such as sharing resources or having timing dependencies between them), or a series of smaller projects make up a larger program. In such a case, you can consolidate these separate projects into one file, either as a series of summary tasks or with all summary tasks and subtasks included.

When you consolidate projects, you can choose to link to the source file. When you do, any changes to the source file are represented and updated in the consolidated file.

If it's your job to keep track of the big picture, you have to understand how consolidated projects are updated, as I describe in the following section.

Consolidating projects

To consolidate projects in Project, you open a blank file and then insert existing projects to build a satisfying master project schedule.

The neat thing about consolidated projects is that you have some choices about the interaction between the consolidated project and the source files you insert in it. For example, you can link to a source file so that changes made in the source file are reflected in the consolidated project. This capability is helpful for a project manager who has to keep her eye on multiple phases or many smaller projects.

You can also create dependencies between inserted projects in the consolidated file. If you have, for example, one project that can't start until another one finishes, you can clearly see in the consolidated file how various separate projects in your organization affect each other.

Another way to relate consolidated projects to their source files is to make the consolidated project a two-way street, allowing changes in it to be reflected in the source files. You can also make the source files read-only so that no changes can affect other people's files.

To create a consolidated file, follow these steps:

1. **Open a blank Project file and display Gantt Chart view.**

2. **Click anywhere in the Task Name column.**

   If you're inserting multiple projects, click the row in which you want the inserted file (or files) to appear. If you want to insert a project between existing tasks, click the task beneath the spot where you want the project to be inserted.

3. **Choose Project ⇨ Subproject in the Insert group.**

   The Insert Project dialog box, shown in Figure 15-11, appears.

Figure 15-11: The Insert Project dialog box.

4. **Using the navigation pane and file list, locate the Project file that you want to insert, and select it.**

5. **(Optional) Click the down arrow on the Insert button if you want to change the default setting to Insert Read Only.**

6. **If you want to link the project in this file to the source file so that the consolidated file is updated automatically whenever you open it, ensure that the Link to Project check box is selected.**

7. **Click the Insert button.**

   The project is inserted into the file, with the summary task showing and all subtasks hidden. To display all tasks in the inserted project, simply click the plus sign to the left of the summary task.

If you want to insert multiple subprojects, leave them all collapsed. This strategy ensures that they're all inserted at the topmost level of the outline in the consolidated project.

Updating consolidated projects

You have two ways to skin the cat known as "updating a consolidated project," and the one you use depends on whether you linked to the source files when you inserted them. If you linked the files and inserted them without using the read-only setting, changes in source files are reflected in the consolidated file (and vice versa). Updating is simply a matter of ensuring that all files are available in their original linked locations (for example, in a folder on the network); then Project updates automatically.

If you haven't linked the files, changes in source files aren't reflected in consolidated files, and the consolidated file information doesn't affect the source information. You may create this type of unlinked consolidated file if you simply want to see a snapshot of how all projects are progressing and don't want to run the risk of your settings changing the source information. In this case, however, if you want to track progress, you have to create a new consolidated project or enter all updates manually.

After you insert projects in a file, you can move them around by using the Cut and Paste tools. When you do, message windows may appear, offering you options to resolve any conflicts that may occur because of dependency links you've created between inserted projects.

Changing linking settings

Changing your mind is a project manager's prerogative. If you've inserted a source file into a consolidated file, and you find that you didn't initially establish a link, you can change that setting so that the files update each other automatically.

Follow these steps to make changes to the inserted project:

1. **Open the consolidated file.**

2. **Display Gantt Chart view.**

3. **Double-click the task name of the inserted project that you want to update.**

   The Inserted Project Information dialog box appears.

4. **Click the Advanced tab.**

5. **Select the Link to Project check box and then click the Browse button.**

   The Inserted Project dialog box appears.

6. **Use the Look In feature to locate the file that you want to link to and then select the file.**

7. **Click the OK button.**

8. **If you want the source file to be read-only, click the Read Only box in the Inserted Project Information dialog box.**

9. **Click OK to save the link.**

Chapter 16

Project Views: Observing Progress

• •

In This Chapter

▶ Viewing your progress with indicators and taskbars

▶ Seeing progress from various Project views

▶ Examining cost and time variances

▶ Understanding earned value

▶ Observing multiple critical paths

• •

Some project managers use Project simply to paint a picture all the effort that their project will entail and then stash the plan in a drawer. That's a mistake. After you enter all the project data, save a baseline, and then track actual activity on the project, you receive in return an amazing array of information from Project that can help you stay on time and on budget.

After you track some actual activity on several tasks, Project lets you view baseline estimates alongside the real-time plan. Project alerts you to tasks that are running late and also shows how the critical path shifts over time. To read about the critical path, review Chapter 12.

Project also provides detailed performance information. In fact, the information you can see about the cost and schedule performance can be quite robust. You can produce a simple cost-and-schedule variance, or you can use more complex metrics, such as a cost performance index using earned-value management techniques. I discuss this particular measurement technique in the later section "Tracking Progress Using Earned Value Management."

Keep the project file close at hand — and take a look at how Project can make you the most informed project manager in town.

Seeing Where Tasks Stand

You've diligently entered resource work hours on tasks, recorded the progress on tasks, and entered fixed costs. Now what? Well, all that information has initiated several calculations and updates to the project schedule. It's time to take a quick look at the changes that all this tracking has produced in the project schedule.

A check mark in the Indicator field tells you that a task is complete. If you see an unfamiliar indicator icon crop up in the project, hold the mouse pointer over the indicator. A text box opens and describes its meaning. To see a list of Project icons and their meanings, click Tell Me What You Want to Do next to the Format tab and type **indicators** in the Search box. Click Search and then click Indicator Fields.

Baseline versus actual progress

One obvious way to view the difference between a baseline estimate and the progress you've tracked in the project is by using a taskbar. After you track progress on several tasks, the Gantt chart shows a black bar superimposed on the baseline taskbar. For example, in Figure 16-1, Tasks 26–39 are complete; you can tell by the solid black bar that extends the full length of the taskbar. Task 40 is only partially complete; the black line that indicates actual progress only partially fills the duration for the task. Task 41 has no recorded activity on it; you see no black line indicating progress — only the normal taskbar.

Figure 16-1:
The solid line on a taskbar represents actual activity in the project.

		Task Name		
24		◢ **Registration**		
25	✓	◢ **Database**		
26	✓	Collect database requirements		Dion Anthony
27	✓	Design database		Dion Anthony
28	✓	Develop database		Dion Anthony
29	✓	Test database		Dion Anthony
30	✓	User acceptance		Bonnie Rush
31	✓	◢ **User Interface**		
32	✓	Collect user interface requirements		Ally Mac
33	✓	Design user interface		Ally Mac
34	✓	Develop user interface		Ally Mac
35	✓	Test user interface		Ally Mac
36	✓	User acceptance		Bonnie Rush
37		◢ **Payment**		
38	✓	Collect payment requirements		Julie Moore
39	✓	Design payment function		Julie Moore
40		Develop payment function		Julie Moore
41		Test payment function		Julie Moore
42		User acceptance		Bonnie Rush
43		◢ **Confirmation**		
44		Collect confirmation requirements		

Lines of progress

Progress lines offer additional visual indicators of how you're doing. As you can see in Figure 16-2, a progress line zigzags among tasks and forms, showing left- or right-pointing peaks. These peaks indicate late or early tasks (calculated according to the status date you set for tracking or another date that you specify). A progress line that points to the left of a task indicates that the task is running late. Progress lines that point to the right show that — wonder of wonders — you're running ahead of schedule. (Treasure these lines: They don't seem to appear often in projects.)

Figure 16-2: Progress lines, seemingly run amok.

In Figure 16-2, progress is measured as of the actual date. You can see that the tasks under the Finish Line Beverage are running behind, because the line points to the left.

Displaying progress lines

By default, Project doesn't display progress lines. You have to turn them on. And while you're at it, you may as well specify when and how they appear. Here's how to display progress lines and change their settings:

1. **Display Gantt Chart view.**

2. **Right-click the chart portion of the view and choose Progress Lines.**

   The Progress Lines dialog box appears, as shown in Figure 16-3.

3. **If you want Project to always show a progress line for the current or status date, select the Display check box in the Current Progress Line section and then select At Project Status Date or At Current Date.**

Figure 16-3:
The
Progress
Lines
dialog box.

4. **If you want progress lines to be displayed at set intervals, do this:**

   a. *Select the Display Progress Lines check box in the Recurring Intervals section and then select Daily, Weekly, or Monthly.*

   b. *Specify the interval settings.*

   For example, if you select Weekly, you can choose every week, every other week, and so on, as well as for which day of the week the line should be displayed on the timescale.

5. **Choose whether you want to display progress lines beginning at the Project start date or on another date.**

   To use the Project start date, simply select the Project Start option in the Begin At section of the dialog box. To select an alternative start date, select the second option and then select a date from the calendar drop-down list.

6. **If you want to display a progress line on a specific date, select the Display check box in the Selected Progress Lines section and then choose a date from the Progress Line Dates drop-down calendar.**

   You can make this setting for multiple dates by clicking subsequent lines in this list and selecting additional dates.

   You can choose to display progress lines in relation to actual or baseline information.

   If a task has been tracked to show 50 percent complete, for example, and you choose to have Project display progress lines based on actual information, the peak appears relative to the 50 percent *actual* line, not to the complete baseline taskbar.

7. **Click the OK button to save these settings.**

Formatting progress lines

In keeping with the almost mind-boggling array of formatting options that Project makes available to you, you can modify how progress lines are formatted.

As with any changes to formatting, you're tampering with the way Project codes visual information for readers. Be cautious about making formatting changes that cause the plan to be difficult to read for those who are accustomed to the default Project formatting.

To modify progress-line formatting:

1. **Display Gantt Chart view.**

2. **Right-click the chart portion of the view and choose Progress Lines.**

   The Progress Lines dialog box appears (refer to Figure 16-3).

3. **Select the Line Styles tab.**

   You see the display options shown in Figure 16-4.

Figure 16-4: Progress line styles.

4. **In the Progress Line Type area, select a line style sample.**

5. **In the Line Type fields, select a style from the samples.**

   You can make two settings: one for the current progress line and one for all other progress lines.

6. **You can change the line color, progress point shape, and progress point color by making different choices in those boxes.**

7. **If you want a date to appear alongside each progress line, select the Show Date for Each Progress Line check box and then select a date from the Format field.**

8. **If you want to change the font that's used for the displayed date, click the Change Font button and make the changes. Click OK in the Font dialog box.**

9. **Click the OK button to save these settings.**

Delving into the Detail

Visual indicators such as taskbars and indicator icons are useful to alert you to delays or variances between estimated and actual performance, but they don't provide detailed information. To get the lowdown on how far ahead (or behind) you are, down to the day or penny, scan the numbers. The numbers that Project provides reveal much about whether you're on schedule and within the budget.

One way to view variances is to show Tracking Gantt view. From the Task tab, go to the View section on the far left side and click the down arrow. Choose Tracking Gantt. This view has, by default, two thin taskbars for each task. The gray bar at the bottom shows the baseline, whereas the top bar shows the current (scheduled) or actual (tracked) schedule. The color of the top bar varies, depending on whether it's a critical task if it's auto-scheduled or a manually scheduled task. As shown in Figure 16-5, in Tracking Gantt view, you can show and tell exactly where a project went off track or picked up steam.

Figure 16-5:
Tracking
Gantt view.

Two tables that you can display in Gantt Chart view bring the options into focus. The Cost table and Variance table provide information about dollars spent and variations in timing between baseline and actual activity.

To display a table, choose View➪Data Group➪Tables and click the table name. Another option is in the Tracking Gantt view, to place the pointer on the blank square immediately above row 1 and to the left of the first column. Then right-click the mouse to display the available tables for easy selection.

In the Cost table shown in Figure 16-6, you can review data that compares baseline estimates to actual costs and the variance between them. These three columns are presented side by side. In the project shown in the figure, you can see the database work came in right on target. The user interface and the payment work packages each had a $50 variance. By looking at the detail, you can identify the exact activities that caused the variance and how much each activity contributed to the total variance.

	Task Name	Fixed Cost	Fixed Cost Accrual	Total Cost	Baseline	Variance	Actual	Remaining
25	⊿ Database	$0.00	Prorated	$14,400.00	$14,400.00	$0.00	$14,400.00	$0.0
26	Collect database requirements	$0.00	Prorated	$2,600.00	$2,600.00	$0.00	$2,600.00	$0.0
27	Design database	$0.00	Prorated	$2,600.00	$2,600.00	$0.00	$2,600.00	$0.0
28	Develop database	$0.00	Prorated	$2,600.00	$2,600.00	$0.00	$2,600.00	$0.0
29	Test database	$0.00	Prorated	$2,600.00	$2,600.00	$0.00	$2,600.00	$0.0
30	User acceptance	$0.00	Prorated	$4,000.00	$4,000.00	$0.00	$4,000.00	$0.0
31	⊿ User Interface	$0.00	Prorated	$10,350.00	$10,300.00	$50.00	$10,350.00	$0.0
32	Collect user interface requirements	$0.00	Prorated	$2,000.00	$2,000.00	$0.00	$2,000.00	$0.0
33	Design user interface	-$300.00	Prorated	$1,600.00	$1,900.00	-$300.00	$1,600.00	$0.0
34	Develop user interface	$200.00	Prorated	$2,200.00	$2,000.00	$200.00	$2,200.00	$0.0
35	Test user interface	$150.00	Prorated	$1,350.00	$1,200.00	$150.00	$1,350.00	$0.0
36	User acceptance	$0.00	Prorated	$3,200.00	$3,200.00	$0.00	$3,200.00	$0.0
37	⊿ Payment	$0.00	Prorated	$5,250.00	$5,200.00	$50.00	$5,250.00	$0.0
38	Collect payment requirements	$25.00	Prorated	$825.00	$800.00	$25.00	$825.00	$0.0
39	Design payment function	$0.00	Prorated	$800.00	$800.00	$0.00	$800.00	$0.0
40	Develop payment function	$0.00	Prorated	$2,000.00	$2,000.00	$0.00	$2,000.00	$0.0
41	Test payment function	$25.00	Prorated	$825.00	$800.00	$25.00	$825.00	$0.0
42	User acceptance	$0.00	Prorated	$800.00	$800.00	$0.00	$800.00	$0.0
43	⊿ Confirmation	$0.00	Prorated	$5,260.00	$5,260.00	$0.00	$5,260.00	$0.0

Figure 16-6: Cost table.

For the Cost table, a variance that's positive indicates that you've spent more than expected. A variance that's negative indicates that you're under budget.

Project assumes that the remaining costs will remain at the budgeted amount. In other words, from the total budgeted amount for the work, it assumes that the remaining work will be completed on budget, and it adds the actual costs to date to produce the total cost. Rarely do future estimates end on budget when the work to date is in a cost-overrun situation, so don't rely on the information in the Total Cost column.

In Figure 16-7, the Variance table shows whether the schedule is on track or has variances (much like the Cost table shows cost variances). The table shows the variance between the start and finish of tasks and the baseline start and finish dates. Notice in the example that the "Define route" task was late by two days, which in turn caused the "Get route approval" task to be delayed as well. Because there is float between the route approval and marking the route, this did not negatively impact the critical path.

	Task Mode	Task Name	Start	Finish	Baseline Start	Baseline Finish	Start Var.	Finish Var.
114		▲ Course Logistics	M 5/2/16	W 11/2/16	T 4/28/16	W 11/2/16	2 days	0 days
115		▲ Route	M 5/2/16	T 11/1/16	T 4/28/16	T 11/1/16	2 days	0 days
116		Define route	M 5/2/16	F 5/13/16	T 4/28/16	W 5/11/16	2 days	2 days
117		Get route approval	M 5/16/16	F 7/15/16	T 5/12/16	W 7/13/16	2 days	2 days
118		Mark route	T 11/1/16	T 11/1/16	T 11/1/16	T 11/1/16	0 days	0 days
119		▲ Signs	T 7/14/16	W 11/2/16	T 7/14/16	W 11/2/16	0 days	0 days
120		Identify signage points	T 7/14/16	T 7/14/16	T 7/14/16	T 7/14/16	0 days	0 days
121		Post signs	W 11/2/16	W 11/2/16	W 11/2/16	W 11/2/16	0 days	0 days
122		Take down signs	T 11/1/16	T 11/1/16	T 11/1/16	T 11/1/16	0 days	0 days
123		▲ Parking	T 7/14/16	W 11/2/16	T 7/14/16	W 11/2/16	0 days	0 days
124		Identify parking areas	T 7/14/16	T 7/14/16	T 7/14/16	T 7/14/16	0 days	0 days
125		Manage parking	W 11/2/16	W 11/2/16	W 11/2/16	W 11/2/16	0 days	0 days

Figure 16-7: Variance table.

If you created contingency reserve to help handle unexpected delays, the total variance shown in the Variance table tells you how many days you may have to deduct from the contingency duration to get back on track. You can read more in Chapter 17 about making adjustments for delays and cost overruns and about contingency reserve in Chapter 12.

Tracking Progress Using Earned Value Management

On large projects, especially large government projects, project managers are required to track progress using the earned value management (EVM) method. I won't bore you with a detailed discussion of EVM, but you should become familiar with some of the most common terms and calculations surrounding this concept because many organizations require information on these specific numbers in project reports. Some common terms are defined in this list:

✔ **Planned value (PV):** The budgeted (or baseline) cost of tasks based on the cost of resources assigned to the task, plus any fixed costs associated with the tasks, at the point of measurement. In some circles, planned value is also known as the budgeted cost of work scheduled, or BCWS. For example, if you're installing 100 fixtures, the baseline cost to install a fixture is $100, and you estimate that you can install 5 fixtures per day, the cumulative planned value for Day 3 is $1,500.

✔ **Earned value (EV):** The value of the work you've completed, expressed in dollars. For example, if you've installed only 13 fixtures at the end of Day 3, the earned value is $1,300. In some circles, earned value is referred to as the budgeted cost of work performed, or BCWP.

✔ **Actual cost (AC):** A calculation that includes tracked resource hours or units expended on the task plus fixed costs. In the example, assume that you had to pay overtime to complete some of the work and that the actual costs at the end of Day 3 are $1,650. AC is also known as actual cost of work performed, or ACWP.

✔ **Budget at completion (BAC):** The sum of the planned value. In the example, the BAC of the project is 100 fixtures × $100, or $10,000.

✔ **Estimate at completion (EAC):** A forecast of the total cost of the project. Project calculates that EAC = BAC − EV + AC. EVM practitioners cringe at the assumption that future costs will stay on budget. However, Project isn't an EVM tool. If you need to get serious about using EVM, you can buy a plug-in that accurately calculates multiple EACs based on assumptions of future performance.

✔ **Variance at completion (VAC):** The difference between the budget at completion (BAC) and the estimate at completion (EAC) is VAC = BAC − EAC.

✔ **Cost variance (CV):** The difference between earned value and actual costs. The equation is CV = EV − AC. This number is expressed as a negative number if the project is over budget and as a positive number if you're under budget.

✔ **Schedule variance (SV):** The difference between earned value and planned value. The equation is SV = EV − PV. This number is expressed as a negative number if you're accomplishing less work than planned; it's a positive number if you're accomplishing more work than planned. Be aware of saying aloud that you're behind or ahead of schedule. If the work isn't on the critical path, the schedule performance doesn't necessarily indicate an ahead-of-schedule status or a behind-schedule status.

To see the Earned Value table, as shown in Figure 16-8, select the View tab on the Ribbon, click Tables in the Data group, select More Tables, and choose Earned Value. You can also look at tables that focus only on Earned Value Cost Indicators or Earned Value Schedule Indicators.

	Task Name	Planned Value - PV (BCWS)	Earned Value - EV (BCWP)	AC (ACWP)	SV	CV	EAC	BAC	VAC	Ac
25	▲ Database	$14,400.00	$14,400.00	$14,400.00	$0.00	$0.00	$14,400.00	$14,400.00	$0.00	
26	Collect database requirements	$2,600.00	$2,600.00	$2,600.00	$0.00	$0.00	$2,600.00	$2,600.00	$0.00	
27	Design database	$2,600.00	$2,600.00	$2,600.00	$0.00	$0.00	$2,600.00	$2,600.00	$0.00	
28	Develop database	$2,600.00	$2,600.00	$2,600.00	$0.00	$0.00	$2,600.00	$2,600.00	$0.00	
29	Test database	$2,600.00	$2,600.00	$2,600.00	$0.00	$0.00	$2,600.00	$2,600.00	$0.00	
30	User acceptance	$4,000.00	$4,000.00	$4,000.00	$0.00	$0.00	$4,000.00	$4,000.00	$0.00	
31	▲ User Interface	$10,300.00	$10,300.00	$10,350.00	$0.00	-$50.00	$10,350.00	$10,300.00	-$50.00	
32	Collect user interface requirements	$2,000.00	$2,000.00	$2,000.00	$0.00	$0.00	$2,000.00	$2,000.00	$0.00	
33	Design user interface	$1,900.00	$1,900.00	$1,600.00	$0.00	$300.00	$1,600.00	$1,900.00	$300.00	
34	Develop user interface	$2,000.00	$2,000.00	$2,200.00	$0.00	-$200.00	$2,200.00	$2,000.00	-$200.00	
35	Test user interface	$1,200.00	$1,200.00	$1,350.00	$0.00	-$150.00	$1,350.00	$1,200.00	-$150.00	
36	User acceptance	$3,200.00	$3,200.00	$3,200.00	$0.00	$0.00	$3,200.00	$3,200.00	$0.00	
37	▲ Payment	$5,200.00	$5,200.00	$5,250.00	$0.00	-$50.00	$5,250.00	$5,200.00	-$50.00	
38	Collect payment requirements	$800.00	$800.00	$825.00	$0.00	-$25.00	$825.00	$800.00	-$25.00	
39	Design payment function	$800.00	$800.00	$800.00	$0.00	$0.00	$800.00	$800.00	$0.00	
40	Develop payment function	$2,000.00	$2,000.00	$2,000.00	$0.00	$0.00	$2,000.00	$2,000.00	$0.00	
41	Test payment function	$800.00	$800.00	$825.00	$0.00	-$25.00	$825.00	$800.00	-$25.00	
42	User acceptance	$800.00	$800.00	$800.00	$0.00	$0.00	$800.00	$800.00	$0.00	
43	▲ Confirmation	$0.00	$0.00	$5,260.00	$0.00	-$5,260.00	$5,260.00	$5,260.00	$0.00	
44	Collect confirmation requirements	$0.00	$0.00	$520.00	$0.00	-$520.00	$520.00	$520.00	$0.00	
45	Design confirmation function	$0.00	$0.00	$1,100.00	$0.00	-$1,100.00	$1,100.00	$1,040.00	-$60.00	

Figure 16-8: Earned value table.

Calculating Behind the Scenes

While you're happily entering resource hours and fixed costs into the project, Project is busy making calculations that can shift around task timing and resource workload in the plan. These calculations relate to how tasks are updated, how the critical path is determined, and how earned value is calculated. If you're a control freak, you'll be happy to know that you can, to some extent, control how Project goes about making these calculations.

To change when Project calculates plan updates, select the File tab on the Ribbon, click the Options button to open the Project Options dialog box, and then examine the Schedule category. Scroll to the bottom until you see a section called Calculation Options for This Project. If you turn off the Calculate Project After Each Edit setting, you must click the Calculate Project button in the Schedule group on the Project tab of the Ribbon whenever you want Project to perform all its calculations. You can also choose to set different modes for only the current project or for all open projects.

Earned-value options

As I mention earlier in this chapter, usually only large projects use earned value management. To find the settings to customize how earned value works in the project, select the File tab, click the Options button, and select Advanced. Scroll down until you see Earned Value Options for This Project. Figure 16-9 shows you the two sample settings for calculating earned value.

Figure 16-9:
Two settings to calculate earned value.

The Default Task Earned Value Method setting provides these two choices:

- ✓ **% Complete:** This setting calculates earned value using the percent complete that you record on each task. The setting assumes that, on a task that's halfway complete, half the work hours have been used.

- ✓ **Physical % Complete:** Use this setting if you want to manually enter a percentage of completion not based on a straight percent-complete calculation. For example, if you have a four-week task to complete a mail survey, 50 percent of the effort may happen in the first 25 percent of the duration of the project: Design, print, and mail the survey. Nothing happens for two weeks while you wait for responses and then you see a flurry of activity when the responses are returned to you. So a straight calculation that 50 percent of the task is completed 50 percent of the way through isn't accurate. If your projects have a lot of tasks of this type, you may consider changing the settings to use this method. Then you can display the Physical % Complete column in the Gantt Chart sheet and enter more accurate (in your opinion) percent-complete information for each task.

The second setting in the earned-value options in the Project section of the Project Options dialog box is the Baseline for Earned Value Calculation drop-down list. The baseline you use to calculate earned value is essentially setting the planned value for the project. If you're using multiple baselines — such as one for reporting and one for managing — pay close attention to the baseline against which you choose to measure the earned value. Choose any of the 11 possible baselines you may have saved in the project. After you make these two choices, click OK to close the Project Options dialog box.

An abundance of critical paths

While I'm talking about the Project Options box, let's take a quick look at some options for calculating the critical path. Three settings in the Project Options dialog box concern critical path calculations. If following one project's critical path is too tame for you, start reviewing multiple critical paths. In Options ➪ Advanced, the very bottom section is Calculation Options for This Project (see Figure 16-10). By selecting the Calculate Multiple Critical Paths check box you set up Project to calculate a different critical path for each set of tasks in the project. Doing so can be helpful if you want to identify tasks that, if delayed, will cause you to miss the final project deadline or the goals of a single phase in the project.

You can establish which factors add a task to the critical path, by specifying the number of days of slack the critical tasks may have. Tasks with no slack are, by default, on the critical path. However, you can change this situation if you want to be alerted that tasks with only one day of slack are critical — figuring that one day isn't much padding and that these tasks are still in jeopardy. The setting labeled Tasks Are Critical If Slack Is Less Than or Equal to (x) Days is immediately beneath the Calculate Multiple Critical Paths check box in the Advanced category.

Figure 16-10:
Selecting
multiple
critical
paths.

Finally, in Options ⇨ Schedule, the Inserted Projects Are Calculated Like Summary Tasks is straightforward. If you insert another project as a task in the project, selecting this setting allows Project to calculate one critical path for the entire project. If you don't select it, any projects that you insert are treated as outsiders — that is, they aren't considered in the master project's critical-path calculations. If an inserted project won't affect the project's timing, you may deselect this option.

Chapter 17

You're Behind — Now What?

In This Chapter

▶ Analyzing plan versions and notes to understand what went wrong

▶ Experimenting with what-if scenarios

▶ Benefitting from more time or more people

▶ Adjusting the timing going forward

---

*L*et's face it: A project rarely proceeds as planned. Every project has issues (situations that must be handled before the project can move forward) and risks (uncertain events that can prevent a project objective from being met). Issues and risks either crop up suddenly or barrel down on you like a freight train coming down the track. Regardless of whether you see risks approaching, at some point you may feel that the floor has dropped out from under you. One day the project is doing just fine, and the next day it's $75,000 over budget. Or it appears that you'll miss the drop-dead finish date by two weeks. All the aspirin in the world won't solve this one.

The first step is to find the cause and then fix it so that you can move forward and try to save the project. To try to save the day when the project rolls off the track you will need to analyze the options and make tough choices. Project can help you analyze possible solutions and anticipate the likely results. After you decide what to do, you will update Project to reflect the solutions.

Using Project with Risk and Issue Logs

You can proactively document problems on the project in a number of ways, especially if you create and maintain an issue log and a risk register on the project. In Chapter 12, I describe how to handle risk, assign contingency reserve, and update the project schedule to include the work, resources, time, and funding necessary to implement risk responses.

An *issue* is a situation that you have to deal with before you can move forward, such as a risk that develops, a decision that has to be made, or an uncooperative stakeholder. Whatever the case, you should record issues in an *issue log* so that you can assign accountability for managing and resolving them in a timely manner.

You can also use Project to run what-if scenarios and develop alternative approaches for responding to issues or risks. You may have developed multiple baselines (described in Chapter 14) to account for various outcomes. It is a good practice to record task notes for those tasks affected by a risk or an issue. (Information on task notes is in Chapter 3.) Storing interim plans, multiple baselines, and task notes in Project helps you more easily explain messy situations to the powers that be.

Printing interim plans and baselines

Interim plans and multiple baselines demonstrate how you've made adjustments for risks or issues. Using these two items indicates that you were attuned to potential problems. You should also update the boss and other stakeholders by generating printouts or reports reflecting potential major issues and risks. I talk more about reports in Chapter 18.

A *baseline* saves pertinent project data, including start and finish dates, duration, work, and cost; an *interim plan* saves only the start and finish dates of tasks in the project. Chapter 14 describes interim plans and baselines in depth.

To view multiple baselines, follow these steps:

1. **Click the Task tab. In the View section, click the down arrow for a list of Views.**

2. **At the bottom of the list, choose More Views.**

3. **In the More Views dialog box, select Multiple Baselines Gantt.**

4. **Click Apply.**

Multiple Baselines Gantt view shows the original Baseline, Baseline 1, and Baseline 2. To customize what you see by including baselines and interim plans in whichever way you want to see them, follow these steps:

1. **Display Task Sheet view.**

2. **Scroll the sheet pane to the right and click the Add New Column column heading.**

   The menu listing available fields appears, as shown in Figure 17-1.

[Type Column Name]
% Complete
% Work Complete
Active
Actual Cost
Actual Duration
Actual Finish
Actual Overtime Cost
Actual Overtime Work
Actual Start
Actual Work
ACWP
Assignment
Assignment Delay
Assignment Owner
Assignment Units
Baseline Budget Cost
Baseline Budget Work
Baseline Cost
Baseline Deliverable Finish
Baseline Deliverable Start
Baseline Duration
Baseline Estimated Duration
Baseline Estimated Finish
Baseline Estimated Start
Baseline Finish
Baseline Fixed Cost
Baseline Fixed Cost Accrual
Baseline Start
Baseline Work
Baseline1 Budget Cost
Baseline1 Budget Work
Baseline1 Cost
Baseline1 Deliverable Finish
Baseline1 Deliverable Start

Figure 17-1:
Adding new
columns.

3. **Scroll down and click the field to insert.**

   For example, you may choose Start 1–10 and Finish 1–10 for any interim plan (or choose Baseline through Baseline 10 for baseline data).

4. **If necessary, repeat Steps 2 and 3 to display additional columns.**

Printing task notes

In addition to printing interim plans and baselines, you can print task notes. They should include information about risk and issues such as vendor problems or late deliveries.

To add a note to a task, either display the Notes column in a task sheet pane or double-click a task and add the note on the Notes tab of the Task Information dialog box.

Project doesn't let you print a single note or only the notes; you have to print the entire project and include the notes. To print task notes, follow these steps:

1. **Click the File tab.**

2. **Click Print.**

3. **Click the Page Setup link.**

   A dialog box appears.

4. **Select the View tab.**

5. **Check the Print Notes check box.**

   Figure 17-2 shows the Page Setup dialog box with the Print Notes check box selected on the View tab.

6. **Click OK to save your changes.**

7. **Click Print.**

Figure 17-2:
Printing
notes.

When a note is associated with a task, a Note icon appears in the leftmost column of the schedule. You can hover the mouse on the icon to show the note content. If the information in the note is explained in greater detail in another project document — such as a risk register, an issue log, or a specification document — you can use the note to indicate where to find the detailed information. The note then serves as an indicator of additional relevant information about that task.

What-If Scenarios

Just as you can be too close to a problem to see its solution, you can be too close to the project to recognize what you need to do. Using the filtering and sorting features in Project, though, you can slice and dice various aspects of the project somewhat differently to see a fresh perspective.

You can also use tools, such as resource leveling, to solve resource conflicts. Resource leveling may not always solve problems to your satisfaction, but it's a good way to let Project show you a what-if scenario that may solve resource problems instantly.

See Chapter 12 for more information about how to use resource leveling.

Sorting tasks

Sometimes when the project isn't going as planned, it's time to sort tasks. In Project, you can sort tasks by several criteria, including start date, finish date, priority, and cost.

To determine how sorting can help you, consider these examples:

- ✔ **To cut costs:** When you sort tasks by cost, you can focus on the most expensive tasks first, to see whether you have room to trim useful-but-pricey items.

- ✔ **To review task timing:** When you sort by duration in descending order, you can see the longest tasks first.

To apply a preset sorting order, simply choose View➪Data Group➪Sort and then choose an option from the submenu, such as By Start Date or By Cost. The sort button has an A over a Z with a down arrow next to it.

If you want to see additional sort criteria or to sort by more than one criterion, follow these steps:

1. **Choose View➪Sort➪Sort By.**

   The Sort dialog box appears, as shown in Figure 17-3. You can use it to sort by as many as three criteria in ascending or descending order. The Then By field is empty without a value selected.

Figure 17-3: Choosing criteria for sorting.

2. **In the Sort By list, select a criterion.**

3. **Select either Ascending (to sort from lowest to highest) or Descending (to sort from highest to lowest).**

   In a date field, the sorting order is from soonest to latest and from latest to soonest, respectively; in a text field, alphabetical is the order.

4. **(Optional) If you want a second criterion, select the first Then By check box and make a selection.**

   For example, if you choose to sort first by cost and then by type, tasks are sorted from least expensive to most expensive and then (within each cost level) by type (Fixed Duration, Fixed Units, and Fixed Work).

5. **(Optional) If you want to add a third criterion, select the second Then By check box and make a selection.**

6. **Click the Sort button.**

To return to the original task order, choose View ⇨ Sort ⇨ By ID. Tasks are now back in *task ID number* order, which is the standard sorting criterion in Project.

Filtering

Filtering, as described in Chapter 11, is a good way to focus on the areas of the project that are at risk. Especially in larger projects, where it can be difficult to scan hundreds of tasks and notice which ones are running late or over budget, filters can home in on exactly where the trouble lies. Filters are on the View tab, in the Data group.

You can choose to remove from the display any tasks that don't meet filter criteria, or you can simply highlight tasks that meet the criteria onscreen.

Table 17-1 lists filters that are useful when you're trying to identify and solve problems with the schedule.

Table 17-1	Filters That Isolate Problems
Filter Name	*What It Displays*
Task Filters	
Critical	Tasks that must be completed according to schedule to meet the final deadline (the critical path)
Cost Overbudget	Tasks that exceed budgeted expenditures
Incomplete Tasks	Tasks that haven't been marked as complete

Filter Name	What It Displays
Late/Overbudget Tasks Assigned To	Tasks assigned to a resource you specify that exceed their baseline estimates and are over budget
Should Start By	Tasks that should have started as of a specified date
Slipped/Late Progress	Tasks that are running late and have no progress recorded
Resource Filters	
Overallocated Resources	Tasks with resources assigned that are overbooked at some point during the life of the task
Slipping Assignments	Tasks involving resource work that should have already begun
Work Incomplete	Tasks whose work should have been recorded already
Work Overbudget	The number of work hours that have exceeded the original estimate

You may not see all these choices in the More Filters dialog box; when you click View and, in the Data group, click Filter and then click More Filters to open it, you have to enable the Task option to see task-related filters and enable the Resource option to see resource-related filters.

You can export Project information to a program such as Excel so that you can use analysis tools, such as pivot tables. If this idea excites you, check out *Excel 2016 For Dummies,* by Greg Harvey. The Save As Type drop-down list at the bottom of the Project Save As dialog box enables you to choose the export format.

Examining the critical path

One useful filter in Project is named Critical; it displays or highlights all tasks that are on the critical path. If you're running late, knowing which tasks can't slip helps you identify areas that have no room for delay — and, conversely, areas where you can delay noncritical tasks and still meet the deadline. You may use the Critical filter to help determine how to free overallocated resources or get a task that's running late back on track.

Ensure that the Gantt chart shows the Gantt bars for critical tasks in red. To do so, make sure you're in the Gantt chart view; then select the Gantt Chart Tools Format tab on the Ribbon and ensure that the Critical Tasks option is selected in the Bar Styles group.

You can look at the critical path in any Gantt Chart or Network Diagram view. Figure 17-4 shows Gantt Chart view of a project sorted for the critical path. Figure 17-5 shows Network Diagram view (with the boxes collapsed) with the same filter applied.

Figure 17-4:
Gantt Chart
sorted for
the critical
path.

Figure 17-5:
Network
Diagram
view of the
critical path.

If you need a closer look at task timing, modify the timescale display to use smaller increments, such as days or hours. To do so, right-click the timescale itself and then choose Timescale, or click View and then, in the Zoom group, click the Zoom drop-down arrow, and select Zoom In.

Using resource leveling (again)

If you use manual resource leveling early in the project to solve resource conflicts prior to baselining, try it again to help you when you need to update the schedule. With changes to tasks and tracked activity, resource leveling may uncover new options to solve conflicts.

If resource leveling is set to Automatic, Project automatically performs this calculation every time you modify the schedule. To see whether the option is set to Automatic or Manual, choose Resource⇨Leveling Options to open the Resource Leveling dialog box, as shown in Figure 17-6. If the Manual radio button is selected, close the dialog box and click Level All in the Leveling group to run resource leveling.

Figure 17-6:
Resource-
leveling
controls.

Determining which factors are driving the timing of a task

You can use the Task Inspector feature to determine what's causing tasks to occur in a certain time frame, such as dependencies, task calendars, or task constraints. You simply select a task and then, on the Task tab, click the Task Inspector button in the Tasks group. A pane then lists all factors that affect the timing of that task. Figure 17-7 shows an example of the Select Vendor task for the Finish Line Food work package. In this figure, the Task Inspector button is circled on the taskbar.

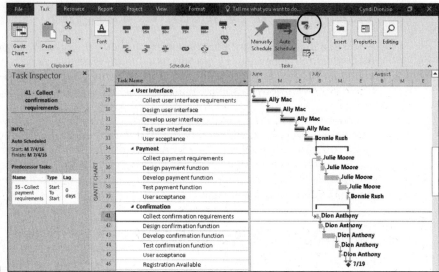

Figure 17-7:
Task
Inspector.

By using this feature (read more about it in Chapter 11), you can determine whether a task that you want to take place earlier can do so if you remove a dependency or constraint that's affecting it. For example, early in the planning phase, you may have believed that collecting payment requirements could start only after the user interface is complete, but now you realize that it can start *while* the user interface is being developed. By understanding what's driving the timing of the task, you can better search for a solution if that timing is causing problems.

How Adding People or Time Affects the Project

Human nature in a corporate environment often causes people to want to throw money and people at projects. In certain cases, that instinct is on target; however, you aren't always able to draw on an endless supply of resources or time. For this reason, you may have to experiment with a combination of options that involve time and resources.

Hurrying up and making modifications

Saving time in Project requires that a task be completed earlier than scheduled or that the timing of the task be adjusted to use up slack. You're likely to find that making this adjustment is similar to trying to solve an intricate puzzle: Correct one piece, and another one begins causing aggravation.

To accomplish work faster, you have these two options:

✔ **Find more resources to help with tasks that are auto-scheduled.** Adding people requires money, so even the schedule gets back on track, it will cost you.

✔ **Modify the scope of tasks.** This strategy may have an effect on the task quality. If you make two inspections rather than three or you shorten the QA cycle by a week, you may run the risk of causing problems down the road.

Changing the timing of tasks and shifting dependencies uses up slack to make up for delays, but it may leave you with no wiggle room. The next time a problem crops up, you'll be up against the wall with no slack.

In reality, combining small modifications for both time and money can often help save the day.

Throwing people at the problem

When auto-scheduled tasks are effort-driven, tasks are accomplished when the specified amount of effort is expended. A task with a duration of three days and based on the Standard calendar, for example, requires three days × eight hours per day to complete (a total of 24 hours of effort). One resource performing this task and working full time takes three days to complete it; three resources working full time take one day to complete the 24 hours of work. When you add resources to a task in this way, Project automatically recalculates its duration.

If you want Project to reduce the duration of a task when you assign more work resources to it, the task must be auto-scheduled, and effort-driven scheduling must be turned on.

Changing how resources are assigned

Beyond simply adding resources to a task, you can modify existing assignments. On any given project, you may have dozens (or even hundreds) of resources working on tasks. All these people are working according to their working calendars, the percentage of resource time assigned to particular tasks, and their ability to do the job. Take a look at how folks were assigned to begin with to see whether you can save time or money by modifying those assignments.

You can modify assignments in several ways:

- ✔ If someone is working at, say, only 50 percent capacity on a task, consider increasing the person's assignment units.

- ✔ If a resource is available who can perform a given task more quickly, switch resources on the task and shorten its duration. Remember that the new Team Planner view can be helpful when making this type of switch.

- ✔ Have certain resources work overtime or let them be overbooked at various points during the project. You may have modified an overbooked resource's assignments earlier to eliminate a conflict, but now you find that you have no choice other than to have the resource work an occasional 10- or 12-hour day.

Calculating the consequences of schedule modifications

Before you get carried away from making changes to resources, stop and think: Adding resources to effort-driven, auto-scheduled tasks can shrink the task and help the project get back on track. However, depending on the resources' hourly rates, this approach may cost more.

Assigning three people to work on a task doesn't necessarily shrink the duration of the task geometrically. That's because those people have to coordinate their efforts, hold meetings, and spend more time communicating than they would if they were working on the task alone. If you add resources, Project shrinks the task geometrically: Consider adding a little time to the task to accommodate the inefficiencies of multiple resources.

Another concern about adding resources to tasks is that it may cause more resource conflicts, with people who are already busy being overbooked on too many tasks that happen in the same time frame. If you have the resources, and they have the skills and the time, though, beefing up the workforce is definitely one way to perform certain tasks more quickly.

To add resources to a task, you can use the Resources tab in the Task Information dialog box, or choose the task and click the Assign Resources button in the Assignments group on the Resource tab of the Ribbon.

Shifting dependencies and task timing

Time is a project manager's greatest enemy. There's never enough time, and the time you have is eaten up quickly.

Follow these suggestions to modify task timing and save time:

- ✔ **Delete a task.** You heard me. If a task represents a step that can be skipped and no actual work for it is tracked, simply delete the task. It doesn't happen often, but sometimes — after you rethink the project — you realize that a few actions are unnecessary or have already been handled by someone else. You also can mark the task as inactive.

- ✔ **Adjust dependencies.** Perhaps the revision of the manual can start a few days before *all* the feedback is returned. Or perhaps the electrical and plumbing chores can take place at the same time rather than one after the other (assuming that the electrician and the plumber can stay out of each other's way). Use the Predecessors tab in the Task Information dialog box, shown in Figure 17-8, to modify dependencies. In the Lag column, you can enter a negative number to allow tasks to overlap.

Figure 17-8:
Modifying task dependencies and applying lag.

- ✔ **Modify constraints.** Perhaps you've set a task to start no earlier than the first of the year because you don't want to spend money on it until the new fiscal year budget kicks in. To save time, consider whether you can allow it to start a week before the end of the year and bill the costs in January. Examine any constraint of this type — especially those created to verify the timing logic.

- ✔ **Verify external dependencies.** If you've created an external link to a task in another project and set dependencies with tasks in the project, see whether the other project manager can speed up certain tasks. Or if the timing relationship isn't absolutely critical, delete the link to the other project. It may be slowing you down more than you realize.

- ✔ **Change the scheduling method or move the task.** Remember that Project usually cannot automatically reschedule a task based on dependency changes if the task is manually scheduled. You can either change the task to be auto-scheduled by using the Auto Schedule button in the Tasks group on the Task tab of the Ribbon, or you can select a manually scheduled task and then click the Respect Links button in the Schedule group on the Task tab to move it to its proper time frame. Or you can use the Move drop-down list on the Task tab to reschedule a task to a particular earlier or future time slot, or to one when resources are available.

If you've set resource leveling to Automatic, Project may have delayed certain tasks until overbooked resources are freed up. On the Resource tab, click the Leveling Options button in the Level group and change the setting to Manual.

When All Else Fails

Okay. You've monkeyed with resource assignments and shifted around task dependencies to save time, and you've deleted tasks and assigned less expensive resources to save money. Still, it's not enough. In this scenario, you have to say to the boss, "You can have it on time, you can have it on budget, or you can have quality work. Choose two."

If the boss throws money at you, add resources to tasks, as discussed in the earlier section "Throwing people at the problem." But keep in mind that not all tasks are effort driven. Some tasks aren't shortened by adding resources.

Taking the time you need

If the boss is willing to give you more time, grab it. However, when you do, you have to update the project a few ways:

- ✔ **Modify task durations.** Add time to tasks that are running late. In Project, you do this by increasing their durations or moving out their start dates.

- ✔ **Review task constraints.** If you've specified that certain tasks can finish no later than a certain date, but now you're extending the project finish date three months, you may be able to remove or adjust those original constraints accordingly.

- ✔ **Add to the contingency reserve.** If you have a contingency reserve task, you can simply add to its duration, giving more waffle room to all other tasks. (See Chapter 12 for more about contingency reserve.)

After you insert the extra time, you should make sure that the new timing of tasks doesn't cause new resource conflicts by looking at Resource Graph view and then reset the baseline to reflect the new schedule. To reset a baseline, select the Project tab and then Set Baseline ⇨ Set Baseline. Choose Baseline 1–10 in the Save Baseline dialog box to save to a different baseline and preserve the original. Click OK after choosing a baseline.

Inform team members of the new timing and provide them an updated version of the plan.

Finding ways to cut corners

If your manager tells you to cut some corners that sacrifice quality, you have license to modify the quality of the deliverables. You can eliminate tasks that may ensure higher quality, such as a final proofreading of the employee manual. You can hire less-experienced and less-expensive workers, for example, and you can use cheaper paper or computer equipment.

To cut corners in Project, you have to

- **Take fewer steps:** Delete tasks. Click the ID of the task in Gantt Chart view, and click Delete. You also can mark the task as Inactive. (Review any dependencies that were broken because you deleted tasks!)

- **Use less-expensive resources:** Delete one set of resource assignments, and assign other resources to tasks in the Assign Resources dialog box.

- **Use less-expensive materials:** Change the unit price of material resources you've created in Resource Sheet view. Or shop around for better pricing on items that are set up as cost resources, and enter the lower prices of tasks to which you've assigned those resources by using the Cost column in the Assign Resources dialog box, as shown in Figure 17-9. To get to the Assign Resources dialog box, right-click a task or a resource. From the right-click drop-down menu choose Assign Resources.

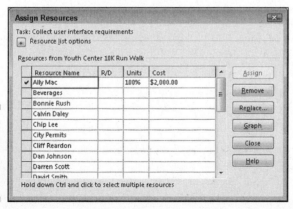

Figure 17-9: Modifying the resource cost.

You can also take a more sweeping approach: Simply redefine the goal of the project. If the goal were to launch a new product line, perhaps you can modify the goal to simply manage the design of the new product and then leave the launch to a later date or another project manager. If you were supposed to produce 10,000 widgets, see whether the company can make do with 7,500. To make this type of change, you may have to slice and dice entire phases of the project — or even start from scratch and build a new plan.

Save the revised project schedule with a new name to provide a head start on the revised project schedule. Clear the baseline (from the Project tab, choose Project ➪ Set Baseline ➪ Clear Baseline, click OK), make modifications, and then save a new baseline.

Chapter 18

Spreading the News: Reporting

In This Chapter

▶ Generating standard reports

▶ Creating custom reports

▶ Dazzling readers with Visual Reports

▶ Adding graphics and formatting to reports

▶ Making printer settings

▶ Sharing a snapshot of the Timeline

▶ Enhancing reports with copy and paste

*H*ere it is — the big payoff. It's your reward for entering all those task names and resource hourly rates, and for tracking activity on dozens of tasks during those late-hour sessions in the first hectic weeks of the project. You're finally ready to print a report or another type of project data, receiving tangible benefits from Project that you can hand out at meetings and show off to impress the boss.

Reports help you communicate information about projects by conveying schedule progress, resource assignments, cost accumulation, and activities that are in progress or scheduled soon. You can take advantage of built-in reports or create new reports to include the data that's most relevant to you. Dashboard Reports and Visual Reports in Project 2016 offer graphical possibilities to help paint a picture of the progress.

Knowing that you want to impress people, Project also makes it possible to apply certain themes, images, shapes, charts, and tables to reports to help make the point.

A report isn't the only tool you use to communicate with. You can customize headers, footers, and legends, and insert graphics into the schedule to make a presentation memorable. Other capabilities, such as customizing and copying Timeline view, enable you to incorporate Project data into reports in other programs.

Generating Standard Reports

Standard reports are already designed for you, offering numerous choices regarding the information you can include. You do little more than click a few buttons to generate them. Essentially, you select a report category, choose a specific report, and print it. If the plain-vanilla version of a report isn't quite right, you can modify standard reports in a variety of ways.

You can also print any view in Project: Simply press Ctrl+P, and then click Print. The entire project is printed in whichever view is onscreen at the time. Or you can choose File⇨Print. In the Print dialog box that appears, you can choose to print only certain pages of the project or only a specific date range from the timescale. Any filter or grouping that you've applied is shown in the printed document.

What's available

On the Report tab, Project has four standard report categories: Dashboards, Resources, Costs, and In Progress. Each category contains several predesigned reports (as you can see on the Report Ribbon, shown in Figure 18-1), for a total 16 standard reports.

Figure 18-1:
The Report Ribbon.

Standard reports vary in content, format (for example, a table, chart, or a comparison report), and sometimes page orientation (landscape or portrait). You can edit a report to change its name, the period it covers, the table of information it's based on, and the filters applied to it. You can also sort information as you generate the report and add formatting, such as themes, images, and shapes.

Overviewing the dashboard reports

One cool feature in Project 2016 is dashboard reporting. The program has five standard dashboard reports: Burndown, Cost Overview, Project Overview, Upcoming Tasks, and Work Overview.

To see a dashboard report, simply click the Report tab, click the Dashboards down arrow, and select the report you want. Figure 18-2 shows an example of a Cost Overview dashboard report.

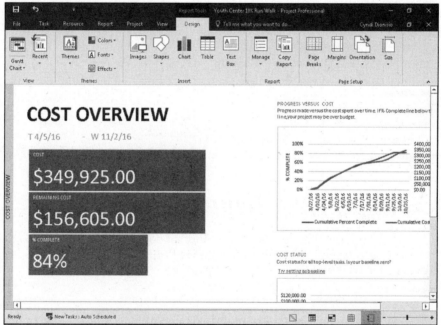

Figure 18-2:
Cost
Overview
report.

A dashboard report you may not be familiar with is a burndown chart. You use it to compare the amount of work remaining to the baseline work remaining and the number of tasks remaining compared with the baseline remaining tasks. On the burndown chart, you can see the rate of work compared with the planned rate of work to determine whether you're accomplishing work at the same rate as planned. If the number of tasks remaining is higher than the baseline rate, you're in jeopardy of delivering late. Figure 18-3 shows a burndown chart.

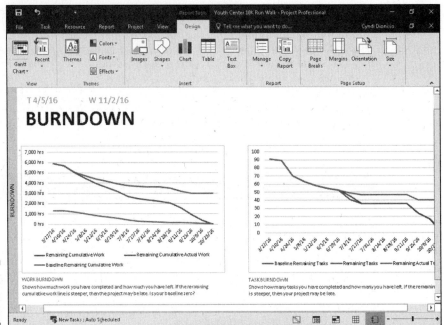

Figure 18-3:
Burndown
report.

Creating New Reports

Suppose that the standard report set doesn't have exactly what you want. No problem! The reporting function in Project 2016 makes it a snap to create a new report. Follow these steps:

1. **From the Report tab, select New Report.**

   Select the type of report you want: Blank, Chart, Table, or Comparison.

2. **When the Report Name dialog box opens, enter a name for the report and click OK.**

   A split window opens: The left side holds the report, and the right side holds a Field List.

3. **In the Select Category section, choose among Time, ID, Name, Resource Names, and Unique ID.**

4. **From the Select Fields scroll list, check the check box next to the fields you want from the various categories (cost, duration, number, or work).**

5. **If you want to apply a filter, such as incomplete tasks or active tasks, select one from the Filter drop-down menu.**

6. **If you want to group information, select the appropriate grouping from the Group By drop-down menu.**

7. **Select at which level you want to see information reported using the Outline Level drop-down menu — for example, Level 1 (the entire project), Level 2, or Level 3.**

8. **Choose how to sort the data.**

   It's the order in which you want to present it based on the fields you selected in Step 4.

After you create a new report, the report is saved on the Custom Report tab.

Gaining a new perspective on data with visual reports

Project offers six categories of visual reports and some custom reports that you can build yourself. Some visual reports are based on *time-phased data* (data distributed over time, such as allocations of resource time or costs), and some aren't. Report categories are described in this list:

- ✔ **Task Usage:** Based on time-phased data for tasks, this report category lets you peek at information such as cash flow and earned value over time.

- ✔ **Resource Usage:** Based on time-phased resource data, this type of report includes resource costs, resource availability, and resource work data.

- ✔ **Assignment Usage:** Also based on time-phased data, this category provides information in areas such as baseline versus actual costs and baseline versus actual work. It also provides an earned value report.

- ✔ **Task Summary, Resource Summary, and Assignment Summary:** These three report categories provide diagram views of a variety of work and cost data. None of these three categories is based on time-phased data.

Use the Visual Reports feature to select the fields you want to view and to modify the reports on the fly.

Additionally, if you enjoy the capabilities offered by pivot table reports in Excel, you'll be glad to know that the same capability is available in Project. Using pivot tables, you can view data from a variety of perspectives beyond the standard Project report capabilities. Pivot tables offer perspectives that are especially useful for data analysis.

All Visual Reports require you to have Microsoft Excel 2010 or higher; some require Visio.

Creating a visual report

Generating a visual report is simplicity itself. Follow these steps:

1. **From the Report tab, choose Visual Reports Export.**

   The Visual Reports – Create Report dialog box appears, as shown in Figure 18-4.

2. **Click the type of report you want from the available tabs.**

3. **Click View.**

Figure 18-4:
The Visual Reports dialog box.

To customize a visual report, you need to know about pivot tables. Because a discussion of pivot tables in those products is beyond the scope of this book, I heartily recommend *Excel 2016 For Dummies,* by Greg Harvey (Wiley).

You can modify the Visual Reports templates or create your own templates by using the New Template and Edit Template buttons in the Visual Reports dialog box. When you edit a template, you add fields to it or remove fields from it. Creating a new template involves specifying the format (Excel or Visio), choosing the data you want to report on, and selecting fields to include.

Fine-Tuning a Report

After you have lots of data available to you in Project reports, it would be a shame not to customize the presentation to maximize its impact. Project 2016 helps you create reports that not only show off the information, but also make the information look good!

As soon as you start creating a report, Project opens a new Ribbon, named Report Tools, and shows a Design tab. From this tab, you can work with themes; insert images, shapes, and charts; and work with Page Setup in the print function. Before getting into all the wonderful ways you can make reports attractive, I cover some of the easy ways you can manipulate the information in the reports.

Dragging, dropping, and sizing

In Project 2016, you can resize and relocate any item on a report by simply clicking the item and then moving it or resizing it. If you want a particular section of the project overview to stand out, enlarge it and shrink the other sections.

You can also change the way almost any report looks by simply right-clicking and working with the pop-up menus that appear. Figure 18-5 shows the Project Overview Dashboard report with the % Complete section after right-clicking. Notice that you can change its fill, outline, plot area, chart type, and fields. I also drew a box around the Design tab that shows where the Report Tools and Chart Tools are located on the Ribbon.

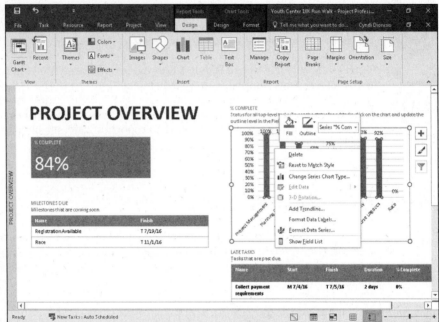

Figure 18-5:
Changing
the report
layout.

You can format the data series in the chart by double-clicking a chart section. Figure 18-6 shows what happens when you double-click the % Complete chart on the Project Overview Dashboard. I've drawn a box around the Ribbon to highlight the fact that you can change the colors, chart data, and chart type. Along the right side of the chart are options to format the plot area by changing the border, color, transparency, width, line format, and dash type.

Looking good!

If you have no creative flair, don't worry — Project does. You can work with the themes that Project provides to present all the reports with flair. From the Report Tools Ribbon on the Design tab, in the Themes group, click Themes. You see 35 different themes that you can apply to reports. Themes include color, type, font, and effect. Play around with a few to find one you like.

If none of the themes works for you, look around on the color, font, and effects drop-down lists until you create *just* the look you're hoping for.

To customize the reports even more, you can add images such as a team logo, shapes, and text boxes. Figure 18-7 shows a portion of a report with a text box and shape added.

Experimenting with customization options can be fun, but as with any other business document, the goal in layout and formatting is readability.

Keep these points in mind when you're formatting Project text:

✔ **Font:** Choose simple sans serif fonts, such as Arial. If you're publishing the project on the web, consider using Verdana, which is a font created for readability online.

✔ **Color:** You have to consider factors such as whether the printout will be in color or black and white, whether the use of too many colors will become confusing for the reader, and whether certain colors (such as yellow) will be difficult to read.

✔ **Font size:** Use a font size that's readable, without making it so big that the taskbar labels become too crowded.

✔ **Effects:** Avoid text effects that can make certain text difficult to read (such as bold, italic, or underlining). Use these effects only to call attention to a few elements of the project.

Spiffing Things Up

These days, image is everything. You and the project may be judged to a certain extent by how professional the printed information looks. Even if the project is a million dollars over budget and four months behind, making reports or other printouts look good can make delivering bad news easier to do. You can make the project presentation look good by adding graphics.

Wouldn't the company logo look spiffy in the header of the report? Or a picture of the new product box in Gantt Chart view of the New Product Launch project?

Graphics can add visual information or make the plan just plain look nicer. You can insert graphics in the project file by using one of these three methods:

✔ **Cut and paste a graphic from another file.** A graphical image that you cut and paste essentially can't be edited by you in Project.

✔ **Insert a link to an existing graphics file.** Linking reduces the Project file.

✔ **Embed a graphic.** Embedding lets you edit the content of the graphic in Project, using the tools of an image program such as Paint.

You can't add graphics willy-nilly, however. You can add graphics in only a few places: the chart pane of any Gantt Chart view; a task note; a resource note; or a header, footer, or legend that's used in reports or printouts of views.

For example, you may put pictures of resources in the Resource Note field so that you can remember who's who, or you may include a photo of the corporate headquarters in the header of the report.

Graphics swell the size of the Project file like a sponge in a pail of water. If you're thinking of using a lot of graphics, don't let them detract from the main information in printouts. Or try linking to them instead of inserting them into the file.

If you want to insert an existing graphics file into a Notes box, follow these steps:

1. **Double-click a task in the Gantt Chart view. Then select the Notes tab in the Task Information or Resource Information dialog box.**

2. **Click the Insert Object button.**

   The Insert Object dialog box, shown in Figure 18-8, appears.

Insert Object button

Figure 18-8:
Browse to
locate a file
on the net-
work or the
hard drive.

3. **Choose the Create from File option.**

4. **Click the Browse button to locate the file.**

5. **To insert to the file, click the Insert button and then click the OK button.**

   You may see a warning before you insert an image. If you want to continue, click Yes.

6. **To link the file, select the Link check box next to the Browse button.**

   If you don't select this option, the object is embedded in the file.

7. **To insert the object as an icon, select the Display as Icon check box.**

   When you display the object as an icon, someone viewing the project on
   a computer can click the icon to view the picture.

8. **Click the OK button.**

If you want to insert an existing graphics file in a header or footer, follow these steps:

1. **Choose File ➪ Print.**

2. **Click the Page Setup link at the bottom of the page.**

3. **Go to the Header or Footer tab in the Page Setup dialog box.**

4. **Click the Insert Picture button, as shown in Figure 18-9.**

   The Insert Picture dialog box appears.

Figure 18-9:
The Page Setup dialog box.

Insert picture

5. **Navigate to the folder that holds the file to insert.**

6. **Click to select the file.**

7. **Click the Insert button.**

   The image appears in the header or footer.

8. **Click OK.**

Call the Printer!

The proof of the report is in the printing, but you should see to several adjustments before you click the button to print. In Project, it's not only margins or page orientation that you need to set (although you have to set them, too); you can also add useful information to headers and footers and set legends to help readers understand the many bars, diamonds, and other graphical elements that many Project views and reports display.

Working with Page Setup

The Page Setup dialog box can be used to control printouts of any displayed Project view. You can open this dialog box by choosing File ⇨ Print ⇨ Page Setup. The Page Setup dialog box, as shown in Figure 18-10, contains six tabs.

Figure 18-10:
Page setup.

Sizing

The Page tab contains several basic page settings that determine the orientation, the paper size, and the way content is scaled to fit the page. By making these settings, you influence how much material can fit on a page and how many pages comprise the document.

You have these choices on the Page tab (refer to Figure 18-10):

- ✔ **Portrait or Landscape orientation:** You've no doubt already dealt with this choice. Portrait orientation is set up like the *Mona Lisa,* with the short edge of the paper running across the top of the page. In landscape orientation, the long edge of the paper runs across the top instead.

- ✔ **Scaling:** You can use the Adjust To setting, which is based on a percentage of the original size, or the Fit To setting, which gives you some control over scaling to fit to the width of a single page or to the height of a single page.

✔ **Other:** This area is a catch-all for two options: Paper Size and First Page Number. All the standard choices for paper size are available in the Paper Size list, including index cards and envelopes. First Page Number can remain as Auto (in which case the first page is numbered 1, the second page is 2, and so on), or you can enter another number there yourself.

Staying within the margins

I won't bore you by defining a margin. However, I'll remind you that a margin serves the dual purpose of controlling how much information can fit on a page and creating a border of white space that frames the document (making it cleaner-looking and easier to read).

To set margins using the Page Setup dialog box, follow these steps:

1. **Click the Margins tab.**

   As you modify margin settings, the preview shows you where they'll appear on the page.

2. **Use the arrows to set the top, bottom, left, and right margins.**

   Click the up arrow for a wider margin, and click the down arrow for a narrower margin.

3. **If you want a border that represents the margin, use the Borders Around options.**

   You can choose to print a border on every page, on only outer pages (print a border on the first and last pages only — available only when printing in Network Diagram view), or on none of the pages.

Setting margins to less than ¼ inch (.25") can cut off the printed output, because printers can print only *so* close to the edge of a page.

Inserting headers and footers

Throughout the life of a project, you print many versions of the project, many reports, and many types of information using various tables. Headers and footers are useful features to help you, and readers, keep track of all this information.

You can use the Header and Footer tabs of the Page Setup dialog box (see Figure 18-11) to set and preview header (top) and footer (bottom) contents.

This list describes the settings you can make on these tabs:

✔ **Text location:** Specify that the text you enter will appear to the left, at the center, or to the right of the header or footer by clicking the corresponding tab and then typing the text.

✔ **Format text:** Use the tool buttons, or quickly insert such elements as the page number, the date, or a picture file.

Figure 18-11:
The Header
and Footer
tabs are
nearly
identical.

✔ **Select standard text:** Insert additional text by using these lists:

General: Includes such options as Total Page Count, Project Title, and Company Name

Project Fields: Includes all fields available in Project

You can use these fields to alert readers to important fields to review or to the nature of the printout. To add General or Project Fields items, select them from their respective lists and then click the Add button to add them to the Left, Center, or Right tab.

Working with a legend

A *legend* acts as a guide to the meanings of various graphical elements, as shown in Figure 18-12. The Legend tab bears a striking resemblance to the Header and Footer tabs except that the legend is generated automatically. All you can specify on this tab is the text that fits in the box to the left of the legend.

The Legend tab of the Page Setup dialog box has a few settings that differ from the Header and Footer tabs:

✔ You can print the legend on every page or on a separate legend page, or you can decide not to print a legend.

✔ You can establish the width of the text area of the legend (the area where you can insert elements such as the page number or the date).

✔ You can edit the text font, style, size, and color of the legend by clicking the Legend Labels box.

Text

Figure 18-12:
Page setup
with legend
information.

Unlike a header or footer, where you have to enter something to make any-thing appear, a legend prints by default. If you don't want a legend to print, click the Legend tab and then set the Legend On option to None.

Deciding what to print

If you're printing a currently displayed view, the View tab of the Page Setup dialog box is available to you, as shown in Figure 18-13.

Figure 18-13:
The View
tab.

You can make these settings on the View tab:

- **Print All Sheet Columns:** Prints every sheet column in the view, regardless of whether it's visible onscreen. With this option deselected, only the columns that show in the view are printed.

- **Print First # Columns on All Pages:** Lets you control a specific number of columns to print.

- **Print Notes:** Prints every task, resource, and assignment note. These items are printed on a separate Notes page.

- **Print Blank Pages:** Lets you print blank pages. For example, use this setting to print a page that represents a time in the project when no tasks are occurring. If you want a smaller number of pages in the printout, ignore this setting.

- **Fit Timescale to End of Page:** Scales the timescale to fit more of the project on the page.

- **Print Column Totals:** Adds a column that contains column totals. It pertains to printouts of Usage views.

- **Print Row Totals for Values within Print Date Range:** Adds a column that contains row totals. It pertains to printouts of Usage views.

Getting a preview

Granted, although software print previews aren't quite as exciting as movie previews, they help you make everything look right before you print the project. When you choose a report or choose File ⇨ Print to print a view, the preview automatically appears in the Backstage. Figure 18-14 has a box around the buttons in the lower-right corner of the preview that enable you to modify the preview so that you can work with the settings more effectively.

You can use the buttons in the Backstage preview to

- Move around the pages of the report by using the first four arrow buttons and the horizontal and vertical scroll bars

- View more detail by clicking the Actual Size button and then clicking the report

- Focus on a single page or all pages in the report by using the One Page and Multiple Pages buttons

Note: Always preview the document before printing it to review the number of pages being printed. One click or one instance of zooming in or out can easily double — or cut in half — the number of pages being sent to the printer. You can easily waste paper if you're not careful.

Figure 18-14:
Backstage
Print view.

Printing, at last!

In this section, I describe how to print the document for which you've made all the eye-pleasing settings discussed in this chapter. For this task, you need to make the print settings to the left of the preview in the Backstage, as shown in Figure 18-14.

This list describes the settings you encounter in this area:

- ✓ **The Copies up arrow and down arrow:** Click the Copies up arrow to print more copies, or click the down arrow to print fewer (but not less than 1).

- ✓ **The Printer area:** This area of the dialog box indicates the printer you will use. You can choose a printer from the list and click the Printer Properties link to control printer settings such as color quality and paper source.

- ✓ **The Settings area:** You can print the entire project or select another option from the drop-down list so that you can print specific dates, print specific pages, or print custom dates and pages. The accompanying options change depending on the choice. You also can use the Settings drop-down list to specify whether to print notes, all sheet columns, or only the left column of pages (to print only the leftmost column on every page).

- ✓ **The remaining settings:** These choices control the orientation and paper size, if you didn't make them elsewhere.

After you make all the settings and you're ready to print, simply click the big Print button in the upper-left corner.

Working on the Timeline

The Timeline gives sort of a 10,000-foot overview of the project schedule. It shows a graphical timeline spanning from the project's start date to its end date, and it highlights the period shown in the main view, such as the time frame shown on the Gantt chart. You can toggle the Timeline on and off as needed. To do so, click the View tab on the Ribbon and select the Timeline check box in the Split View group.

The Timeline even has its own toolbar, Timeline Tools, as shown in Figure 18-15.

Figure 18-15:
The Time-
line Tools
toolbar.

From the Timeline Tools toolbar, you can format text and dates, format the display of tasks on the toolbar, and copy the Timeline in various presentation formats.

Adding tasks to the Timeline

You can add summary tasks, detailed tasks, and milestones to the Timeline. For example, the Timeline shown in Figure 18-16 shows milestones, the Volunteers summary task, and a callout for the Obtain City Permits task. Yes, you can do all these wonderful things!

Figure 18-16:
The
Timeline,
with tasks,
summary
tasks, and
milestones.

You can add information to the Timeline in a number of ways. To add several tasks at a time, follow these simple steps:

1. **Open the Timeline from the View tab.**

   Go to the Task Views tool group and click the Timeline view. The time-line will be visible in the chart area, and the Timeline Tools toolbar will show up above the Format tab.

2. **Click Timeline Tools to show the Timeline Tools toolbar (refer to Figure 18-15).**

3. **Click Existing Tasks in the Insert group.**

   The Add Tasks to Timeline dialog box opens, as shown in Figure 18-17, showing an outline of all tasks in the project. You can select as many as you like. They appear on the Timeline as individual tasks, summary tasks, or milestones, depending on how they're entered in Project.

4. **Click OK.**

Figure 18-17:
Adding
tasks to the
Timeline.

You can also add a new task by clicking the Task button in the Insert group to open the Task Information dialog box and then entering the task information, adding the predecessor and successor information, and assigning resources. When you select the Display on Timeline check box, the task appears on the Timeline.

If you want to change the way a task appears on the Timeline, follow these steps:

1. **Click to select the task.**

2. **In the Current Selection group, select either Display as Bar to show a bar that indicates the duration or Display as Callout to create a callout box that holds the task information. If you want to remove a task from the Timeline, select Remove from Timeline.**

3. **Reposition the callout box to improve readability, if you have several tasks close together.**

You can right-click a task and click Add to Timeline to make the task show up on the Timeline.

Customizing the Timeline

Project lets you customize the Timeline to make it truly fit your needs. For example, you can freeze the Timeline or move it around so that it focuses on a particular time frame. When you move the timeframe in Timeline, the Gantt chart moves in parallel. To move the Timeline, follow these steps:

1. **Click the Timeline so that the Timeline Tools toolbar appears.**

2. **In the Show/Hide group, select Pan & Zoom.**

   A green frame surrounds the current time frame.

3. **Position the cursor on the edge to drag the time frame to the size you like.**

4. **To shift the time frame to a different one, move the cursor to the top of the frame, wait for the four-way arrow, and drag the green frame to the time frame you want.**

You can also change the date format from the Show/Hide group on the Timeline Tools toolbar. Simply click the down arrow and select the way you want to see the date displayed on the Timeline.

The Timeline can be displayed with details about tasks, such as the task name and dates, or without the detail and just milestones and bars that represent tasks, but no names associated with the tasks. If you want a detailed view, select the Detailed Timeline check box in the Show/Hide group.

Copying the Timeline

Because that vendor you're trying to coordinate with doesn't use Project, you need to share the graphical Timeline information via another file format. Project builds in the special capability to take a snapshot of the Timeline so that you can paste it into an email message; a presentation; or another program, such as a word processor.

Follow these steps to copy and use the Timeline:

1. **Create the email message or document where you want to use the Timeline image.**

2. **From the Timeline Tools, choose Copy Timeline and then select a format.**

   The available format choices are For E-Mail, For Presentation, and Full Size.

3. **In the program where you want to insert the Timeline, position the curser where you want the Timeline image to appear.**

4. **Press Ctrl+V.**

   The image appears in the message or document.

Enhanced Copy and Paste

Though it has long been possible to copy and paste information to and from Project and other Office applications, sometimes the results were, well, messy. Now, copy-and-paste operations between applications retain much more information. For example, when you copy tasks from Project and paste them into Word or Excel, you automatically see outline-level formatting and column headings. And formatting from information copied from another application into Project is retained. There's no need to reinvent the wheel every time you need to copy data between apps — and that's a sweet, sweet thing.

Chapter 19

Getting Better All the Time

In This Chapter

▶ Reviewing your successes and failures

▶ Comparing versions of the same project

▶ Creating a template for future projects

*H*ave you ever finished a project and then wondered how in the heck it turned out the way it did? The budgeted totals mystically appear to be several thousand dollars over the original estimates; you missed the final deadline by three weeks; and somewhere along the line, you lost track of three people who were supposed to be working on tasks. But you delivered the deliverables (somehow), and you can finally stuff the project file in the bottom of a drawer. Or can you?

Don't think of Microsoft Project as simply a giant electronic to-do list; rather, it's a sophisticated tool that's used to manage projects. And the logical byproduct of that management is a fantastic treasure-trove of information you can use to become a more highly skilled Project user — and, thus, a more competent project manager.

After you send the last memo related to the project and accept the final kudos or criticism from your boss, take a moment to look over the Project schedule one more time.

Reviewing the Project

When I teach classes in project management, my students are often over-whelmed by all the information they have to collect, analyze, and report. Add to these elements a product such as Microsoft Project, and many times students begin reeling from all the data that they have to input and all the information that Project spews at them. They can't see straight for all the views, reports, tables, and filters that they have to use to access information about their projects.

I tell them this secret: You won't understand every aspect of managing your first, second, or even third project. But you will become more comfortable with your skills. Similarly, you won't understand every nuance of the Project schedule on your first project. You won't even uncover every capability of Project on your second project. But gradually, as you master the ins and outs of managing projects and using Project, you'll more effectively apply project management skills and more easily absorb the information that Project generates — and you'll more quickly understand how it can help you avoid mistakes on future projects.

Review every project at the end of each phase and at the end of the project to see what you did right and what you did wrong. Then you can use what you discover to improve your skills on the next project.

Learning from your mistakes

You know what they say: If you don't study history, you're doomed to repeat it. And repeating a mistake is the last thing you want to do when managing a project.

Consider these strategies when reviewing your last project:

- ✓ **Compare the original baseline plan against the final actual activity, as shown in Figure 19-1.** Even if you created interim or baseline plans to adjust for drastic changes, look at the widest gap between what you expected to happen in the initial plan and what did happen. This strategy can be the best way to see areas where you tend to underestimate the most or where changes in the project's scope caused dramatic changes. For a refresher on baselines, refer to Chapter 14.

Figure 19-1:
Baseline and actual figures.

Task Name	Start	Finish	Baseline Start	Baseline Finish
⊿ **Youth Center 10K Run Walk**	T 4/5/16	W 11/2/16	T 4/5/16	T 11/29/16
⊿ **Project Management**	T 4/5/16	T 4/5/16	T 4/5/16	T 11/29/16
Charter signed	T 4/5/16	T 4/5/16	T 4/5/16	T 4/5/16
⊿ **Planning Phase**	W 4/6/16	W 4/27/16	W 4/6/16	W 4/27/16
On board project management team	W 4/6/16	T 4/19/16	W 4/6/16	T 4/19/16
Project kick off	W 4/20/16	W 4/20/16	W 4/20/16	W 4/20/16
Develop scope statement	T 4/21/16	W 4/27/16	T 4/21/16	W 4/27/16
Develop schedule	T 4/21/16	W 4/27/16	T 4/21/16	W 4/27/16
Develop budget	T 4/21/16	W 4/27/16	T 4/21/16	W 4/27/16
Develop registration plan	T 4/21/16	W 4/27/16	T 4/21/16	W 4/27/16
Develop PR and advertising Plan	T 4/21/16	W 4/27/16	T 4/21/16	W 4/27/16
Develop volunteer management plan	T 4/21/16	W 4/27/16	T 4/21/16	W 4/27/16
Develop food and beverage plan	T 4/21/16	W 4/27/16	T 4/21/16	W 4/27/16
Develop safety plan	T 4/21/16	W 4/27/16	T 4/21/16	W 4/27/16
Develop course logistics plan	T 4/21/16	W 4/27/16	T 4/21/16	W 4/27/16
Planning complete	W 4/27/16	W 4/27/16	W 4/27/16	W 4/27/16

✔ **Review the notes you made about tasks to remind yourself of changes or problems that cropped up.** Insert the column named Notes into the Gantt Chart sheet and read all notes in one sitting.

✔ **Note which resources failed to deliver as promised; if you manage them, provide them constructive feedback.** If you don't manage resources, maintain notes on their working speed and quality to assist in future assignments. Also note which outside vendors failed to perform as expected (and move them to the bottom of the contracting list).

✔ **Assess your own communications in saved emails or memos.** Determine whether you gave the team enough information to perform effectively and whether you informed management about project issues in a timely way.

✔ **Assess feedback from your boss, your customers, and other stakeholders.** Determine whether any overall constraints, such as the project budget or deliverables, changed dramatically during the course of the project. Ask whether end users were satisfied with the rate at which you completed the project and delivered the final product. Inquire about the team's performance from their perspective and about whether they would rely on you to lead another, similar project.

Debriefing the team

No project is the province of a single person. Even if no one else ever touched the Project plan, your team still provided input for that plan via the hours of activity they reported and the information they provided to you during the course of the project.

Follow these suggestions for refining the communications process:

✔ **Ask team members about the success of actual activity reporting.** Did you send email, schedule notes, or use the Project Web App tools, such as TimeSheet, to gather resource information? Did you consider taking advantage of all the benefits of online collaboration? Should you do so on the next project?

✔ **Determine whether your team rates your communications as frequent and thorough.** Did you share with resources too little information about the project, or did you inundate them with too much? Did you send simple reports on specific aspects of the project or send entire (cumbersome) Project files? Did the management team feel that your reporting on the project was sufficient for their needs? Should you learn to take better advantage of other software, such as Excel and Visio, accessed via Visual Reports?

Debrief yourself

To evaluate the success of a project, assess whether team members gave you the information you needed to operate efficiently, or whether you should lay down more stringent ground rules for reporting in the next project. If you were swamped with work throughout the project, consider having someone update entries for you the next time around. Determine whether management apprised you of company changes in a timely way so that you could make adjustments to maintain the schedule.

In the heat of the project battle, many team members often have no time to stop and change processes or to find the help they need. Review the Project Notes areas to see what types of mix-ups occurred and when (or which ones made you want to pull your hair out). Then institute changes before you begin the next project.

Comparing Versions of a Project

Project managers sometimes prefer to save new versions of project plans rather than work with interim plans. This approach can work, but it doesn't enable the project history to be captured in a single project file. No matter — Project's Compare Versions feature lets you see the differences between two Project plan files. These files can be either two different versions of the plan for a single project or files for two separate projects that happen to be similar.

You can use this method to either review events from a completed project or compare similar new projects as you're building them. The finished comparison report shows you the project differences graphically and provides a legend to identify report features.

To compare two files in Project, follow these steps:

1. **Open the file that you want to compare.**

   The active file is considered the current project.

2. **From the Report tab, click the Compare Projects button in the Project group.**

   The Compare Project Versions dialog box appears, as shown in Figure 19-2.

Figure 19-2:
Comparing
project
versions.

3. **If the file to compare doesn't appear in the drop-down list labeled Compare the Current Project** *(filename)* **to This Previous Version, click the Browse button to search for and select the appropriate file.**

   The file you select is considered the previous project.

4. **To compare tables other than the default tables that are shown, select the appropriate tables from the Task Table and Resource Table drop-down lists.**

5. **Click the OK button.**

6. **If you see a message indicating that you have too many columns to compare, click OK to continue.**

   Project runs the comparison and displays the comparison report, as shown in Figure 19-3. The comparison report appears in the upper pane, and the individual project files show up in the two lower panes. The legend at the left describes the symbols in the Indicators column of the report.

7. **Click Resource Comparison in the View group on the Compare Projects tab.**

   The Comparison Report pane changes to display resource information.

8. **Click the Close Comparison (X) button on the Legend for Comparison Report pane to close the pane.**

   Click the Save button on the Quick Access toolbar and name the file so that the next time you want to view this comparison report, the projects and fields will already be set up.

Figure 19-3:
Comparing
projects.

Building on Success

Although human nature often makes people focus unnecessarily on the shortcomings resulting from a project, the fact is that you've likely done *many* things well. Before you start planning another project, you want to store the positive aspects somewhere that you can easily find later.

Creating a template

One option for saving information from your current project is to create a *template,* which is simply a file you save that contains the settings you want to replicate. When you open a template, you can save it as a Project document with a new name and all those settings already built in.

Project contains its own templates for common types of projects, but you can save any project as a template. If you often repeat the same set of tasks in a project — as people in many industries do — save yourself the time of re-creating all those tasks.

Templates can contain, in addition to any tasks in the project, any or all of these types of information for those tasks:

- ✔ All information for each baseline
- ✔ Actual values
- ✔ Rates for all resources
- ✔ Fixed costs

You can save all this information or only selected items. For example, if you create numerous fixed costs (such as equipment) and resources with associated rates (and you use them in most projects), you can save a template with only fixed costs and resource rates.

To save a file as a template, follow these steps:

1. **Open the file you want to save and then choose File ➪ Save As.**

2. **In the Save and Sync pane, select where you want to save the template.**

   You can save it in SharePoint, on your computer, in the cloud, or in another location that you add.

3. **Navigate to where you want to save the template.**

   The Save As dialog box appears, as shown in Figure 19-4.

Figure 19-4:
Saving a
file as a
template.

4. **From the Save As Type drop-down list, select Project Template (*.mpt).**

5. **Click the Save button.**

You will be asked to select the type of data you want to remove from the template, such as values of all baseline, actual values, and so on. Check the boxes you want to save in the template, and click Save.

Microsoft saves templates in the central folder named Templates.

Mastering the Organizer

The marvelously flexible nature of Project lets you customize many settings such as tables, filters, views, and reports. For example, you can create separate tables of data to display in views that contain sheet panes. You can also create separate filters, reports, and calendars. If you have any kind of a life, you may not want to spend evenings re-creating all these elements on the next project. Instead, use the Organizer to copy them to other Project files.

You can use the Organizer to copy information from one file to another file. These are some of the most common types of items you can copy with Organizer:

- ✔ Calendar
- ✔ Field
- ✔ Filter
- ✔ Form
- ✔ Group
- ✔ Report
- ✔ Table
- ✔ Toolbar
- ✔ View

 If you want to make a custom item that you've created in the current file available for use in all Project plan files, use the Organizer to copy the item into the global template Global.MPT. Though some items are copied to the Organizer by default, it never hurts to ensure that crucial items are saved there.

Follow these steps to use the Organizer:

1. **Open the project that you want to copy items from and the project to copy items to.**

2. **In the file you want to copy to, choose File ⇨ Info.**

   Backstage view opens, showing the overall file choices.

3. **Click the Organize Global Template button.**

   The Organizer dialog box appears, as shown in Figure 19-5.

Figure 19-5:
The
Organizer
dialog box.

4. **Click the tab for the type of information you want to copy.**

5. **In the left column, click the line to copy from.**

   By default, Project selects the Global.MPT template for the list on the left and the file from which you open the Organizer for the list on the right. If you want to copy items from another open file instead, choose it by clicking the drop-down list below the file list on the right. (Depending on the tab you display, the drop-down list may be named Views Available In, Groups Available In, Reports Available In, and so forth.)

6. **Click the Copy button.**

   The item appears in the list on the right.

7. **(Optional) To rename a custom item that you've created,**

   a. Click it and then click the Rename button.

   b. Enter a new name in the Rename dialog box that appears and then click the OK button.

8. To copy additional items on the same tab, repeat Steps 5 and 6.

9. To copy an item on a different tab, repeat Steps 4–8.

10. When you finish copying items from one file to another, click the Close (X) button.

Don't rename default items in the Organizer. Renaming them can cause errors and malfunctions, such as the inability to display a particular view.

Part V
The Part of Tens

the
part of
tens

 Discover ten project management pitfalls and how to avoid them at www.dummies.com/extras/project2016.

In this part . . .

- ✔ Check out the ten golden rules of project management.
- ✔ Follow ten cool shortcuts in Project 2016.

Chapter 20

Ten Golden Rules of Project Management

In This Chapter

▶ Following good project-management practices

▶ Scheduling projects efficiently

▶ Benefitting from mistakes

A s you begin to use Project 2016, the common sayings (or aphorisms, axioms, and precepts) in this chapter can help you recall basic project-management principles. Tack them on your office wall so that you can review them throughout the workday.

Roll with It

Rolling wave planning is an excellent way to simplify the management of a project. Plan no further into the future than you can reasonably see — and don't plan in more detail than makes sense. When a project is first chartered, you only have milestone dates. As you begin to understand more about the project, you can define the project life cycle and the key deliverables to be created in each of its phases.

Build the project in phases. Start with the initial phases, and fill in detailed tasks, sequences, resources, and durations. Leave the later phases at a high level of detail; that way, you'll have less work to redo on later tasks that simply can't be anticipated at the beginning of the project. You'll also have less need to manipulate the baseline of those later tasks: If tasks are too far in the future, their time requirements won't match up with the resources you originally set aside for them.

When it's early in the game, avoid delving into detail on tasks that are far in the future.

Project can help you with rolling wave planning when you use these features of the program:

- ✔ **Network Diagram view:** Helps you visualize project phases graphically
- ✔ **Timeline:** Shows milestones, deliverables, and phases at a high level
- ✔ **Task expansion and collapse:** Lets you hide or display project phases

See Chapter 3 for more about the best ways to collapse and expand summary tasks and subtasks.

Put Your Ducks in a Row

Before you start creating the project, do your homework. If you don't have all the information you need when you sit down at the computer to work with Project, you'll continually stop, midplan, and run off to find the information — not an efficient way to work.

Before you sit down to build a project schedule, think about the following project information:

- ✔ **Reality check of basic expectations:** Based on your experience in managing similar projects over time, determine whether the deliverables, budget, and preliminary schedule are within reason. Decide whether to discuss changes to the scope and budget to avoid a project that's unrealistic from the start.

- ✔ **Resource information:** If the resource is human, record the resource's full name, contact information, skills, cost, schedule, timing conflicts, manager's name, and manager's contact information. For equipment or facilities, find its availability and cost.

- ✔ **Team structure:** Determine whether one team member records everyone else's progress or all resources do their own tracking. Decide who updates the schedule after changes are made, who receives copies of which reports, and who has access to the master schedule online.

- ✔ **Management expectations:** Ask whether management expects to see regularly scheduled basic reports or another type of report instead. Ask how, and from whom, to get budget approval at various phases in the project planning, and ask whether any cross-enterprise interests will require reports or approval from multiple sources. (See Chapter 18 for the lowdown on reports.)

✔ **Company policies:** These documents may spell out working hours and overtime policies, holiday calendars, charges for overhead costs or project markups, and the sharing (or not) of information with clients and vendors.

After you contemplate the issues in this list, you're ready to sit down and start entering information into a Project project. (Do you hear an echo in here?)

Expect the Unexpected

You know he's out there — Murphy and his darn law stipulating that anything that can go wrong *will* go wrong. Most projects, especially lengthier and more complex projects, aren't completed on time or on budget. Your job as the project manager is to plan as accurately as you can and then make prudent adjustments whenever someone throws a wrench into the works — and Project gives you lots of tools to do it. But beyond all the automated features of Project, you can anticipate change by simply planning for it.

The critical path determines the project duration. Every wise project manager builds contingency reserve time and funds into his or her projects. When a project wraps up a week late and $5,000 over budget, only the project manager knows that it was *four* weeks later and $25,000 costlier than originally scheduled, with no contingency reserve. (I introduce contingency reserve in Chapter 12.)

Add contingency reserve before major deliverables or the end of a phase to account for unexpected events. You can even add a Contingency task and resource it with Murphy.

Use the cost resource type (rather than a work or material resource) to add a set amount of contingency reserve to a task or phase.

Don't Put Off until Tomorrow . . .

Though Project management software can simplify many aspects of your work life, most people using Project for the first time become overwhelmed by the amount of time they spend entering and updating data. These tasks can certainly be cumbersome, but the reward from mastering the automated updating and reporting capabilities in Project more than makes up for any labor they endure up front.

Whenever possible, import tasks from Outlook or Excel into Project to help speed data entry in the planning phase.

Track as often as you can — at least once a week. If you don't tend to the task of tracking progress on a project, you may wind up behind the proverbial eight ball. This strategy not only saves you from having to enter a mountain of tracking data, but also lets you — and your team — see the status of the project at any time. That way, you can promptly spot disaster approaching and make preventive adjustments.

Delegate, Delegate, Delegate

Avoid the urge to attempt to do everything on a project yourself. Although creating and maintaining the Project file on your own might seem to give you more control over the result, flying solo in a larger project is nearly impossible (and possibly a full-time job). Of course, you can't allow dozens of people to make changes to the plan, because you would risk losing track of who did what and when. However, following these few simple practices can convert a few fingers in the project pie from harmful to helpful:

- **Designate one person to handle all data.** This person's mission is to enter all tracking data into the master file.

- **Break the project into a few subprojects, and assign people whom you trust to act as managers of those subprojects.** Let them handle their own tracking and adjustments, and then assemble these projects into a master project so that you can monitor overall status.

- **Set uniform procedures for the team up front.** Don't let one team member report time on an interoffice memo sheet, another send you his progress by email, and others record their work hours in the time sheet willy-nilly. Work out a strategy that uses Project features to communicate consistently.

You can track progress at a high level, such as 25 percent, 50 percent, 75 percent, and 100 percent complete. (I discuss tracking in Chapter 15.)

Document It

Most people have heard the project management warning "Cover your assumptions," and Project helps you do it easily. Use these features to document the details of the project:

- ✔ **Notes area:** Use it for both tasks and resources to make a record of background information, changes, or special issues.

- ✔ **Reports:** Customize them to incorporate all pertinent information and help document trends and changes, as detailed in Chapter 18.

- ✔ **Visual Reports:** Use this new feature to paint the picture of the project status for visually oriented stakeholders; see Chapter 18.

Save multiple versions of the project, especially if you change the baseline in later versions. This way, you have a record of every step in the project planning to refer to when questions arise down the road.

Keep the Team in the Loop

I've worked in offices where I spent more time wrestling with the question of whom to keep informed about what than I did working. If I didn't include marketing and finance in every email on a new product launch, I'd be called on the carpet the next day, or (worse) a vital action step would fall through the cracks because someone didn't know to take action. Follow these methods of keeping communication channels open:

- ✔ **Use Project features that integrate with Outlook or other email programs.** Use them to send Project files or other types of communications.

- ✔ **Update the communications management plan.** Document who needs what information, when, and how often. I discuss this plan in Chapter 15.

- ✔ **Review progress with team members by meeting regularly in person, over the phone, or via meeting software.** Ensure that all team members have the latest version of the Project schedule to refer to during these meetings.

- ✔ **Display the work breakdown structure (WBS) code on reports.** Then you can easily refer to specific tasks in large projects without confusion. Work breakdown structures are covered Chapter 2.

Measure Success

When you begin the project, you should have an idea of what constitutes success, and you should know how to measure that success. You've heard this one: "You can have the deliverable on time, on budget, or done right. Choose two." Success can involve attaining many goals, such as

- ✔ Customer satisfaction
- ✔ Management satisfaction
- ✔ Meeting budget constraints
- ✔ Being on time

To determine how you'll measure success, ask these questions:

- ✔ Will success in budgeting mean not exceeding the original estimates by more than 10 percent?
- ✔ Will the project be considered on time if you work on it the estimated number of weeks minus a two-month period when you were on hold for a union strike, or is the total working time less important than meeting a specific deadline?
- ✔ How will you measure customer satisfaction?
- ✔ Does a successful product launch include high sales figures after the launch, or was the project successful merely because you moved it out the door?

Place milestones in the project that reflect the achievement of each type of success. When you reach one, you can pat your team on the back. Knowing what success looks like helps you motivate your team to get there.

Maintain a Flexible Strategy

Stuff happens. There's never been a project that didn't require accommodations for surprises along the way. The mark of a good project manager is that she's alert to these changes and makes adjustments to deal with them quickly.

Making adjustments to accommodate bad news isn't easy; in fact, it can be truly difficult to deliver bad news. However, avoiding a problem in the project and hoping that it will simply disappear has a nasty habit of snowballing into an even worse problem. The following tools can help you stay alert to changes and make adjustments:

- ✔ The work contour option can help you change the contour of the work to front-load, back-load, or otherwise change the spread of work over the duration of the task, as described in Chapter 9.

- ✔ Use the Task Inspector, detailed in Chapter 17, to see what's driving a task. You can look for options such as adding resources, revising task dependency relationships, and using reserve.

- ✔ Turn on critical path formatting to see the critical path of the project and track how much slack remains. Adjusting tasks to efficiently use up their slack can keep you on schedule in a crisis, as I describe in Chapter 17.

Learn from Your Mistakes

One great gift that Project offers is the capability to look back after completing a project so that you can learn from your mistakes. You can review the original schedule, and every version after it, to see how well you estimated time and money, and then figure out how to do it better.

By using records of the project, you can spot trends to find out, for example, where you always seem to miss on timing, or why you always allow much too little time for market research and much too much time for questions and answers. Perhaps you always forget to budget for temporary help during rush periods, or you overstaff early on, when you need only a few people.

Use the wealth of information in Project schedules to educate yourself on your own strengths and weaknesses as a project planner and manager and to improve your skills with each project you take on.

Chapter 21

Ten Cool Shortcuts in Project 2016

In This Chapter

▶ Viewing task and resource information

▶ Keeping shortcuts close at hand

▶ Changing the view for better focus

▶ Adding tasks to the Timeline

I'm always amazed to watch people work who are adept at using a specific type of software. Their fingers seem to fly over the keyboard; without ever touching the mouse, they create documents, presentations, and other artifacts. In this chapter, I show you ten cool shortcuts that can help you handle Project 2016 like a pro.

Task Information

From Gantt Chart view, you can double-click any task in the project to open the Task Information dialog box. You can then use it, as shown in Figure 21-1, to enter or modify durations, predecessor information, resources, notes, task types, and constraints.

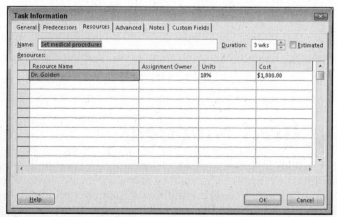

Figure 21-1:
The Task
Information
dialog box.

In Chapter 2, I give you more information about the Task Information dialog box.

Resource Information

If you want to know anything about a resource, you can find the information in the Resource Information dialog box, as shown in Figure 21-2. From any Resource Sheet view, double-click a resource name to see contact information, availability, cost rates, and any notes you've entered about the resource.

Figure 21-2:
The
Resource
Information
dialog box.

You can use the Resource Information dialog box to enter, edit, or update resource information for people, supplies, equipment, and locations considered to be resources. In Chapter 7, I detail how to work with resources in Project.

When the Assign Resources dialog box is open, double-click a resource name to display the Resource Information dialog box.

Frequently Used Functions

Most user actions in Project are fairly standard, so you shouldn't have to visit the Ribbon every time you want to give a command. Instead, you can simply right-click a task to display a floating menu of options that let you (for example)

✔ Cut, copy, and paste text

✔ Insert and delete tasks

✔ Assign resources

✔ Navigate to the Task Information dialog box

✔ Add notes

✔ Add the task to the timeline

Figure 21-3 shows a typical menu of options you see after right-clicking a task.

Figure 21-3:
Floating
menu bar.

Subtasks

Sometimes, you need to see portions of the project expanded to show all tasks in detail while other portions remain rolled up to a summary task level. In addition to the standard method of clicking the triangle next to the summary task to expand or summarize tasks, you can use keystrokes.

To hide a subtask, press Alt+Shift+hyphen (–). To show subtasks, press Alt+Shift+plus sign (+).

Indenting and Outdenting

In Chapter 2, I introduce the work breakdown structure (WBS), which lets you show the parent-child relationship in a task by indenting its subtasks to create the outline (the WBS) of the project. Instead of selecting all the tasks you want to work with and then indenting or outdenting them from the Ribbon, you can select them and then press Alt+Shift+right arrow to indent them. To outdent a task, press Alt+Shift+left arrow.

Fill Down

Suppose that all the tasks in a series have the same resource or the same duration. Rather than repeatedly enter the same resource or duration, you can enter the duration on the topmost task in the list, select the rest of the tasks, and then press Ctrl+D. Project "fills down" the resource to the rest of the selected tasks.

Navigation

The Alt key is a helpful tool for navigating to the beginning or end of the project. Simply press Ctrl+Home to move to the beginning of the project or press Ctrl+End to move to the end.

You can also press the Alt key to navigate around the timescale. To move to the right (forward in time), press Alt+right arrow. To move to the left (backward in time), press Alt+left arrow.

Hours to Years

Sometimes, you want to see the big-picture view of the project by viewing the timescale at the level of months and years. At other times, you need to see details about when tasks will occur. In Project, you can set the timescale to show time in years, all the way down to hours. To show incrementally larger timescale units, press Ctrl+/ (slash). To show smaller, more detailed timescale units, press Ctrl+Shift+* (asterisk).

Timeline Shortcuts

Even the Timeline has shortcuts. When you first show the Timeline, it displays the text Add tasks with dates to the timeline. Double-click the text to open the Add Tasks to Timeline dialog box (shown in Figure 21-4). Every task is accompanied by a check box; simply select the ones you want to show on the Timeline.

Figure 21-4:
Adding
tasks to the
Timeline.

Double-clicking the initial text to open the Add Tasks to Timeline dialog box only works the first time you open the Timeline. After you begin entering information on the Timeline, the text that appears on it the first time you open it disappears, and you have to enter tasks by right-clicking them first and choosing Add to Timeline from the shortcut menu.

Quick Find

To find information quickly within the project, press Ctrl+F to open the Quick Find dialog box. Then type the word you want to find in the Find What box.

Appendix

Glossary

· ·

activity: Also known as *task,* an individual step performed to reach a project's goal.

actual: Final reporting data for a task, such as the date when the task really started versus its planned start date or the amount of work completed versus the planned amount of work.

ACWP (actual cost of work performed): Cost of the actual, real work done on a task, work package, or project to date.

ALAP (as late as possible): A constraint put on a task's timing to make the task occur as late as possible in the project schedule, taking into account any dependency relationships.

analogous estimate: An estimating method that takes information from past similar projects into consideration when developing estimates for the current project.

ASAP (as soon as possible): A constraint put on a task's timing to make the task occur as early as possible in the project schedule, taking into account any dependency relationships. This is the default constraint type.

automatically scheduled (auto-scheduled): A task mode where Project calculates the schedule as needed based on task dependencies, constraints, and resource availability.

BAC (budget at completion): The sum total of all costs involved in completing a task, work package, or project. *See also* baseline cost.

Backstage view: The area that presents files and options when you click the File tab.

baseline: The formally agreed-upon dates for starting, finishing, duration, work, and cost data in the project. Later, actual schedule and duration, work, and cost data are tracked so they can be compared with the baseline data.

baseline cost: The formally agreed-upon planned costs for a project's tasks, used to compare with actual costs as they are incurred.

BCWP (budgeted cost of work performed): Also called *earned value;* the value of work that has been completed on a task, work package, or project. For example, a task with $1,000 of costs accrues a BCWP of $750 when it's 75 percent complete.

BCWS (budgeted cost of work scheduled): The budget for the scheduled task, work package, or project.

booking type: A category for resources that specifies whether they're committed to the project or simply proposed to be involved.

calendar: The various settings for hours in a workday, days in a workweek, holidays, and nonworking days on which a project schedule is based. You can set Project, Task, and Resource calendars.

Change Highlighting: A feature that highlights duration, start, and finish data changes caused by any other changes you've made in your project since you last saved it.

charter: A document that formally authorizes or recognizes a project.

circular dependency: A timing relationship among tasks that creates an endless loop that can't be resolved.

collapse: To close a project outline to hide subtasks from view.

combination view: A Project view with task/resources details appearing at the bottom of the screen.

constraint: A parameter that forces a task to fit a specific timing. For example, a task can be constrained to start as late as possible in a project. Constraints interact with dependency links to determine a task's timing.

contingency reserve: Time or money that's factored into your schedule or budget to mitigate identified risks.

cost: The amount of money associated with a task when you assign *resources,* which are equipment, materials, or people with associated fees or hourly rates, and any additional fixed costs.

cost variance (CV): The difference between the baseline costs and the combination of actual costs to date and estimated costs remaining *(scheduled costs).* The cost variance is either *positive* (over budget) or *negative* (under budget). When using earned value management, CV is the difference between the earned value and the actual cost, shown as EV–AC = CV.

critical path: The series of tasks that must occur on time for the overall project to meet its deadline. The end date of the critical path is the earliest a project can be completed. Any slip on the critical path causes a slip in the due date.

critical task: A task on the critical path. *See also* critical path.

crosstab: A report format that compares two intersecting sets of data. For example, you can generate a crosstab report that shows the costs of critical tasks that are running late.

cumulative cost: The planned total cost to date on a particular task. This calculation adds the costs already incurred on a task to any planned costs remaining for the uncompleted portion of the task.

cumulative work: The planned total work on a particular task. This calculation adds the work completed on a task to any planned work remaining for the uncompleted portion of the task.

current date line: The vertical line in a Gantt chart that indicates today's date and time. *See also* Gantt Chart view.

deadline date: A date you assign to a task that doesn't constrain the task's timing. However, if a deadline date is assigned, Project displays an indicator symbol if the task runs past the deadline.

deliverable: A product or capability necessary to complete the project.

dependency: A timing relationship between two tasks in a project. A *dependency link* causes a task either to occur before or after another task, or to begin or end at some point during the life of the other task.

duration: The total number of work periods it takes to complete a task.

duration variance: The difference between the planned (baseline) task duration and the current estimated task duration, based on activity to date and any remaining activity still to be performed.

EAC (estimate at completion): The total planned cost for a specific task, work package, or project. This calculation combines the costs incurred to date with costs estimated for a task's remaining work.

earned value: A reference to the value of work completed. A task with $1,000 of associated costs has an earned value of $750 when it's 75 percent complete. *See also* BCWP.

earned value management: A project management technique that compares scope, schedule, and cost to measure project performance.

effort: The number of labor units required to complete a task.

effort-driven: A setting for an auto-scheduled task that requires an assigned amount of effort to be completed. When you add resources to an effort-driven task, the assigned effort is distributed among the task resources equally.

enterprise custom fields: Custom fields stored in a global file. These fields can be used to standardize Project plan content across an organization.

Enterprise Resource Pool: A Project Server feature that allows you to save all resource information for resources used across an organization in one location.

exception: A specified date or date range that isn't governed by the default working time calendar.

expand: To open a project outline to reveal both summary tasks and subtasks.

expected duration: An estimate of the actual duration of a task, based on work performance to date.

external task: A task in another project. You can set links between tasks in your project and external tasks.

File tab: The tab at the far left end of the Ribbon that you can click to access file- and program-related actions, such as opening a file or setting Project options, in the Backstage view. *See also* Backstage view.

finish date: The date on which a project or task is estimated to be — or actually is — completed.

finish-to-finish relationship: A dependency relationship in which the finish of one task determines the finish of another task.

finish-to-start relationship: A dependency relationship in which the finish of one task determines the start of another task.

fixed duration: For auto-scheduled tasks, a task type setting that specifies that the length of time required to complete a task remains constant no matter how many resources are assigned to the task. A half-day seminar is an example of a fixed-duration task.

fixed-unit: A task type setting for auto-scheduled tasks that specifies that the resource units are constant; if you change the duration of the task, resource units don't change. This is the default task type.

fixed-work: A task type setting for auto-scheduled tasks for which the number of resource hours assigned to the task determines its length. Fixed work tasks can't be effort-driven.

float: The amount of time that you can delay a task before the task becomes critical. Float is used up when any delay in a task will delay the overall project deadline.

Gantt Chart view: A standard Project view that displays columns of task information alongside a chart that shows task timing in bar-chart format.

generic resources: A type of resource that allows you to make skill-based assignments based on a skill/code profile.

grouping: The organization of tasks by a customized field to summarize costs or other factors.

ID number: The number automatically assigned to a task by Project based on its vertical sequence in the project list. The ID number appears at the far left of the task's row.

inactive: A task that still appears in the task list but is struck out and no longer considered in schedule calculations. Marking a task as inactive enables you to document planned activities that ultimately weren't required for the project.

indent: To move a task to a lower level of detail in the project's outline hierarchy.

lag: The set amount of delay that occurs between the end of one task and the beginning of another. Lag is built into a dependency relationship between tasks when you indicate that a certain amount of time must pass before the second task can begin. In other words, adding lag time creates a delay between tasks.

leveling: A calculation used by Project that modifies resource work assignments for the purpose of resolving resource conflicts.

linking: To establish a connection between tasks in separate schedules so that task changes in the first schedule are reflected in the second; also, to establish dependencies among project tasks.

manually scheduled: A new task mode where Project does not recalculate the task schedule based on changes in dependent tasks. You must manually reschedule tasks when using this mode. This is the default task scheduling mode in new project files.

material resources: The supplies or other items used to complete a task (one of two resource categories; the other is work resources).

milestone: A task that usually has zero duration, which marks an event in a schedule. By default, the Gantt chart shows a diamond marker for a milestone task.

mini-toolbar: A toolbar that appears along with a shortcut menu to offer options such as formatting choices.

network diagram: A visual display of how all the tasks relate to one another.

Network Diagram view: An illustration that graphically represents workflow among a project's tasks; one of the Microsoft Project standard views.

node: In Network Diagram view, a box that contains information about individual project tasks.

nonworking time: The time when a resource isn't available to be assigned to work on any task in a project.

outdent: To move a task to a higher level in a project's outline hierarchy.

overallocation: When a resource is assigned to spend more time on a single task or a combination of tasks occurring at the same than that resource's work calendar permits.

overtime: Any work scheduled beyond a resource's standard work hours. You can assign a different rate from a resource's regular rate to overtime work.

parametric estimate: An estimating method that uses a mathematical model to determine project duration.

percent complete: The amount of work on a task that has already been accomplished, expressed as a percentage.

PERT (Program Evaluation and Review Technique) chart: A standard project management chart that indicates workflow among project tasks. This is a *network diagram* in Project. *See also* Network Diagram view.

predecessor: In a dependency link, the task designated to occur before another task. *See also* dependency *and* successor.

priority: A ranking of importance assigned to tasks. When you use resource leveling to resolve project conflicts, priority is a factor in the leveling calculation. A higher-priority task is less likely than a lower-priority task to incur a delay during the leveling process. *See also* resource leveling.

progress lines: Gantt Chart view bars that overlap the baseline taskbar and allow you to compare the baseline plan with a task's tracked progress.

project: A unique venture undertaken to produce distinct deliverables, products, or outcomes.

project calendar: The calendar assigned to the project file. All new tasks use this calendar by default unless you assign a different calendar to a particular task. The project calendar can be one of the default calendars built into Project — Standard, 24 Hours, or Night Shift — or a custom calendar that you create.

project management: The practice of organizing, managing, and controlling project variables to meet the project outcomes and mission.

Project Server: A network-based tool for managing projects across the enterprise. A project manager can use Project Professional to publish a project to Project Server. The project manager, team members, and stakeholders can then view and work with the project data stored in Project Server via a tool called Project Web App.

Project Web App: A web-based companion product of Microsoft Project Server that enables team members to enter information about their tasks into an overall project schedule without having Project installed on their own computers.

Quick Access toolbar: A small, customizable toolbar above the Ribbon that offers buttons for the most frequently used commands.

recurring task: A task that will occur several times during the life of a project. Regular project team meetings or quarterly inspections are examples of recurring tasks.

resource: A cost associated with a task. A resource can be a person, a piece of equipment, materials, or a fee.

resource-driven: A task whose timing is determined by the number of resources assigned to it.

resource leveling: A process used to modify resource assignments to resolve resource conflicts.

resource pool: A group of resources created in a centralized location that multiple project managers can access and assign to their projects.

resource sharing: A feature that allows you to use resources you created in a resource pool in your current plan.

Ribbon: The bar at the top of Project that organizes commands on tabs.

risk: An uncertain event or condition that, if it occurs, affects the schedule (or another project objective, such as cost, resources, or performance).

roll up: The calculation by which all subtask values are *rolled up* — summarized — in a single summary task.

rolling wave planning: Progressively elaborating the amount of detail in the plan for near-term work and keeping farther-out work at a higher level.

schedule variance (SV): The difference between the planned and actual duration or the planned and actual finish dates. When using earned value management, SV is the difference between the earned value and the planned value, shown as EV–PV = SV.

scope: The work needed to produce the deliverables, products, or outcomes for the project.

shortcut menu: A contextual menu that presents applicable commands when you right-click an item in Project.

slack: The amount of time that you can delay a task before the task becomes critical. Slack is used up when any delay in a task will delay the overall project deadline.

split tasks: Tasks that have one or more breaks in their timing. When you split a task, you stop it partway and then start it again at a later time.

stakeholder: Those people who are affected by or can affect the project.

start date: The date on which a project or task begins.

start-to-finish relationship: A dependency relationship in which the start of one task determines the finish of another task.

start-to-start relationship: A dependency relationship in which the start of one task determines the start of another task.

subproject: A copy of a second project inserted into a project. The inserted project becomes a phase of the project into which it is inserted.

subtask: A task that details a specific step in a project phase. This detail is rolled up into a higher-level summary task. A subtask is also called a *subordinate task*. *See also* roll up.

successor: In a dependency relationship, the task whose schedule is dependent on the linked predecessor task's schedule. *See also* dependency.

summary task: In a project outline, a task that has subordinate tasks. A summary task rolls up the details of its subtasks and has no timing of its own. *See also* roll up.

tab: A part of the Ribbon that you can click to display related tools and commands.

task: Also known as an *activity,* an individual step performed to reach a project's goal.

taskbar: A bar that graphically shows a task's schedule according to the Timeline on the chart portion of Gantt Chart view. A taskbar is also called a *Gantt bar.*

Team Planner view: A view that enables you to see and change assignments in a Timeline-like format.

template: A format in which a file can be saved. The template saves elements such as calendar settings, formatting, and tasks. New project files can be based on a template to save the time involved in reentering settings.

three-point estimate: An estimating method that accounts for uncertainty by averaging the optimistic, pessimistic, and most likely estimates. A three-point estimate may be modified by averaging the one optimistic, one pessimistic, and four most likely estimates.

Timeline view: A view that appears along with some other views to give a simplified picture of the overall schedule.

timescale: The area of Gantt Chart view that displays units of time. When the timescale is placed against those units of time, taskbars graphically represent the timing of tasks.

tracking: Recording the actual progress of work completed and the costs accrued for a project's tasks.

user-controlled scheduling: A feature that enables you to select a task mode that controls how a task will be scheduled. *See also* automatically scheduled *and* manually scheduled.

variable rate: A shift in resource cost that can be set to occur at specific times during a project. For example, if a resource is expected to receive a raise or if equipment lease rates are scheduled to increase, you can assign variable rates for those resources.

WBS (work breakdown structure): A hierarchical representation of the project work. Each level represents a lower level of detail.

workload: The amount of work that any resource is performing at any given time, taking into account all tasks to which the resource is assigned.

work resources: The people or equipment that performs work necessary to accomplish a task. *See also* material resources.

Index

• Symbols and Numerics •

– (minus symbol), 191
% Complete setting, 247
+ (plus sign), 191
^ (upward-facing arrow), 16
24 Hours calendar option, 120

• A •

AC (actual cost), 245
accessing filters, 159
accrual, of costs, 146–147
activity, 315
actual, 315
actual cost (AC), 245
actual cost of work performed (ACWP), 315
actual progress, *versus* baseline plan, 238
ACWP (actual cost of work performed), 315
Add Progress Line tool, 217
Add Tasks to Timeline dialog box, 313
adding
  to contingency reserve, 264
  custom fields, 135–136
  dependency links, 58–60
  notes to tasks, 253
  people to tasks, 261–262
  tasks to Timeline, 285–287
  text, 198
  up costs, 146–147
adjusting
  constraints, 263
  dependencies, 263
  gridlines, 195–196
  layout, 192–195
  linking settings, 235
  Network Diagram layout, 99–100

Network Diagram view, 96–100
resource assignments, 178–179, 261–262
resource calendars, 127–129
scheduling method, 263–264
settings for task calendars, 126
task durations, 264
timescale, 92–95
Visual Reports template, 273
ALAP (as late as possible), 315
analogous estimating, 70–71, 315
applying
  contingency reserve, 172–173
  predefined groups, 163–164
  preset sorting order, 255
  tracking methods, 215
as late as possible (ALAP), 315
as soon as possible (ASAP), 315
Assign Resources dialog box, 138–139,
    179–180, 310
assigning
  material resources, 151–152
  resources, 49, 110–111, 133–143
  resources to recurring tasks, 49
Assignment Summary category, 271
Assignment Usage category, 271
assignments, in Project files, 82
assignment-time phased approach, 215, 218
AutoFilter feature, 159–161
automatic scheduling
  compared with manual scheduling, 26–28
  defined, 315
  specifying remaining durations for
    tasks, 225–227
availability
  estimating, 111–112
  managing for resources, 111–113
  setting, 111–112
avoiding fixed costs, 148–149

• B •

BAC (budget at completion), 245, 315
Backstage view, 14, 315
Bar Styles dialog box, 187–189
base calendars, 119–122, 120
baseline, 315
baseline cost, 316
baseline plan
  about, 201–202
  versus actual progress, 238
  clearing, 205–206
  defined, 146
  printing, 252–253
  resetting, 205–206
  saving, 202–203
  saving more than one, 203–205
BCWP (budgeted cost of work
      performed), 316
behaviors, limiting, 69
booking type, 316
bottom line, 147
Box Styles dialog box, 97
budget at completion (BAC), 245, 315
budgeted cost of work performed
      (BCWP), 316
building, on successes, 294–298

• C •

calculations, 246–249, 262
Calendar view
  about, 82, 90–91
  layout options in, 194
  scrolling in, 84
calendars
  about, 119
  base, 119–122
  creating custom templates, 129–130
  defined, 316
  how they relate to each other, 121–122
  how they work, 120–121
  options for, 122–124
  project, 119–122
  resource, 119–122, 126–129
  sharing copies of, 130–131
  task, 119–122, 126–129
  working times, 124–125
change, as a project variable, 8
Change Highlighting feature, 316
Change Working Time dialog box, 124–125
changing
  constraints, 263
  dependencies, 263
  gridlines, 195–196
  layout, 192–195
  linking settings, 235
  Network Diagram layout, 99–100
  Network Diagram view, 96–100
  resource assignments, 178–179, 261–262
  resource calendars, 127–129
  scheduling method, 263–264
  settings for task calendars, 126
  task durations, 264
  timescale, 92–95
  Visual Reports template, 273
chart, 13, 85
charter, 316
Cheat Sheet (website), 3
checking
  dependencies, 174
  external dependencies, 263
  resource availability, 177–178
child tasks. *See* subtasks
circular dependency, 316
Clear Baseline dialog box, 205–206, 208–209
clearing
  baseline plans, 205–206
  interim plans, 208–209
collapsing
  defined, 316
  task outline, 45–47, 302
color, for reports, 275
columns
  displaying, 95–96
  hiding, 95
  inserting, 95
combination view, 316
communication, project manager and, 9
communications management plan,
      developing, 213–218

companion website, 3
company policies, 303
comparing versions of projects, 292–294
completing tasks in less time, 174–176
considerations, for project planning,
 302–303
consolidated projects, 232–235
consolidated resource, 110
constraints
 about, 171
 controlling timing with, 73–76
 costs, 176
 defined, 73, 316
 establishing, 74–75
 how they work, 73–74
 modifying, 263
 negotiating, 171–184
 rescheduling, 183–184
 resources workload, 176–183
 time, 171–176
contingency reserve
 adding to, 264
 applying, 172–173
 defined, 316
controlling
 availability of resources, 174–175
 resource availability, 111–113
 task warnings and suggestions,
  167–170
 timing with constraints, 73–76
copy-and-paste method, 44–45, 288
copying Timeline, 288
Cost Overbudget filter, 256
cost resources
 about, 105
 defined, 145
 determining, 137
cost variance (CV), 245, 316–317
cost-per-use rates, entering, 149–151
costs
 accrual of, 146–147
 adding up, 146–147
 assigning material resources, 151–152
 bottom line, 147
 cost-per-use rates, 149–151
 cutting, 176, 255

defined, 316
determining, 145–153
 effect of settings on, 152–153
 fixed, 148–149
 hourly, 149–151
 overtime, 149–151
 project manager and, 9
 as a project variable, 8
 specifying information for, 148–152
 trading time for, 175–176
Costs category, 268
crashing, 175
Create Report dialog box, 272–273
creating
 custom calendar templates,
  129–130
 custom text fields, 198–200
 do-it-yourself filters, 161–163
 groups, 164–166
 images, 197–198
 project charter, 20–21
 recurring tasks, 48–49
 reports, 270–273
 resources, 103–117
 standard reports, 268–270
 subtasks, 39–43
 summary tasks, 39–43
 task notes, 51–52
 templates, 294–296
 visual reports, 272–273
Critical filter, 256
critical path
 abundance of, 248–249
 defined, 317
 displaying, 189–190
 examining, 257–258
critical path tasks, 158
critical tasks, 97, 317
cross-project link, 61
crosstab, 317
cumulative cost, 317
cumulative work, 317
current date line, 317
custom fields
 adding, 135–136
 creating, 198–200

customer, 9
customizing
  column displays of tables, 87
  Quick Access Toolbar, 17–18
  Timeline, 287
  views, 91–100
cut-and-paste method, moving tasks with,
    44–45
cutting costs, 176, 255
CV (cost variance), 245, 316–317

• D •

dashboard reports, 269–270
data, gathering, 214
deadline date, 317
deadlines, setting, 75–76
debriefing
  your team, 291
  yourself, 292
decomposition, 22
Default Task Earned Value Method
    setting, 247–248
delegating, 304
deleting
  dependencies, 62–63
  resource assignments, 178–179
  tasks, 50–51, 175, 263, 265
deliverable, 8, 317
demoting, 35–36
dependencies
  about, 53–54
  adjusting, 263
  checking, 174
  defined, 317
  deleting, 62–63
  external, 54, 61, 263
  how tasks become dependent, 54–58
  lag time, 57–58
  lead time, 58
  mandatory, 53
  setting connections, 58–63
  shifting, 262–264
  types of, 55–57
dependency links, 54, 58–60
dependent tasks, 54–55

determining
  cost resources, 137
  material resources, 137
  percent complete, 220–221
  project cost, 145–153
  timing factors, 259–260
developing communications management
    plan, 213–218
dialog boxes
  Assign Resources, 138–139, 179–180, 310
  Bar Styles, 187–189
  Box Styles, 97
  Change Working Time, 124–125
  Clear Baseline, 205–206, 208–209
  Create Report, 272–273
  Format Box, 192
  Format Drawing, 198
  Gridlines, 196
  Group Definition, 166
  Insert Object, 277–278
  Layout, 193–194
  Level Resources, 180–183
  More Filters, 161–163
  More Groups, 164–166
  Move Project, 183–184
  Options, 123
  Page Setup, 279–283
  Quick Find, 313
  Resource Information, 108–109, 113,
    152, 310
  Resource Leveling, 259
  Set Baseline, 203, 204, 207–208
  Task Information, 30–31, 59–60, 63, 69,
    72–77, 138, 140, 220–221, 253, 286,
    309–310
  Zoom, 90
discretionary dependency, 53
displaying
  columns, 95–96
  critical path, 189–190
  Layout dialog box, 193
  preset tables of sheet data, 96
  progress lines, 239–240
  Resource Sheet view, 117
  tables, 243
  text labels, 93

tools, 17–18
Type column, 67
views, 83
documenting, 305
do-it-yourself filters, creating, 161–163
drag-and-drop method, moving
tasks with, 44
dragging, in reports, 273–274
dropping, in reports, 273–274
duration
defined, 70, 317
estimating, 70–73
fixed, 66
setting for tasks, 72–73
duration variance, 317

• E •

EAC (estimate at completion), 245, 317
earned value (EV), 245, 318
earned value management (EVM),
244–246, 318
earned-value options, 247–248
editing layouts in Network
Diagram view, 100
effects, for reports, 276
effort
defined, 70, 318
estimating, 70–73
effort-driven, 318
effort-driven tasks, 67, 69
entering
cost-per-use rates, 149–151
fixed-cost updates, 227–228
hourly rates, 149–151
hours for overtime, 224–225
overtime rates, 149–151
project information, 24–26
resource hours, 222–224
task start date, 77
tasks, 30–32
Work Breakdown Structure (WBS), 28–30
enterprise custom fields, 318
Enterprise Resource Pool, 318
enterprise resources, 115
environment, as a project variable, 8

establishing constraints, 74–75
estimate at completion (EAC), 245, 317
estimating
analogous, 70–71
availability, 111–112
duration, 70–73
effort, 70–73
parametric, 71
resource requirements, 106–107
task time, 65–79
three-point, 71–72
EV (earned value), 245, 318
EVM (earned value management),
244–246, 318
examples, task type, 68
Excel 2016 For Dummies (Harvey),
257, 273
exceptions
defined, 121, 318
setting to working times, 124–125
expanding
defined, 318
task outline, 45–47, 302
expectations, basic, 302–303
expected duration, 318
expecting the unexpected, 303
external dependency, 54, 61, 263
external task, 318

• F •

F5 key, 85–86
fast tracking, 58, 174
File tab, 14, 318
file tabs
about, 12–13
navigating, 14–17
files, saving as templates, 295–296
'fill down,' 312
filtering, 256–257
filters
about, 157–158
accessing, 159
AutoFilter feature, 159–161
creating do-it-yourself, 161–163
predesigned, 158–159

financial information, in Project files, 82
Find feature, 133–136
finding
  help, 179–180
  resources, 133–136
  ways to cut corners, 265–266
fine-tuning
  about, 157
  filters, 157–163
  Group feature, 163–166
  reports, 273–276
  Task Inspector pane, 166–167
  task warnings and suggestions,
    167–170
finish date, 318
finish information, recording, 222
finish-to-finish relationship, 56–57, 318
finish-to-start relationship, 56, 59, 318
fixed costs
  about, 176
  avoiding, 148–149
  entering updates, 227–228
fixed duration, 66, 319
fixed units, 66, 319
fixed work, 66, 319
flat-loaded, 180
float, 158, 319
font, for reports, 275
font size, for reports, 276
footers, inserting, 280–281
Format Box dialog box, 192
Format Drawing dialog box, 198
Format file tab, 16
formatting
  about, 185–186
  adjusting layout, 192–195
  creating custom text fields,
    198–200
  Gantt Chart, 186–191
  images, 197–198
  modifying gridlines, 195–196
  Network Diagram boxes, 98–99
  progress lines, 241–242
  task bars, 186–189
  task boxes, 191–192
  text, 280
frequently used functions, 310–311
functions, frequently used, 310–311

• G •

Gantt Chart
  about, 86–87
  formatting, 186–191
  restyling, 190–191
Gantt Chart Tools Format contextual tab,
    197–198
Gantt Chart view
  about, 14–15, 82
  defined, 319
  entering tasks in, 30
  layout options in, 195
gathering data, 214
generic resources, 319
Go To feature, 85–86
graphics, for reports, 276–278
gridlines, modifying, 195–196
Gridlines dialog box, 196
Group Definition dialog box, 166
grouping, 319
groups
  about, 12–13
  creating, 164–166
Groups feature
  about, 163
  applying predefined groups, 163–164
  creating groups, 164–166

• H •

hanger task, 62
hard logic, 53
Harvey, Greg (author)
  Excel 2016 For Dummies, 257, 273
Header and Footer tab (Page Setup
    dialog box), 280–281
headers, inserting, 280–281
help, finding, 179–180
Help function, 18
hiding
  columns, 95
  subtasks, 311
  View bar, 83
history, resources and, 107
hourly rates, entering, 149–151
hyperlinks, inserting, 33–34

• I •

icons, explained, 2–3
ID number, 319
identifying
  resources, 109–110
  task types, 66–67
images, creating, 197–198
Import Outlook Tasks feature, 32–35
importing
  resources from Outlook, 116–117
  tasks from Outlook, 32–35
In Progress category, 268
inactive tasks, 50–51, 319
Incomplete Tasks filter, 256
indent, 312, 319
Insert Object dialog box, 277–278
inserting
  columns, 95
  footers, 280–281
  headers, 280–281
  hyperlinks, 33–34
  projects into other projects, 34–35
inspecting tasks, 166–167
interim plans
  about, 201, 206–207
  clearing, 208–209
  printing, 252–253
  resetting, 208–209
  saving, 207–208
issue logs, 251–254

• K •

keystroke combinations, for navigating
  timescale, 95

• L •

lag, 319
lag time, 57–58
landscape orientation, 279
Late/Overbudget Tasks Assigned To
  filter, 257
layout, adjusting, 192–195
Layout dialog box, 193–194
lead time, 58

learning from mistakes, 290–291, 307
legend, 281–282
Legend tab (Page Setup dialog box),
  281–282
Level Resources dialog box, 180–183
leveling
  defined, 319
  resources, 180–183
levels, of tasks, 41
limiting behaviors, 69
lines, of progress, 239–242
linking settings
  changing, 235
  defined, 320
lookup table, 198

• M •

maintaining flexible strategies, 306–307
management expectations, 302–303
managing
  availability of resources, 174–175
  resource availability, 111–113
  task warnings and suggestions, 167–170
  timing with constraints, 73–76
mandatory dependency, 53
manual scheduling
  compared with automatic scheduling,
    26–28
  defined, 320
margins, for printing, 280
Margins tab (Page Setup dialog box), 280
Mark on Track tool, 216, 220
material resources
  about, 105
  assigning, 151–152
  defined, 320
  determining, 137
materials
  less-expensive, 265
  tracking, 231–232
measuring success, 306
Mendez, Monica (engineer), 111
Microsoft Project. See Project 2016
milestones
  about, 191
  defined, 320
  setting, 49–50

mini-toolbar, 320
minus symbol (–), 191
mistakes, learning from, 290–291, 307
modifications, timing and, 260–261
modifying
  constraints, 263
  dependencies, 263
  gridlines, 195–196
  layout, 192–195
  linking settings, 235
  Network Diagram layout, 99–100
  Network Diagram view, 96–100
  resource assignments, 178–179, 261–262
  resource calendars, 127–129
  scheduling method, 263–264
  settings for task calendars, 126
  task durations, 264
  timescale, 92–95
  Visual Reports template, 273
More Filters dialog box, 161–163
More Groups dialog box, 164–166
Move Project dialog box, 183–184
Move Task tool, 217, 228–229
moving
  objects, 198
  tasks, 43–45, 228–229

navigating
  about, 312
  file tabs, 14–17
  Ribbon, 14–17
  tabs, 82–84
  views, 82–84
negotiating project constraints, 171–184
network diagram, 62, 320
Network Diagram view
  about, 82, 89–90
  changing formatting of task boxes in,
    191–192
  defined, 302, 320
  layout options in, 194
  modifying, 96–100
Night Shift calendar option, 120
node, 90, 320

noncritical tasks, 97
nonworking, 122
nonworking time, 320
Notes area, 305

objects, 198
observing progress. *See* Project views
Options dialog box, 123
Organizer, 296–298
organizing work, 22–24
outdent, 312, 320
outdent-and-indent shuffle, 35–36
Outlook
  importing resources from, 116–117
  importing tasks from, 32–35
Overallocated Resources filter, 257
overallocation
  about, 111, 143
  beating, 179
  defined, 320
  of resources, 158
Over-Budget Work filter, 158
overtime
  defined, 320
  entering hours for, 224–225
  entering rates for, 149–151
  reducing, 176

Page Setup dialog box, 279–283
Page tab (Page Setup dialog box), 279
panes
  resizing, 92
  view, 92–96
  in views, 84–85
parametric estimating, 71, 320
parent tasks. *See* summary tasks
pausing tasks, 76–79
people, adding to tasks, 261–262
percent complete
  defined, 320
  determining, 220–221

% Complete setting, 247
Percent Complete tool, 216
PERT (Program Evaluation and Review
    Technique chart), 321
PERT chart, 89–90
Physical % Complete setting, 247–248
planned value (PV), 244–245
planning, considerations for, 302–303
plus sign (+), 191
portrait orientation, 279
positioning text, 280
precedence diagram, 62
predecessor, 321
predefined groups, applying, 163–164
predesigned filters, setting, 158–159
preview, print, 283–284
printing
  about, 278–279
  baseline plans, 252–253
  interim plans, 252–253
  Page Setup, 279–283
  print preview, 283–284
  Project view, 186
  settings, 284–285
  task notes, 253–254
priority, 321
Program Evaluation and Review Technique
    (PERT) chart, 321
progress
  observing. *See* Project views
  in Project files, 82
progress lines, 239–242, 321
Project 2016. *See also specific topics*
  about, 10–11
  defined, 120
  shortcuts in, 309–313
project calendars
  about, 119–122
  defined, 120, 321
project charter, creating, 20–21
project constraints
  about, 171
  controlling timing with, 73–76
  costs, 176
  defined, 73, 316
  establishing, 74–75

how they work, 73–74
modifying, 263
negotiating, 171–184
rescheduling, 183–184
resources workload, 176–183
time, 171–176
project costs
  accrual of, 146–147
  adding up, 146–147
  assigning material resources, 151–152
  bottom line, 147
  cost-per-use rates, 149–151
  cutting, 176, 255
  defined, 316
  determining, 145–153
  effect of settings on, 152–153
  fixed, 148–149
  hourly, 149–151
  overtime, 149–151
  project manager and, 9
  as a project variable, 8
  specifying information for, 148–152
  trading time for, 175–176
Project file tab, 16
Project files, components of, 82
project information, entering, 24–26
project management
  about, 7–8
  defined, 8, 321
  Project 2016, 10–11
  project manager, 8–10
  rules of, 301–307
  schedule, 11–13
project manager
  about, 8–9
  role of, 9–10
project plan. *See* scheduling
Project Server, 321
project summary task, 41–43
project views
  about, 15, 81, 237
  Backstage, 14, 315
  baseline *versus* actual progress, 238
  calculating, 246–249
  Calendar, 82, 84, 90–91, 194
  combination, 316

project views *(continued)*
  customizing, 91–100
  delays, 242–244
  displaying, 83
  earned value management (EVM), 244–246
  Gantt Chart, 14–15, 30, 82, 86–87, 195, 319
  lines of progress, 239–242
  navigating, 82–84
  Network Diagram, 82, 89–90, 96–100, 191–192, 194, 302, 320
  panes in, 84–85
  printing, 186
  resetting, 100
  Resource Graph, 177–178
  Resource Sheet, 88, 117
  Resource Usage, 84, 142, 177–178, 271
  scrolling, 84–85
  Task Sheet, 82, 217–218
  Task Usage, 82, 217–218, 271
  Team Planner, 88, 142–143, 323
  Timeline, 82, 88–89, 323
  for tracking, 217–218
  variances, 242–244
Project views
  about, 237
  baseline *versus* actual progress, 238
  calculating, 246–249
  delays, 242–244
  earned value management (EVM), 244–246
  lines of progress, 239–242
  printing, 186
  variances, 242–244
Project Web App, 321
project work, 22
projects
  comparing versions of, 292–294
  consolidated, 232–235
  defined, 120, 321
  rescheduling, 183–184
  reviewing, 289–291
  saving, 36–37
  starting. *See* starting projects
  updating, 229–231, 264–265
  variables, 8

promoting, 35–36
PV (planned value), 244–245

• Q •

Quick Access Toolbar
  about, 12–13
  customizing, 17–18
  defined, 321
Quick Find dialog box, 313

• R •

recording start and finish information, 222
recurring tasks, 48–49, 321
reducing overtime, 176
redundant predecessor, 55
Remember icon, 2
Report file tab, 15, 268
reporting
  about, 267
  copy-and-paste, 288
  creating new reports, 270–273
  fine-tuning reports, 273–276
  generating standard reports, 268–270
  graphics, 276–278
  printing reports, 278–285
  Timeline, 285–288
reports
  about, 305
  dashboard, 269–270
requirements, estimating for resources, 106–107
rescheduling, 179, 183–184
resetting
  baseline plans, 205–206
  interim plans, 208–209
  views, 100
resizing
  objects, 198
  panes, 92
resource calendars
  about, 119–122
  changing, 127–129
  setting, 126–127
  working with, 126–129

Resource column, assigning resources from, 137, 138
resource dependency, 53
Resource file tab, 15
Resource Graph view, 177–178
resource hours, entering, 222–224
Resource Information dialog box, 108–109, 113, 152, 310
Resource Information form, 107
resource leveling
  about, 62
  defined, 322
  using, 259
Resource Leveling dialog box, 259
resource pool, 114–116, 322
resource sharing, 322
Resource Sheet view, 88, 117
Resource Summary category, 271
Resource Usage view, 84, 142, 177–178, 271
resource workload, 176–183
resource-driven, 322
resources
  about, 103–105, 107
  assigning, 110–111, 133–143
  assigning to recurring tasks, 49
  changing assignments of, 261–262
  checking availability of, 177–178
  creating, 103–117
  creating one at a time, 108–109
  defined, 104, 322
  deleting assignments, 178–179
  determining material and cost-resource units, 137
  effect on task timing, 105–106
  estimating availability of, 111–112
  estimating requirements for, 106–107
  finding, 133–136
  identifying, 109–110
  importing from Outlook, 116–117
  information on, 302–303
  less-expensive, 176, 265
  leveling, 180–183
  life span of, 112–113
  making assignments of, 137–140
  managing availability of, 111–113, 174–175
  modifying assignments, 178–179
  overallocation of, 158

  in Project files, 82
  project manager and, 9
  as a project variable, 8
  setting availability of, 111–112
  shaping work contours, 140–142
  sharing, 114–117
  Team Planner view, 142–143
  types of, 105
Resources category, 268
restyling Gantt Chart, 190–191
reviewing
  projects, 289–291
  task constraints, 264
  task timing, 255
Ribbon
  about, 12–13
  defined, 322
  navigating, 14–17
  View tab, 82
risk
  defined, 172, 322
  logs, 251–254
  as a project variable, 8
  working with, 173
roll up, 322
rolling wave planning, 41, 202, 301–302, 322

• S •

saving
  baseline plans, 202–203
  files as templates, 295–296
  interim plans, 207–208
  more than one baseline plan, 203–204
  projects, 36–37
scaling, for printing, 279
schedule model, 11
schedule variance (SV), 245, 322
scheduling
  automatic, 26–28, 225–227, 315
  with calendars, 122–125
  changing method of, 263–264
  project manager and, 9
scope
  defined, 322
  project manager and, 9
  as a project variable, 8

scrolling views, 84–85
selecting
  resources from Resource column, 138
  text, 281
Set Baseline dialog box, 203, 204, 207–208
setting(s)
  availability, 111–112
  calendar options, 122–124
  deadlines, 75–76
  dependency connections, 58–63
  effect on costs of, 152–153
  exceptions to working times, 124–125
  milestones, 49–50
  modifying for task calendars, 126
  predesigned filters, 158–159
  print, 284–285
  resource calendars, 126–127
  resource rates per hour, 150
  status date, 219–220
  task duration, 72–73
  timescale, 312
shaping work contours, 140–142
sharer files, 114
sharing
  copies of calendars, 130–131
  resources, 114–117
sheet, 13, 85
shifting dependencies, 262–264
shortcut menu, 322
shortcuts, 309–313
Should Start By filter, 257
showing
  columns, 95–96
  critical path, 189–190
  Layout dialog box, 193
  preset tables of sheet data, 96
  progress lines, 239–240
  Resource Sheet view, 117
  tables, 243
  text labels, 93
  tools, 17–18
  Type column, 67
  views, 83
sizing
  in reports, 273–274
  when printing, 279–280

skills
  considerations for, 135–136
  resources and, 107
slack, 322
Slipped/Late Progress filter, 257
Slipping Assignments filter, 257
Slipping Tasks filter, 158
soft logic, 53
sorting tasks, 255–256
specifying
  cost information in projects, 148–152
  remaining durations for auto-scheduled
    tasks, 225–227
  status date, 219–220
split tasks, 78–79, 322
stakeholders
  defined, 9, 322
  as a project variable, 8
Standard calendar option, 120
standard reports, generating, 268–270
start date
  defined, 323
  entering for tasks, 77
start information, recording, 222
starting projects
  about, 19–20
  creating project charter, 20–21
  demoting, 35–36
  entering project information, 24–26
  entering tasks, 30–32
  entering WBS, 28–30
  importing tasks from Outlook, 32–35
  indent, 35–36
  manual scheduling *versus* automatic
    scheduling, 26–28
  organizing work, 22–24
  outdent, 35–36
  promoting, 35–36
  saving, 36–37
  Work Breakdown Structure (WBS), 21–22
starting tasks, 76–79
start-to-finish relationship, 57, 323
start-to-start relationship, 56, 323
Status bar, 13, 18
status date, specifying, 219–220
strategies, maintaining flexible, 306–307

subprojects, 323
subtasks
about, 191, 311
creating, 39–43
defined, 323
successes
building on, 294–298
measuring, 306
successor, 54, 323
summary task duration, 42, 323
summary tasks, 39–43, 191
SV (schedule variance), 245, 322

• *T* •

tables
defined, 86, 149
displaying, 243
tabs
defined, 323
navigating, 82–84
task bars
defined, 323
formatting, 186–189
task boxes, formatting, 191–192
task calendars
about, 119–122
working with, 126–129
task constraints, reviewing, 264
task drivers, 166–167
task durations, modifying, 264
Task file tab, 14–15
Task Filters filter, 256
Task Form view, 82
task ID, 86
Task Information dialog box
about, 309–310
adding notes to tasks, 253
adding tasks to Timeline with, 286
assigning resources from, 138, 140
dependencies and, 59–60, 63
determining percent complete,
220–221
Effort Driven setting, 69
entering task start dates, 77
entering tasks via, 30–31

establishing constraints, 74–75
setting deadlines, 75–76
setting task duration, 72–73
Task Inspector pane, 166–167
task notes, printing, 253–254
Task Sheet pane, 60
Task Sheet view, 82, 217–218
Task Summary category, 271
Task tab, 28
Task Usage view, 82, 217–218, 271
task warnings and suggestions,
handling, 167–170
tasks. *See also* dependencies
about, 39
adding people to, 261–262
adding to Timeline, 285–287
collapsing outline, 45–47, 302
completing in less time, 174–176
creating task notes, 51–52
deleting, 50–51, 175, 263, 265
dependent, 54–55
effort-driven, 67, 69
entering, 30–32
estimating time for, 65–79
expanding outline, 45–47, 302
importing from Outlook, 32–35
inactive, 50–51
inspecting, 166–167
moving, 43–45
pausing, 76–79
in Project files, 82
project summary, 41–43
recurring, 48–49
setting milestones, 49–50
sorting, 255–256
splitting, 78–79
starting, 76–79
subtasks, 39–43
summary, 39–43
timing of, 262–264
types of, 66–67
task-time phased approach, 215, 218
task-total method, 215
team
keeping in the loop, 305
structure of, 302–303

Team Planner view
  about, 88
  benefits of, 142–143
  defined, 323
techniques, estimating, 70–72
Tell Me What You Want to Do feature, 18
templates
  about, 11–12
  calendar, 129–130
  creating, 294–296
  defined, 323
text
  adding, 198
  formatting, 280
  positioning, 280
  selecting, 281
text labels, displaying, 93
themes, for reports, 274–276
three-point estimating, 71–72, 323
time
  as a project constraint, 171–176
  as a project variable, 8
  trading for cost, 175–176
Timeline
  about, 13, 18, 285
  adding tasks to, 285–287
  copying, 288
  customizing, 287
  defined, 302
  shortcuts for, 313
Timeline view, 82, 88–89, 323
time-phased data, 271
timescale
  changing, 92–95
  defined, 85, 92, 324
  setting, 312
timing
  about, 65–66
  controlling with constraints, 73–76
  effect of resources on task,
      105–106
  modifications and, 260–261
  in Project files, 82
  resources driving, 259–260
  of tasks, 262–264
Tip icon, 2

tools
  displaying, 17–18
  tracking, 216–217
tracking
  about, 213
  applying methods for, 215
  consolidated projects, 232–235
  defined, 324
  determining percent complete, 220–221
  developing communications management
      plans, 213–218
  entering fixed-cost updates, 227–228
  entering specific hours, 222–224
  gathering data, 214
  importance of, 303–304
  materials, 231–232
  moving tasks, 228–229
  overtime, 224–225
  recording, 218–228
  recording start and finish
      information, 222
  remaining on track, 220
  specifying remaining durations for
      auto-scheduled tasks, 225–227
  specifying status date, 219–220
  tools for, 216–217
  updating projects, 229–231
  views for, 217–218
Tracking Gantt view, 242
trading time for cost, 175–176
24 Hours calendar option, 120
Type column, displaying, 67

• U •

unexpected, expecting the, 303
units, fixed, 66
Units setting, 112
Update Project feature, 217, 229–231
Update Tasks tool, 216
updating
  consolidated projects, 234
  projects, 229–231, 264–265
upward -facing arrow (^), 16
upward-facing arrow (^), 16
user-controlled scheduling, 27, 324

• V •

VAC (variance at completion), 245
variable rate, 324
variables, project, 8
variance at completion (VAC), 245
variances, viewing, 242
verifying
  dependencies, 174
  external dependencies, 263
  resource availability, 177–178
versions, comparing for projects, 292–294
View bar, hiding, 83
View file tab, 16
view panes, working with, 92–96
View tab, 82, 282–283
viewing
  baselines, 204
  dashboard reports, 269
  multiple baselines, 252
  unassigned tasks, 143
  variances, 242
views
  about, 15, 81, 237
  Backstage, 14, 315
  baseline *versus* actual progress, 238
  calculating, 246–249
  Calendar, 82, 84, 90–91, 194
  combination, 316
  customizing, 91–100
  delays, 242–244
  displaying, 83
  earned value management
    (EVM), 244–246
  Gantt Chart, 14–15, 30, 82, 86–87, 195, 319
  lines of progress, 239–242
  navigating, 82–84
  Network Diagram, 82, 89–90, 96–100,
    191–192, 194, 302, 320
  panes in, 84–85
  printing, 186
  resetting, 100
  Resource Graph, 177–178
  Resource Sheet, 88, 117
  Resource Usage, 84, 142, 177–178, 271

  scrolling, 84–85
  Task Sheet, 82, 217–218
  Task Usage, 82, 217–218, 271
  Team Planner, 88, 142–143, 323
  Timeline, 82, 88–89, 323
  for tracking, 217–218
  variances, 242–244
Visual Reports feature
  about, 271–272, 305
  creating, 272–273

• W •

Warning! icon, 2
WBS. *See* Work Breakdown
    Structure (WBS)
Web Extras (website), 3
websites
  Cheat Sheet, 3
  companion, 3
  Web Extras, 3
what-if scenarios, 254–260
work
  fixed, 66
  organizing, 22–24
Work Breakdown Structure (WBS)
  about, 21–22
  defined, 324
  entering, 28–30
work contours, shaping, 140–142
Work Incomplete filter, 257
Work Overbudget filter, 257
work resources, 105, 324
workday, 121
working times
  defined, 122
  setting exceptions to, 124–125
workload, 324

• Z •

Zoom command, 86
Zoom dialog box, 90
Zoom menu, 94
zooming, 94

About the Author

Cynthia Snyder is a well-known project management speaker, consultant, and trainer. She is the project manager of the team that updated PMI's *Project Management Body of Knowledge,* 6th Edition, and she is the author of many books, including *PMP Certification All-in-One For Dummies, A Project Manager's Book of Forms: A Companion to the PMBOK Guide,* and *A User's Manual to the PMBOK Guide* (all from Wiley). Her books have been translated into several languages. Cynthia provides consulting services focusing on project management maturity, and she is a much-sought-after trainer in the private, public, and educational sectors. She makes her home in the Pacific Northwest, with her husband and a menagerie of animals.

Author's Acknowledgments

Publishing a book is not a solo endeavor. It takes many people to transfer information from the author's head into the reader's hands. If you're reading this, it is because the following people at *For Dummies* and Wiley have been instrumental in getting this information to you.

I am grateful to my acquisitions editor, Steve Hayes, for giving me the opportunity to write this book. Elizabeth Kuball is an excellent project editor — I appreciate her time and effort associated with keeping the schedule on track and helping me with the artwork.

Finally, I would like to acknowledge all the students I have had the opportunity to teach. Project management is a wonderful profession, but it is not for the faint of heart. Thank you for allowing me to light the way for you.

Publisher's Acknowledgments

Executive Editor: Steve Hayes

Project Editor: Elizabeth Kuball

Copy Editor: Elizabeth Kuball

Technical Editor: Ciprian Rusen

Production Editor: Antony Sami

Cover Image: © adventtr/iStockphoto

Dummies products make life easier!

- DIY
- Consumer Electronics
- Crafts

- Software
- Cookware
- Hobbies

- Videos
- Music
- Games
- and More!

For more information, go to **Dummies.com** and search the store by category.

FOR DUMMIES

A Wiley Bran